ntury 21

SOUTH-WESTERN
Accounting 9E

Advanced Working Papers, Chs. 1–10

D1072837

Claudia Bienias Gilbertson, CPA
Teaching Professor
North Hennepin Community College
Brooklyn Park, Minnesota

Mark W. Lehman, CPA
Associate Professor
School of Accountancy
Mississippi State University

Dan Passalacqua, MA
Oak Grove High School
San Jose, California

SOUTH-WESTERN
CENGAGE Learning

Australia · Brazil · Canada · Mexico · Singapore · Spain · United Kingdom · United States

SOUTH-WESTERN
CENGAGE Learning˙

Working Papers, Chs. 1–10, Advanced, Century 21 Accounting, 9E

Claudia Bienias Gilbertson, CPA;
Mark W. Lehman, CPA;
Dan Passalacqua, MA

VP/Editorial Director: Jack W. Calhoun

VP/Editor-in-Chief: Karen Schmohe

VP/Director of Marketing: Bill Hendee

Sr. Marketing Manager: Courtney Schulz

Marketing Coordinator: Gretchen Wildauer

Marketing Communications Manager: Terron Sanders

Production Manager: Patricia Matthews Boies

Content Project Manager: Diane Bowdler

Consulting Editor: Bill Lee

Special Consultants: Robert E. First, Sara Wilson

Manufacturing Buyer: Kevin Kluck

Production Service: LEAP Publishing Services, Inc.

Compositor: GGS Book Services

Cover Designer: Nick & Diane Gliebe, Design Matters

Cover Images: Getty Images, Inc.

For product information and technology assistance, contact us at **Cengage Learning Academic Resource Center, 1-800-423-0563**

For permission to use material from this text or product, submit all requests online at **www.cengage.com/permissions** Further permissions questions can be emailed to **permissionrequest@cengage.com**

ISBN-13: 978-0-538-44792-8
ISBN-10: 0-538-44792-3

South-Western Cengage Learning
5191 Natorp Boulevard
Mason, OH 45040
USA

Cengage Learning products are represented in Canada by Nelson Education, Ltd.

For your course and learning solutions, visit **school.cengage.com**

Printed in the United States of America
6 7 8 9 10   21 20 19 18 17

TO THE STUDENT

These *Working Papers* are to be used in the study of Chapters 1–10 of CENTURY 21 ACCOUNTING ADVANCED, 9E. Forms are provided for:

1. Study Guides
2. Work Together Exercises
3. On Your Own Exercises
4. Application Problems
5. Mastery Problems
6. Challenge Problems
7. Reinforcement Activity 1

Printed on each page is the number of the problem in the textbook for which the form is to be used. Also shown is a specific instruction number for which the form is to be used.

You may not be required to use every form that is provided. Your teacher will tell you whether to retain or dispose of the unused pages.

The pages are perforated so they may be removed as the work required in each assignment is completed. The pages will be more easily detached if you crease the sheet along the line of perforations and then remove the sheet by pulling sideways rather than upward.

Name		Perfect Score	Your Score
Identifying Accounting Terms		24 Pts.	
Analyzing Accounting Principles, Concepts, and Procedures		20 Pts.	
	Total	44 Pts.	

Part One—Identifying Accounting Terms

Directions: Select the one term in Column I that best fits each definition in Column II. Print the letter identifying your choice in the Answers column.

Column I	Column II	Answers
A. account	**1.** Anything of value that is owned. (p. 7)	1. _____
B. accounting equation	**2.** An amount owed by a business. (p. 7)	2. _____
	3. Financial rights to the assets of a business. (p. 7)	3. _____
C. asset	**4.** The amount remaining after the value of all liabilities is subtracted from the value of all assets. (p. 7)	4. _____
D. cash discount		
	5. The owners' equity in a corporation. (p. 7)	5. _____
E. contra account	**6.** An equation showing the relationship among assets, liabilities, and owners' equity. (p. 7)	6. _____
F. controlling account		
	7. Business papers from which information is obtained for a journal entry. (p. 7)	7. _____
G. debit memorandum		
H. departmental accounting system	**8.** The recording of debit and credit parts of a transaction. (p. 8)	8. _____
	9. A form for recording transactions in chronological order. (p. 8)	9. _____
I. double-entry accounting		
	10. A journal used to record only one kind of transaction. (p. 8)	10. _____
J. equities	**11.** A record summarizing all the information pertaining to a single item in the accounting equation. (p. 9)	11. _____
K. file maintenance	**12.** A group of accounts. (p. 10)	12. _____
L. general ledger	**13.** A ledger that contains all accounts needed to prepare financial statements. (p. 10)	13. _____
M. journal	**14.** A ledger that is summarized in a single general ledger account. (p. 10)	14. _____
N. ledger		
O. liability	**15.** An account in a general ledger that summarizes all accounts in a subsidiary ledger. (p. 10)	15. _____
P. merchandising business	**16.** The procedure for arranging accounts in a general ledger, assigning account numbers, and keeping records current. (p. 10)	16. _____
Q. owners' equity	**17.** An accounting system showing accounting information for two or more departments. (p. 12)	17. _____
R. petty cash	**18.** A business that purchases and sells goods. (p. 12)	18. _____
S. posting	**19.** Transferring transaction information from a journal entry to a ledger account. (p. 14)	19. _____

Column I	**Column II**	**Answers**
T. purchases discount	**20.** A form prepared by the customer showing the price deduction for purchase returns and allowances. (p. 16)	**20.** _____
U. source documents	**21.** An account that reduces a related account on a financial statement. (p. 16)	**21.** _____
V. special journal	**22.** A deduction that a vendor allows on the invoice amount to encourage prompt payment. (p. 18)	**22.** _____
W. stockholders' equity	**23.** A cash discount on purchases taken by a customer. (p. 18)	**23.** _____
X. subsidiary ledger	**24.** An amount of cash kept on hand and used for making small payments. (p. 22)	**24.** _____

Part Two—Analyzing Accounting Principles, Concepts, and Procedures

Directions: Place a *T* for True or an *F* for False in the Answers column to show whether each of the following statements is true or false.

Answers

1. The accounting equation may be stated as assets = liabilities. (p. 7)

    1. _____

2. A business with many daily transactions may use special journals. (p. 8)

    2. _____

3. Liability accounts have normal credit balances. (p. 9)

    3. _____

4. An owners' equity account has a normal credit balance. (p. 9)

    4. _____

5. Revenue accounts have normal debit balances. (p. 9)

    5. _____

6. Expense accounts have normal credit balances. (p. 9)

    6. _____

7. Increases in asset accounts are recorded on the debit side. (p. 9)

    7. _____

8. Increases in liability accounts are recorded on the debit side. (p. 9)

    8. _____

9. Increases in owners' equity accounts are recorded on the debit side. (p. 9)

    9. _____

10. Decreases in revenue accounts are recorded on the credit side. (p. 9)

    10. _____

11. Decreases in expense accounts are recorded on the credit side. (p. 9)

    11. _____

12. In a departmental accounting system, gross profit is calculated for each department. (p. 12)

    12. _____

13. A departmental purchases journal should contain a Purchases Debit column for each department. (p. 12)

    13. _____

14. Individual amounts in the Accounts Payable Credit column of the purchases journal are posted at the end of each month. (p. 14)

    14. _____

15. When a customer returns merchandise for credit, the customer issues a debit memorandum for the amount of the return. (p. 16)

    15. _____

16. Using a check as the source document for a cash payment transaction is an application of the accounting concept Objective Evidence. (p. 18)

    16. _____

17. A purchases discount is usually stated as a percentage. (p. 18)

    17. _____

18. A discount is calculated on the original purchase price, even if a purchase return or allowance has been granted. (p. 20)

    18. _____

19. The petty cash fund is replenished on the last business day of each fiscal period. (p. 22)

    19. _____

20. Amounts in the General Debit and General Credit columns of a cash payments journal are posted individually. (p. 23)

    20. _____

1-1 WORK TOGETHER, p. 11

Determining the normal balance, increase, and decrease sides for accounts

Determining the normal balance, increase, and decrease sides for accounts

1-2 WORK TOGETHER, p. 17

Journalizing and posting purchases on account and purchases returns and allowances [1, 2, 4]

PURCHASES JOURNAL   PAGE 3

	DATE		ACCOUNT CREDITED	PURCH. NO.	POST. REF.	ACCOUNTS PAYABLE CREDIT (1)	PURCHASES DEBIT	
							DISCS (2)	TAPES (3)
1									1
2									2
3									3
4									4
5									5
6									6
7									7
8									8
9									9
10									10
11									11

[1, 3]

GENERAL JOURNAL   PAGE 3

	DATE		ACCOUNT TITLE	DOC. NO.	POST. REF.	DEBIT	CREDIT	
1								1
2								2
3								3
4								4
5								5
6								6
7								7
8								8
9								9
10								10
11								11
12								12
13								13
14								14
15								15

Journalizing and posting purchases on account and purchases returns and allowances [1, 2, 4]

PURCHASES JOURNAL   PAGE 4

	DATE	ACCOUNT CREDITED	PURCH. NO.	POST. REF.	ACCOUNTS PAYABLE CREDIT	PURCHASES DEBIT	
						DISCS	TAPES
1								1
2								2
3								3
4								4
5								5
6								6
7								7
8								8
9								9
10								10
11								11

[1, 3]

GENERAL JOURNAL   PAGE 4

	DATE	ACCOUNT TITLE	DOC. NO.	POST. REF.	DEBIT	CREDIT	
1							1
2							2
3							3
4							4
5							5
6							6
7							7
8							8
9							9
10							10
11							11
12							12
13							13
14							14
15							15

1-2 **WORK TOGETHER**
ON YOUR OWN (continued)

GENERAL LEDGER

[2–4]

ACCOUNT Accounts Payable   ACCOUNT NO. 2105

DATE		ITEM	POST. REF.	DEBIT	CREDIT	BALANCE	
						DEBIT	CREDIT
Mar.²⁰⁻⁻	1	Balance	✓				2 1 7 0 00

ACCOUNT Purchases—Discs   ACCOUNT NO. 5105

DATE	ITEM	POST. REF.	DEBIT	CREDIT	BALANCE	
					DEBIT	CREDIT

ACCOUNT Purchases Returns and Allowances—Discs   ACCOUNT NO. 5115

DATE	ITEM	POST. REF.	DEBIT	CREDIT	BALANCE	
					DEBIT	CREDIT

ACCOUNT Purchases—Tapes   ACCOUNT NO. 5205

DATE	ITEM	POST. REF.	DEBIT	CREDIT	BALANCE	
					DEBIT	CREDIT

ACCOUNT Purchases Returns and Allowances—Tapes   ACCOUNT NO. 5215

DATE	ITEM	POST. REF.	DEBIT	CREDIT	BALANCE DEBIT	BALANCE CREDIT

ACCOUNTS PAYABLE LEDGER

VENDOR Artex Music   VENDOR NO. 210

DATE		ITEM	POST. REF.	DEBIT	CREDIT	CREDIT BALANCE
20-- Mar.	1	Balance	✔			4 8 0 00

VENDOR Castle Records and Tapes   VENDOR NO. 220

DATE		ITEM	POST. REF.	DEBIT	CREDIT	CREDIT BALANCE
20-- Mar.	1	Balance	✔			7 6 0 00

VENDOR Dade, Inc.   VENDOR NO. 230

DATE		ITEM	POST. REF.	DEBIT	CREDIT	CREDIT BALANCE
20-- Mar.	1	Balance	✔			5 7 0 00

1-2 WORK TOGETHER
ON YOUR OWN (concluded)

[2–4]

VENDOR Park Recording Company   VENDOR NO. 260

DATE		ITEM	POST. REF.	DEBIT	CREDIT	CREDIT BALANCE
20-- Mar.	1	Balance	✔			3 6 0 00

VENDOR Quality Tapes   VENDOR NO. 270

DATE	ITEM	POST. REF.	DEBIT	CREDIT	CREDIT BALANCE

VENDOR Raymond Wholesalers   VENDOR NO. 280

DATE	ITEM	POST. REF.	DEBIT	CREDIT	CREDIT BALANCE

Journalizing and posting departmental cash payments [1–3]

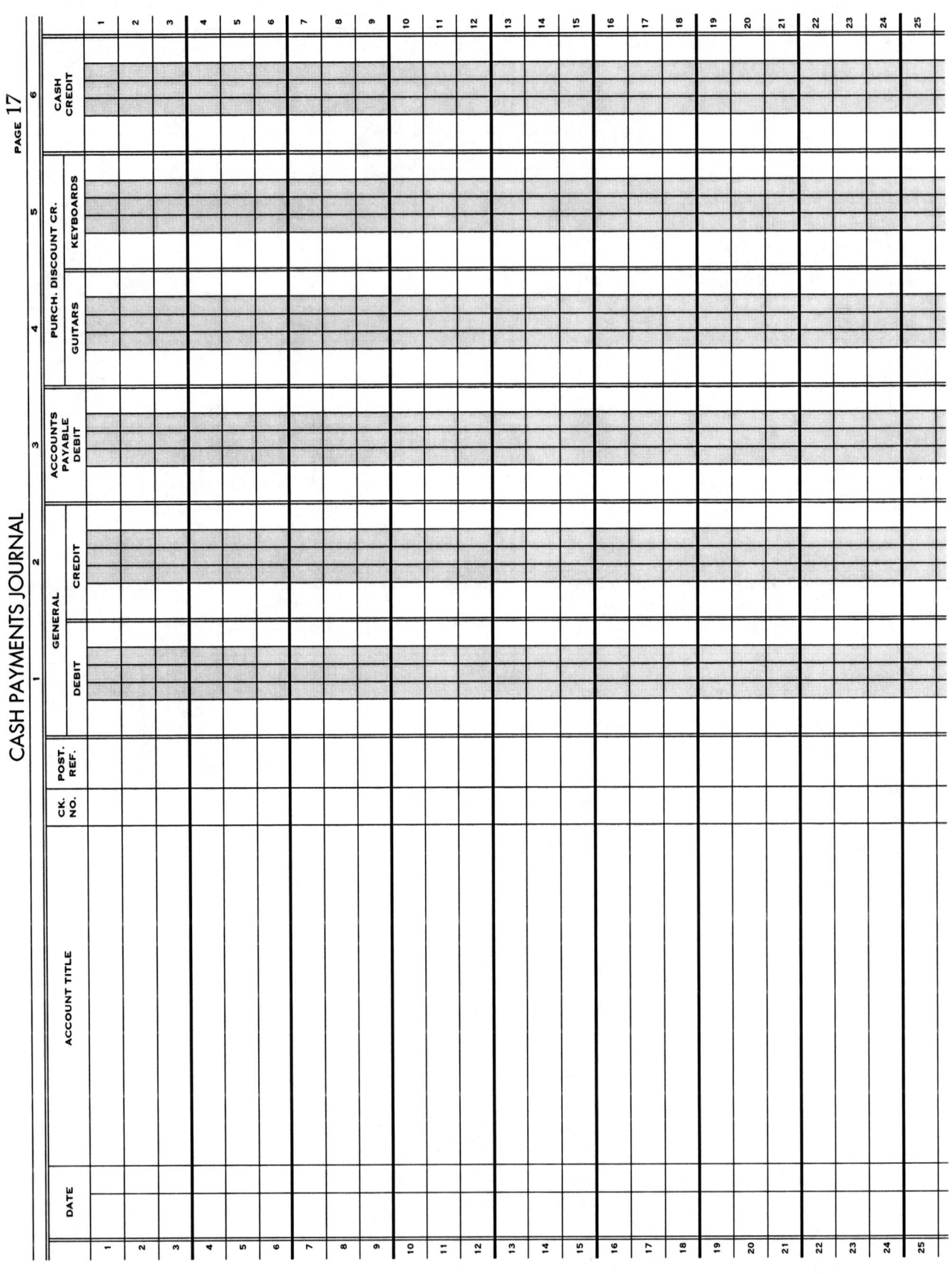

CASH PAYMENTS JOURNAL

PAGE 17

1-3 **WORK TOGETHER (continued)**

[2, 3]

GENERAL LEDGER

ACCOUNT Cash   ACCOUNT NO. 1105

DATE		ITEM	POST. REF.	DEBIT	CREDIT	BALANCE	
						DEBIT	CREDIT
Sept.	1	Balance	✔			23 1 2 0 00	

ACCOUNT Petty Cash   ACCOUNT NO. 1110

DATE		ITEM	POST. REF.	DEBIT	CREDIT	BALANCE	
						DEBIT	CREDIT
Sept.	1	Balance	✔			3 0 0 00	

ACCOUNT Supplies—Administrative   ACCOUNT NO. 1315

DATE		ITEM	POST. REF.	DEBIT	CREDIT	BALANCE	
						DEBIT	CREDIT
Sept.	1	Balance	✔			2 5 6 0 00	

ACCOUNT Accounts Payable   ACCOUNT NO. 2105

DATE		ITEM	POST. REF.	DEBIT	CREDIT	BALANCE	
						DEBIT	CREDIT
Sept.	1	Balance	✔				8 5 9 3 00

ACCOUNT Purchases Discount—Guitars   ACCOUNT NO. 5110

DATE	ITEM	POST. REF.	DEBIT	CREDIT	BALANCE DEBIT	BALANCE CREDIT

ACCOUNT Purchases Discount—Keyboards   ACCOUNT NO. 5210

DATE	ITEM	POST. REF.	DEBIT	CREDIT	BALANCE DEBIT	BALANCE CREDIT

ACCOUNT Advertising Expense   ACCOUNT NO. 7105

DATE	ITEM	POST. REF.	DEBIT	CREDIT	BALANCE DEBIT	BALANCE CREDIT

1-3 WORK TOGETHER (concluded)

[2, 3]

ACCOUNT Miscellaneous Expense   ACCOUNT NO. 7120

DATE		ITEM	POST. REF.	DEBIT	CREDIT	BALANCE DEBIT	BALANCE CREDIT

ACCOUNTS PAYABLE LEDGER

VENDOR Carmel Music   VENDOR NO. 210

DATE		ITEM	POST. REF.	DEBIT	CREDIT	CREDIT BALANCE
20-- Sept.	1	Balance	✔			1 9 6 3 00

VENDOR Magic Keyboards   VENDOR NO. 220

DATE		ITEM	POST. REF.	DEBIT	CREDIT	CREDIT BALANCE
20-- Sept.	1	Balance	✔			3 8 0 0 00

VENDOR Peninsula Guitar   VENDOR NO. 230

DATE		ITEM	POST. REF.	DEBIT	CREDIT	CREDIT BALANCE
20-- Sept.	1	Balance	✔			2 8 3 0 00

Journalizing and posting departmental cash payments [1-3]

CASH PAYMENTS JOURNAL

PAGE 18

| | | | | GENERAL | | ACCOUNTS PAYABLE DEBIT | PURCH. DISCOUNT CR. | | CASH CREDIT |
DATE	ACCOUNT TITLE	CK. NO.	POST. REF.	DEBIT	CREDIT		CARPET	FURNITURE	
				1	2	3	4	5	6

1-3 **ON YOUR OWN (continued)**

[2, 3]

GENERAL LEDGER

ACCOUNT Cash   ACCOUNT NO. 1105

DATE		ITEM	POST. REF.	DEBIT	CREDIT	BALANCE DEBIT	BALANCE CREDIT
Sept.	1	Balance	✔			23 7 2 0 00	

ACCOUNT Petty Cash   ACCOUNT NO. 1110

DATE		ITEM	POST. REF.	DEBIT	CREDIT	BALANCE DEBIT	BALANCE CREDIT
Sept.	1	Balance	✔			3 0 0 00	

ACCOUNT Supplies—Carpet   ACCOUNT NO. 1315

DATE		ITEM	POST. REF.	DEBIT	CREDIT	BALANCE DEBIT	BALANCE CREDIT
Sept.	1	Balance	✔			2 0 6 0 00	

ACCOUNT Accounts Payable   ACCOUNT NO. 2105

DATE		ITEM	POST. REF.	DEBIT	CREDIT	BALANCE DEBIT	BALANCE CREDIT
Sept.	1	Balance	✔				13 8 7 5 00

ACCOUNT Purchases Discount—Carpet   ACCOUNT NO. 5110

DATE		ITEM	POST. REF.	DEBIT	CREDIT	BALANCE	
						DEBIT	CREDIT

ACCOUNT Purchases Discount—Furniture   ACCOUNT NO. 5210

DATE		ITEM	POST. REF.	DEBIT	CREDIT	BALANCE	
						DEBIT	CREDIT

ACCOUNT Advertising Expense   ACCOUNT NO. 7105

DATE		ITEM	POST. REF.	DEBIT	CREDIT	BALANCE	
						DEBIT	CREDIT

ACCOUNT Miscellaneous Expense   ACCOUNT NO. 7120

DATE		ITEM	POST. REF.	DEBIT	CREDIT	BALANCE	
						DEBIT	CREDIT

1-3 ON YOUR OWN (concluded)

[2, 3]

ACCOUNTS PAYABLE LEDGER

vendor Duro Weave, Inc.   vendor no. 210

DATE		ITEM	POST. REF.	DEBIT	CREDIT	CREDIT BALANCE
20-- Oct.	1	Balance	✔			2 6 0 0 00

vendor Luxor Carpet, Inc.   vendor no. 220

DATE		ITEM	POST. REF.	DEBIT	CREDIT	CREDIT BALANCE
20-- Oct.	1	Balance	✔			4 1 7 5 00

vendor Sophos Furniture Co.   vendor no. 230

DATE		ITEM	POST. REF.	DEBIT	CREDIT	CREDIT BALANCE
20-- Oct.	1	Balance	✔			7 1 0 0 00

Determining the normal balance, increase, and decrease sides for accounts

1	2	3	4	5	6	7	8
Account	Account Classification	Account's Normal Balance		Increase Side		Decrease Side	
		Debit	Credit	Debit	Credit	Debit	Credit

1-2 APPLICATION PROBLEM, p. 26

Journalizing and posting departmental purchases on account and purchases returns and allowances

[1, 2]

PURCHASES JOURNAL   PAGE 11

	DATE	ACCOUNT CREDITED	PURCH. NO.	POST. REF.	ACCOUNTS PAYABLE CREDIT	PURCHASES DEBIT		
						CELLULAR PHONES	PAGERS	
1								1
2								2
3								3
4								4
5								5
6								6
7								7
8								8
9								9
10								10
11								11

[1]

GENERAL JOURNAL   PAGE 3

	DATE	ACCOUNT TITLE	DOC. NO.	POST. REF.	DEBIT	CREDIT	
1							1
2							2
3							3
4							4
5							5
6							6
7							7
8							8
9							9
10							10
11							11
12							12
13							13
14							14
15							15

GENERAL LEDGER

ACCOUNT Accounts Payable   ACCOUNT NO. 2105

DATE		ITEM	POST. REF.	DEBIT	CREDIT	BALANCE DEBIT	BALANCE CREDIT
20-- Oct.	1	Balance	✔				2 6 3 5 00

ACCOUNT Purchases—Cellular Phones   ACCOUNT NO. 5105

DATE	ITEM	POST. REF.	DEBIT	CREDIT	BALANCE DEBIT	BALANCE CREDIT

ACCOUNT Purchases Returns and Allowances—Cellular Phones   ACCOUNT NO. 5115

DATE	ITEM	POST. REF.	DEBIT	CREDIT	BALANCE DEBIT	BALANCE CREDIT

ACCOUNT Purchases—Pagers   ACCOUNT NO. 5205

DATE	ITEM	POST. REF.	DEBIT	CREDIT	BALANCE DEBIT	BALANCE CREDIT

ACCOUNT Purchases Returns and Allowances—Pagers   ACCOUNT NO. 5215

DATE	ITEM	POST. REF.	DEBIT	CREDIT	BALANCE DEBIT	BALANCE CREDIT

1-2 APPLICATION PROBLEM (continued)

[1, 2]

ACCOUNTS PAYABLE LEDGER

VENDOR CarPhone Wholesalers　　　　　　　　　　　VENDOR NO. 210

DATE		ITEM	POST. REF.	DEBIT	CREDIT	CREDIT BALANCE
20-- Oct.	1	Balance	✔			6 5 0 00

VENDOR Cell Advantage, Inc.　　　　　　　　　　　VENDOR NO. 220

DATE		ITEM	POST. REF.	DEBIT	CREDIT	CREDIT BALANCE

VENDOR ComSystems　　　　　　　　　　　VENDOR NO. 230

DATE		ITEM	POST. REF.	DEBIT	CREDIT	CREDIT BALANCE
20-- Oct.	1	Balance	✔			4 3 0 00

VENDOR ExecuPhone　　　　　　　　　　　VENDOR NO. 240

DATE		ITEM	POST. REF.	DEBIT	CREDIT	CREDIT BALANCE

[1, 2]

VENDOR PageMax, Inc.   VENDOR NO. 250

DATE	ITEM	POST. REF.	DEBIT	CREDIT	CREDIT BALANCE

VENDOR Phone Solution   VENDOR NO. 260

DATE	ITEM	POST. REF.	DEBIT	CREDIT	CREDIT BALANCE
Oct. 1	Balance	✔			8 5 0 00

VENDOR Telecom Corporation   VENDOR NO. 270

DATE	ITEM	POST. REF.	DEBIT	CREDIT	CREDIT BALANCE

VENDOR Western Distributors   VENDOR NO. 280

DATE	ITEM	POST. REF.	DEBIT	CREDIT	CREDIT BALANCE
Oct. 1	Balance	✔			7 0 5 00

1-3 APPLICATION PROBLEM, p. 27

Journalizing and posting departmental cash payments

[1, 2]

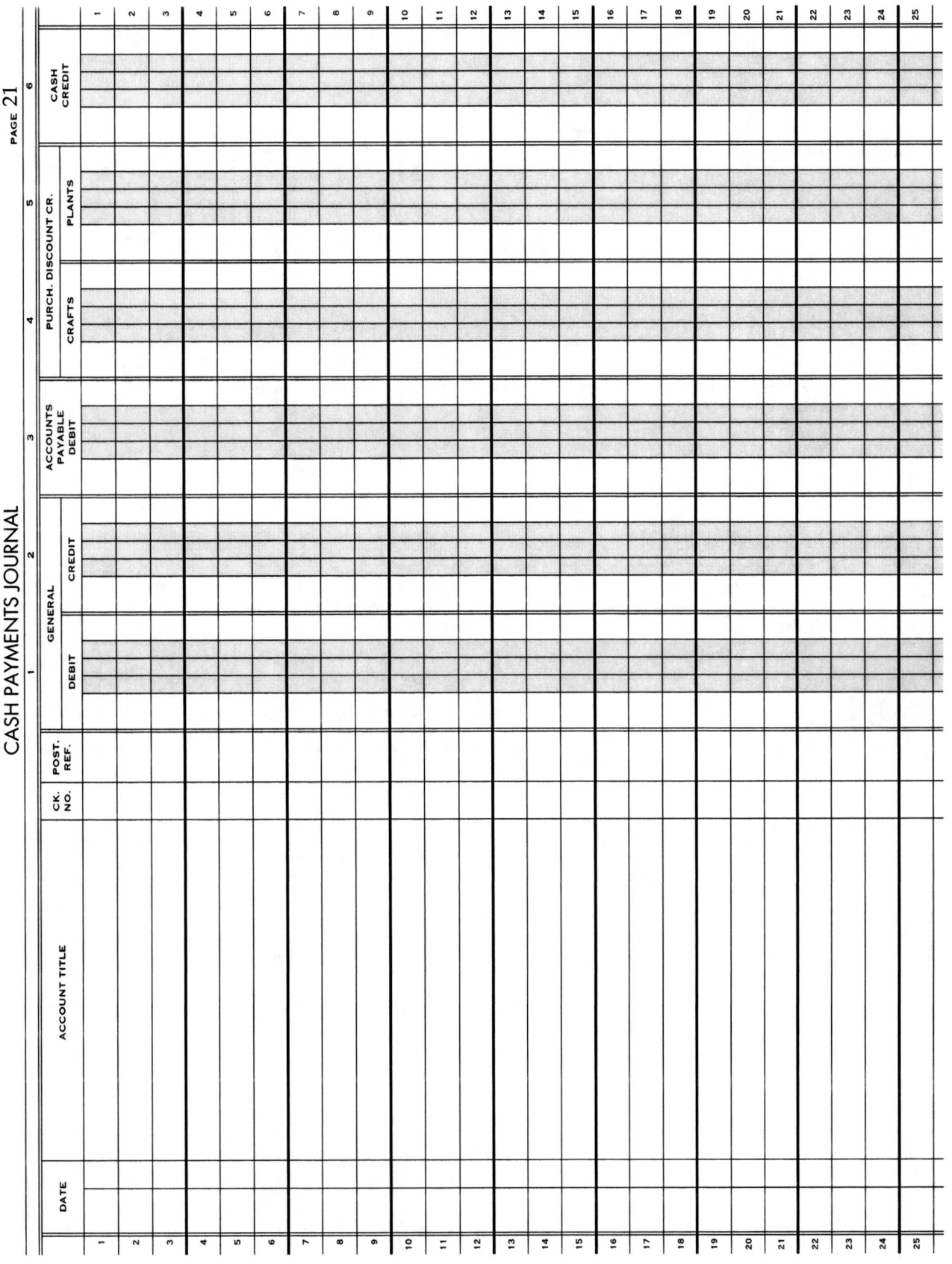

CASH PAYMENTS JOURNAL

PAGE 21

GENERAL LEDGER

ACCOUNT Cash   ACCOUNT NO. 1105

DATE	ITEM	POST. REF.	DEBIT	CREDIT	BALANCE DEBIT	BALANCE CREDIT
Nov. 1	Balance	✔			18 3 8 0 00	

ACCOUNT Petty Cash   ACCOUNT NO. 1110

DATE	ITEM	POST. REF.	DEBIT	CREDIT	BALANCE DEBIT	BALANCE CREDIT
Nov. 1	Balance	✔			5 0 0 00	

ACCOUNT Supplies—Administrative   ACCOUNT NO. 1315

DATE	ITEM	POST. REF.	DEBIT	CREDIT	BALANCE DEBIT	BALANCE CREDIT
Nov. 1	Balance	✔			1 2 6 0 00	

ACCOUNT Accounts Payable   ACCOUNT NO. 2105

DATE	ITEM	POST. REF.	DEBIT	CREDIT	BALANCE DEBIT	BALANCE CREDIT
Nov. 1	Balance	✔				8 8 5 00
30		P11		5 5 1 3 00		6 3 9 8 00

ACCOUNT Purchases Discount—Crafts   ACCOUNT NO. 5110

DATE	ITEM	POST. REF.	DEBIT	CREDIT	BALANCE DEBIT	BALANCE CREDIT

1-3 APPLICATION PROBLEM (continued)

[2]

ACCOUNT Purchases Discount—Plants   ACCOUNT NO. 5210

DATE	ITEM	POST. REF.	DEBIT	CREDIT	BALANCE DEBIT	BALANCE CREDIT

ACCOUNT Advertising Expense   ACCOUNT NO. 7105

DATE	ITEM	POST. REF.	DEBIT	CREDIT	BALANCE DEBIT	BALANCE CREDIT

ACCOUNT Miscellaneous Expense   ACCOUNT NO. 7120

DATE	ITEM	POST. REF.	DEBIT	CREDIT	BALANCE DEBIT	BALANCE CREDIT

ACCOUNT Rent Expense   ACCOUNT NO. 7135

DATE	ITEM	POST. REF.	DEBIT	CREDIT	BALANCE DEBIT	BALANCE CREDIT

ACCOUNTS PAYABLE LEDGER

VENDOR Century Crafts, Inc.   VENDOR NO. 210

DATE	ITEM	POST. REF.	DEBIT	CREDIT	CREDIT BALANCE
20-- Nov. 6		P11		9 6 3 00	9 6 3 00

VENDOR Evergreen Trees & Shrubs   VENDOR NO. 220

DATE	ITEM	POST. REF.	DEBIT	CREDIT	CREDIT BALANCE
20-- Nov. 16		P11		1 8 4 0 00	1 8 4 0 00
20		P11		1 4 6 0 00	3 3 0 0 00

VENDOR Northtown Plants   VENDOR NO. 230

DATE	ITEM	POST. REF.	DEBIT	CREDIT	CREDIT BALANCE
20-- Nov. 3		P11		1 2 5 0 00	1 2 5 0 00

VENDOR Wholesale Crafts, Inc.   VENDOR NO. 240

DATE	ITEM	POST. REF.	DEBIT	CREDIT	CREDIT BALANCE
20-- Nov. 1	Balance	✔			8 8 5 00

1-4 MASTERY PROBLEM, p. 28

Journalizing departmental purchases and cash payments [1–3]

PURCHASES JOURNAL   PAGE 11

	DATE	ACCOUNT CREDITED	PURCH. NO.	POST. REF.	ACCOUNTS PAYABLE CREDIT	PURCHASES DEBIT	
						BACKPACKS	ACCESSORIES
1							
2							
3							
4							
5							
6							
7							
8							
9							
10							
11							

[1]

GENERAL JOURNAL   PAGE 8

	DATE	ACCOUNT TITLE	DOC. NO.	POST. REF.	DEBIT	CREDIT	
1							
2							
3							
4							
5							
6							
7							
8							
9							
10							
11							
12							
13							
14							
15							

CASH PAYMENTS JOURNAL

PAGE 21

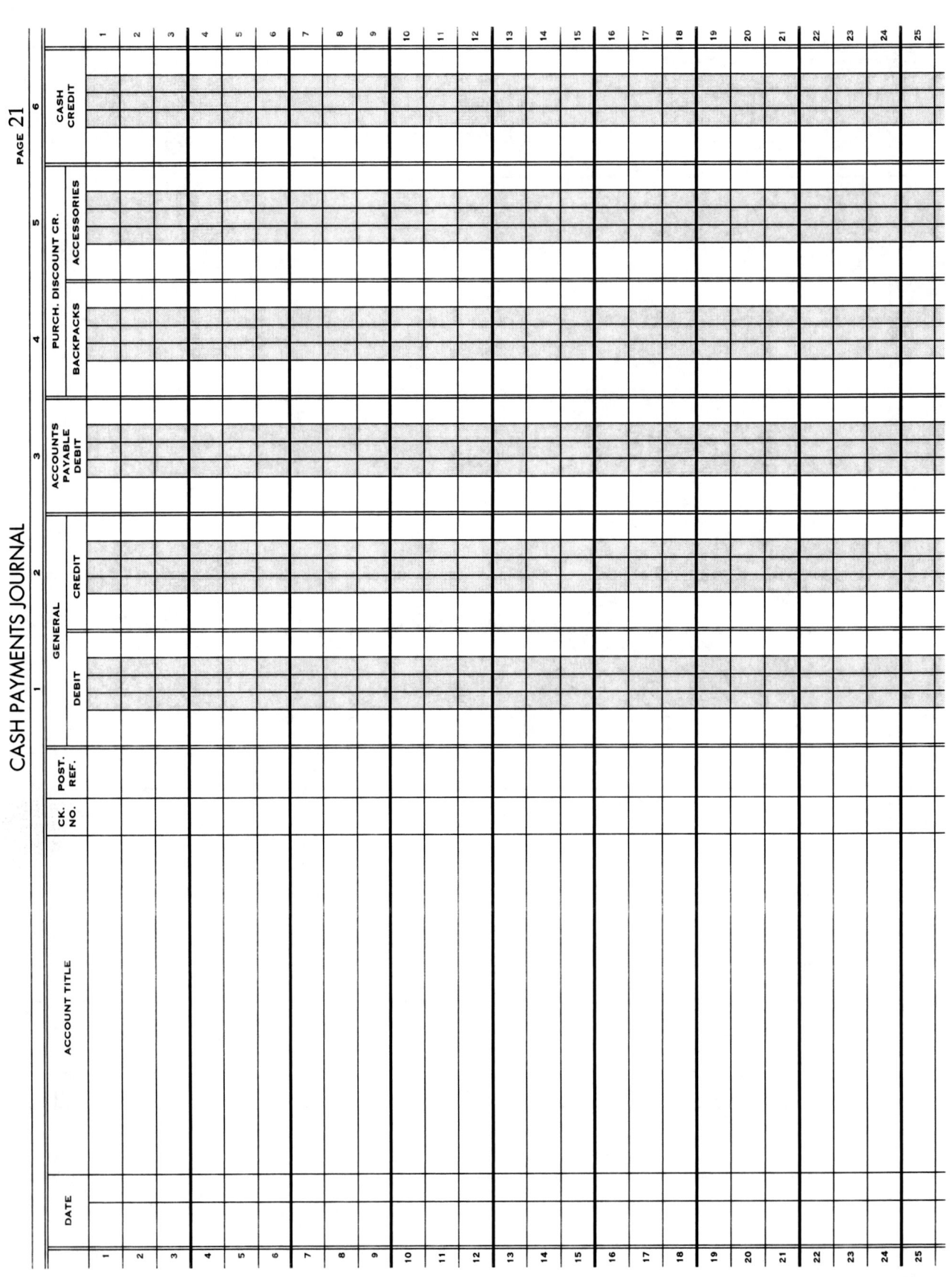

1-4 **MASTERY PROBLEM (continued)**

[1, 3]

GENERAL LEDGER

ACCOUNT Cash   ACCOUNT NO. 1105

DATE		ITEM	POST. REF.	DEBIT	CREDIT	BALANCE	
						DEBIT	CREDIT
20-- Apr.	1	Balance	✔			10 9 4 0 00	

ACCOUNT Supplies—Administrative   ACCOUNT NO. 1315

DATE		ITEM	POST. REF.	DEBIT	CREDIT	BALANCE	
						DEBIT	CREDIT
20-- Apr.	1	Balance	✔			8 5 0 00	

ACCOUNT Accounts Payable   ACCOUNT NO. 2105

DATE		ITEM	POST. REF.	DEBIT	CREDIT	BALANCE	
						DEBIT	CREDIT
20-- Apr.	1	Balance	✔				1 3 5 7 50

ACCOUNT Purchases—Accessories   ACCOUNT NO. 5105

DATE		ITEM	POST. REF.	DEBIT	CREDIT	BALANCE	
						DEBIT	CREDIT
20-- Apr.	1	Balance	✔			6 1 4 0 00	

ACCOUNT Purchases Discount—Accessories   ACCOUNT NO. 5110

DATE		ITEM	POST. REF.	DEBIT	CREDIT	BALANCE DEBIT	BALANCE CREDIT
Apr.	1	Balance	✔				1 0 1 50

ACCOUNT Purchases Returns and Allowances—Accessories   ACCOUNT NO. 5115

DATE		ITEM	POST. REF.	DEBIT	CREDIT	BALANCE DEBIT	BALANCE CREDIT
Apr.	1	Balance	✔				8 5 2 00

ACCOUNT Purchases—Backpacks   ACCOUNT NO. 5205

DATE		ITEM	POST. REF.	DEBIT	CREDIT	BALANCE DEBIT	BALANCE CREDIT
Apr.	1	Balance	✔			12 8 1 0 00	

ACCOUNT Purchases Discount—Backpacks   ACCOUNT NO. 5210

DATE		ITEM	POST. REF.	DEBIT	CREDIT	BALANCE DEBIT	BALANCE CREDIT
Apr.	1	Balance	✔				1 2 7 00

1-4 **MASTERY PROBLEM (continued)**

[1, 3]

ACCOUNT Purchases Returns and Allowances—Backpacks   ACCOUNT NO. 5215

DATE		ITEM	POST. REF.	DEBIT	CREDIT	BALANCE DEBIT	BALANCE CREDIT
20-- Apr.	1	Balance	✔				3 1 5 00

ACCOUNT Advertising Expense   ACCOUNT NO. 7105

DATE		ITEM	POST. REF.	DEBIT	CREDIT	BALANCE DEBIT	BALANCE CREDIT
20-- Apr.	1	Balance	✔			2 1 5 00	

ACCOUNT Miscellaneous Expense   ACCOUNT NO. 7125

DATE		ITEM	POST. REF.	DEBIT	CREDIT	BALANCE DEBIT	BALANCE CREDIT
20-- Apr.	1	Balance	✔			2 5 1 00	

ACCOUNT Rent Expense   ACCOUNT NO. 7140

DATE		ITEM	POST. REF.	DEBIT	CREDIT	BALANCE DEBIT	BALANCE CREDIT
20-- Apr.	1	Balance	✔			3 7 5 0 00	

ACCOUNTS PAYABLE LEDGER

VENDOR CampAll, Inc.   VENDOR NO. 210

DATE	ITEM	POST. REF.	DEBIT	CREDIT	CREDIT BALANCE

VENDOR CampWorld Supplies   VENDOR NO. 220

DATE	ITEM	POST. REF.	DEBIT	CREDIT	CREDIT BALANCE
20-- Apr. 1	Balance	✔			6 4 5 00

VENDOR PackGear   VENDOR NO. 230

DATE	ITEM	POST. REF.	DEBIT	CREDIT	CREDIT BALANCE
20-- Apr. 1	Balance	✔			5 0 0 00

VENDOR Sequoia Sporting Goods   VENDOR NO. 240

DATE	ITEM	POST. REF.	DEBIT	CREDIT	CREDIT BALANCE
20-- Apr. 1	Balance	✔			1 3 2 50

1-4 MASTERY PROBLEM (concluded)

[1, 3]

VENDOR SierraPack   VENDOR NO. 250

DATE	ITEM	POST. REF.	DEBIT	CREDIT	CREDIT BALANCE

VENDOR TahoeDesigns   VENDOR NO. 260

DATE	ITEM	POST. REF.	DEBIT	CREDIT	CREDIT BALANCE

Journalizing purchases at net amount and using the account Discounts Lost [1, 2]

PURCHASES JOURNAL PAGE 11

					1	2	3	
	DATE	ACCOUNT CREDITED	PURCH. NO.	POST. REF.	ACCOUNTS PAYABLE CREDIT	PURCHASES DEBIT		
						BACKPACKS	ACCESSORIES	
1								1
2								2
3								3
4								4
5								5
6								6
7								7
8								8
9								9
10								10
11								11

[1]

GENERAL JOURNAL PAGE 8

	DATE	ACCOUNT TITLE	DOC. NO.	POST. REF.	DEBIT	CREDIT	
1							1
2							2
3							3
4							4
5							5
6							6
7							7
8							8
9							9
10							10
11							11
12							12
13							13
14							14
15							15

1-5 CHALLENGE PROBLEM (concluded)

[1, 2]

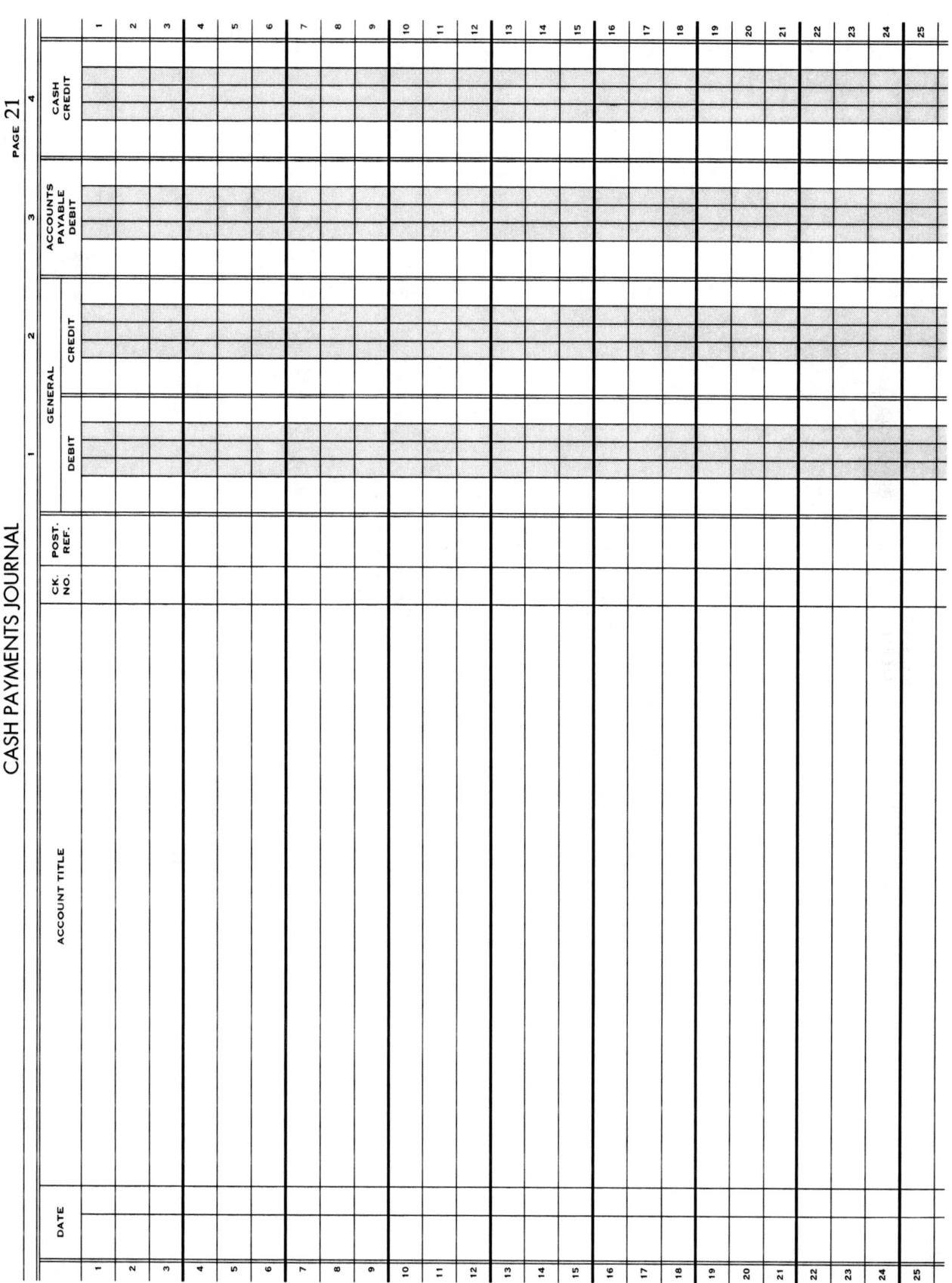

CASH PAYMENTS JOURNAL

PAGE 21

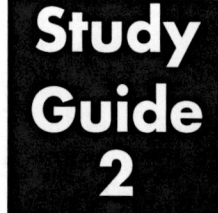

Name	Perfect Score	Your Score
Analyzing Departmental Accounting Procedures	15 Pts.	
Analyzing Departmental Sales and Cash Receipts	13 Pts.	
Total	28 Pts.	

Part One—Analyzing Departmental Accounting Procedures

Directions: Place a *T* for True or an *F* for False in the Answers column to show whether each of the following statements is true or false.

Answers

1. Records of departmental operating expenses are necessary to determine departmental gross profit from operations. (p. 34) — 1. _____

2. In a departmental business, each sales invoice shows the amount of merchandise sold by department. (p. 36) — 2. _____

3. Preparing two copies of a sales invoice provides a copy for the customer and a copy for the business to use for journalizing the transaction. (p. 36) — 3. _____

4. Each departmental sales journal entry is posted individually as a credit to the appropriate customer's account. (p. 38) — 4. _____

5. After posting a line of departmental sales journal, the customer number is recorded in the journal's Post. Ref. column. (p. 38) — 5. _____

6. An account showing deductions from a sales account is known as a contra cost account. (p. 40) — 6. _____

7. The vendor prepares a debit memorandum for a sales returns and allowances transaction. (p. 40) — 7. _____

8. A cash discount on sales is called a sales discount. (p. 44) — 8. _____

9. A departmental cash receipts journal contains a Cash Debit column for each department. (p. 45) — 9. _____

10. Both the debit part and the credit part of a cash or credit card sales transaction are entered in special amount columns in a departmental cash receipts journal. (p. 47) — 10. _____

11. Each amount in the Accounts Receivable Credit column of a departmental cash receipts journal is posted individually to the accounts receivable ledger. (p. 48) — 11. _____

12. Each amount in the Sales Credit columns of a departmental cash receipts journal is posted often to the appropriate account in the general ledger. (p. 48) — 12. _____

13. Each amount in the Cash Debit column of a departmental cash receipts journal is posted individually to the debit side of the cash account. (p. 48) — 13. _____

14. The total of the Sales Credit column of a departmental cash receipts journal is posted to a general ledger account. (p. 48) — 14. _____

15. After the totals of special amount columns have been posted, the general ledger account numbers are written in parentheses below the special columns in the cash receipts journal. (p. 48) — 15. _____

Part Two—Analyzing Departmental Sales and Cash Receipts

Directions: For each item below, select the choice that best completes the sentence. Print the letter identifying your choice in the Answers column.

1. One item of information available through a departmental accounting system is the (A) net income or net loss for each department (B) gross profit from operations for each department (C) administrative expenses for each department (D) total operating expenses for each department. (p. 34)

    1. _____

2. The source document for recording a transaction in a departmental sales journal is (A) a cash register tape (B) a memorandum (C) a sales invoice (D) an adding machine tape. (p. 36)

    2. _____

3. Recording all sales at the time of sale, regardless of when payment is made, is an application of the (A) Going Concern concept (B) Realization of Revenue concept (C) Matching Expenses with Revenue concept (D) Historical Cost concept. (p. 36)

    3. _____

4. When audio equipment subject to sales tax is sold on account, Accounts Receivable is (A) debited for the amount of merchandise sold (B) debited for the amount of merchandise sold plus the sales tax on the merchandise (C) credited for the amount of merchandise sold (D) not affected. (p. 37)

    4. _____

5. In a departmental business, when audio equipment is sold on account, (A) Sales is debited (B) Sales—Audio is debited (C) Sales is credited (D) Sales—Audio is credited. (p. 37)

    5. _____

6. Each amount in the Accounts Receivable Debit column of a departmental sales journal is (A) posted as a debit to a customer's account (B) posted as a credit to a customer's account (C) posted to a controlling account (D) not posted. (p. 38)

    6. _____

7. The total of each column in a departmental sales journal is (A) posted daily (B) posted weekly (C) posted at the end of the month (D) not posted. (p. 39)

    7. _____

8. The account credited when a customer returns merchandise or is granted an allowance is (A) Accounts Payable (B) Sales Returns (C) the appropriate departmental sales account (D) none of these. (p. 40)

    8. _____

9. The source document for a sales returns and allowances transaction is (A) a sales invoice (B) a debit memorandum (C) a credit memorandum (D) none of these. (p. 40)

    9. _____

10. Sales returns and allowances are posted (A) monthly to a customer's account in the general ledger (B) frequently to a customer's account in the general ledger (C) monthly to a customer's account in the accounts receivable ledger (D) frequently to a customer's account in the accounts receivable ledger. (p. 42)

    10. _____

11. A business offers a sales discount (A) because of state laws (B) to encourage early payment (C) to get repeat business from the customer (D) none of these. (p. 44)

    11. _____

12. The terms 2/10, n/30 mean (A) a 2% sales discount may be deducted if sales on account are paid within 30 days of the invoice date (B) a 2% sales discount may be deducted if sales on account are paid within 10 days (C) all sales on account must be paid within 30 days (D) B and C. (p. 44)

    12. _____

13. Businesses post transactions affecting vendor and customer accounts (A) often during the month (B) only at the end of the month (C) only when financial statements must be prepared (D) at the end of a fiscal period. (p. 49)

    13. _____

2-1 WORK TOGETHER, p. 43

**Journalizing and posting departmental sales on account and
sales returns and allowances**

[1, 2]

SALES JOURNAL

PAGE 9

	DATE	ACCOUNT DEBITED	SALE NO.	POST. REF.	ACCOUNTS RECEIVABLE DEBIT	SALES TAX PAYABLE CREDIT	SALES CREDIT	
					1	2	SWIMWEAR 3	ACCESSORIES 4
1								1
2								2
3								3
4								4
5								5
6								6
7								7
8								8
9								9
10								10
11								11

[1]

GENERAL JOURNAL

PAGE 18

	DATE	ACCOUNT TITLE	DOC. NO.	POST. REF.	DEBIT	CREDIT	
1							1
2							2
3							3
4							4
5							5
6							6
7							7
8							8
9							9
10							10
11							11
12							12
13							13
14							14
15							15

GENERAL LEDGER

ACCOUNT Accounts Receivable   ACCOUNT NO. 1205

DATE		ITEM	POST. REF.	DEBIT	CREDIT	BALANCE	
						DEBIT	CREDIT
Sept. 20--	1	Balance	✔			1 5 5 8 75	

ACCOUNT Sales Tax Payable   ACCOUNT NO. 2230

DATE		ITEM	POST. REF.	DEBIT	CREDIT	BALANCE	
						DEBIT	CREDIT
Sept. 20--	1	Balance	✔				1 2 3 20

ACCOUNT Sales—Swimwear   ACCOUNT NO. 4105

DATE		ITEM	POST. REF.	DEBIT	CREDIT	BALANCE	
						DEBIT	CREDIT

ACCOUNT Sales Returns and Allowances—Swimwear   ACCOUNT NO. 4115

DATE		ITEM	POST. REF.	DEBIT	CREDIT	BALANCE	
						DEBIT	CREDIT

ACCOUNT Sales—Accessories   ACCOUNT NO. 4205

DATE		ITEM	POST. REF.	DEBIT	CREDIT	BALANCE	
						DEBIT	CREDIT

ACCOUNT Sales Returns and Allowances—Accessories   ACCOUNT NO. 4215

DATE		ITEM	POST. REF.	DEBIT	CREDIT	BALANCE	
						DEBIT	CREDIT

2-1 **WORK TOGETHER (concluded)**

ACCOUNTS RECEIVABLE LEDGER

CUSTOMER Emily Branford   CUSTOMER NO. 110

DATE		ITEM	POST. REF.	DEBIT	CREDIT	DEBIT BALANCE
20-- Sept.	1	Balance	✔			5 5 00

CUSTOMER Roger Minkow   CUSTOMER NO. 120

DATE		ITEM	POST. REF.	DEBIT	CREDIT	DEBIT BALANCE
20-- Sept.	1	Balance	✔			1 3 6 00

CUSTOMER Sara Nunez   CUSTOMER NO. 130

DATE		ITEM	POST. REF.	DEBIT	CREDIT	DEBIT BALANCE
20-- Sept.	1	Balance	✔			4 8 50

CUSTOMER Oak Grove High School Swim Team   CUSTOMER NO. 140

DATE		ITEM	POST. REF.	DEBIT	CREDIT	DEBIT BALANCE
20-- Sept.	1	Balance	✔			7 0 00

**Journalizing and posting departmental sales on account and
sales returns and allowances**   [1, 2]

SALES JOURNAL   PAGE 10

	DATE	ACCOUNT DEBITED	SALE NO.	POST. REF.	1 ACCOUNTS RECEIVABLE DEBIT	2 SALES TAX PAYABLE CREDIT	3 SALES CREDIT EQUIPMENT	4 SALES CREDIT SUPPLIES	
1									1
2									2
3									3
4									4
5									5
6									6
7									7
8									8
9									9
10									10
11									11

[1]

GENERAL JOURNAL   PAGE 20

	DATE	ACCOUNT TITLE	DOC. NO.	POST. REF.	DEBIT	CREDIT	
1							1
2							2
3							3
4							4
5							5
6							6
7							7
8							8
9							9
10							10
11							11
12							12
13							13
14							14
15							15

2-1 **ON YOUR OWN (continued)**

[1, 2]

GENERAL LEDGER

account Accounts Receivable   ACCOUNT NO. 1205

DATE		ITEM	POST. REF.	DEBIT	CREDIT	BALANCE	
						DEBIT	CREDIT
Oct.	1	Balance	✔			2 1 5 0 00	

account Sales Tax Payable   ACCOUNT NO. 2230

DATE		ITEM	POST. REF.	DEBIT	CREDIT	BALANCE	
						DEBIT	CREDIT
Oct.	1	Balance	✔				1 1 0 3 00

account Sales—Equipment   ACCOUNT NO. 4105

DATE		ITEM	POST. REF.	DEBIT	CREDIT	BALANCE	
						DEBIT	CREDIT

account Sales Returns and Allowances—Equipment   ACCOUNT NO. 4115

DATE		ITEM	POST. REF.	DEBIT	CREDIT	BALANCE	
						DEBIT	CREDIT

account Sales—Supplies   ACCOUNT NO. 4205

DATE		ITEM	POST. REF.	DEBIT	CREDIT	BALANCE	
						DEBIT	CREDIT

account Sales Returns and Allowances—Supplies   ACCOUNT NO. 4215

DATE		ITEM	POST. REF.	DEBIT	CREDIT	BALANCE	
						DEBIT	CREDIT

ACCOUNTS RECEIVABLE LEDGER

CUSTOMER Dunford, Inc.　　　　　　　　　　　　　　　　　　　　　　CUSTOMER NO. 110

DATE		ITEM	POST. REF.	DEBIT	CREDIT	DEBIT BALANCE
20-- Oct.	1	Balance	✔			6 5 5 00

CUSTOMER Libby Products Co.　　　　　　　　　　　　　　　　　　　CUSTOMER NO. 120

DATE		ITEM	POST. REF.	DEBIT	CREDIT	DEBIT BALANCE
20-- Oct.	1	Balance	✔			1 1 3 6 00

CUSTOMER Professional Services Corp.　　　　　　　　　　　　　　CUSTOMER NO. 130

DATE		ITEM	POST. REF.	DEBIT	CREDIT	DEBIT BALANCE
20-- Oct.	1	Balance	✔			1 0 4 8 50

CUSTOMER United Charities　　　　　　　　　　　　　　　　　　　CUSTOMER NO. 140

DATE		ITEM	POST. REF.	DEBIT	CREDIT	DEBIT BALANCE
20-- Oct.	1	Balance	✔			7 0 00

2-2 WORK TOGETHER, p. 50

Journalizing and posting departmental cash receipts [1, 2]

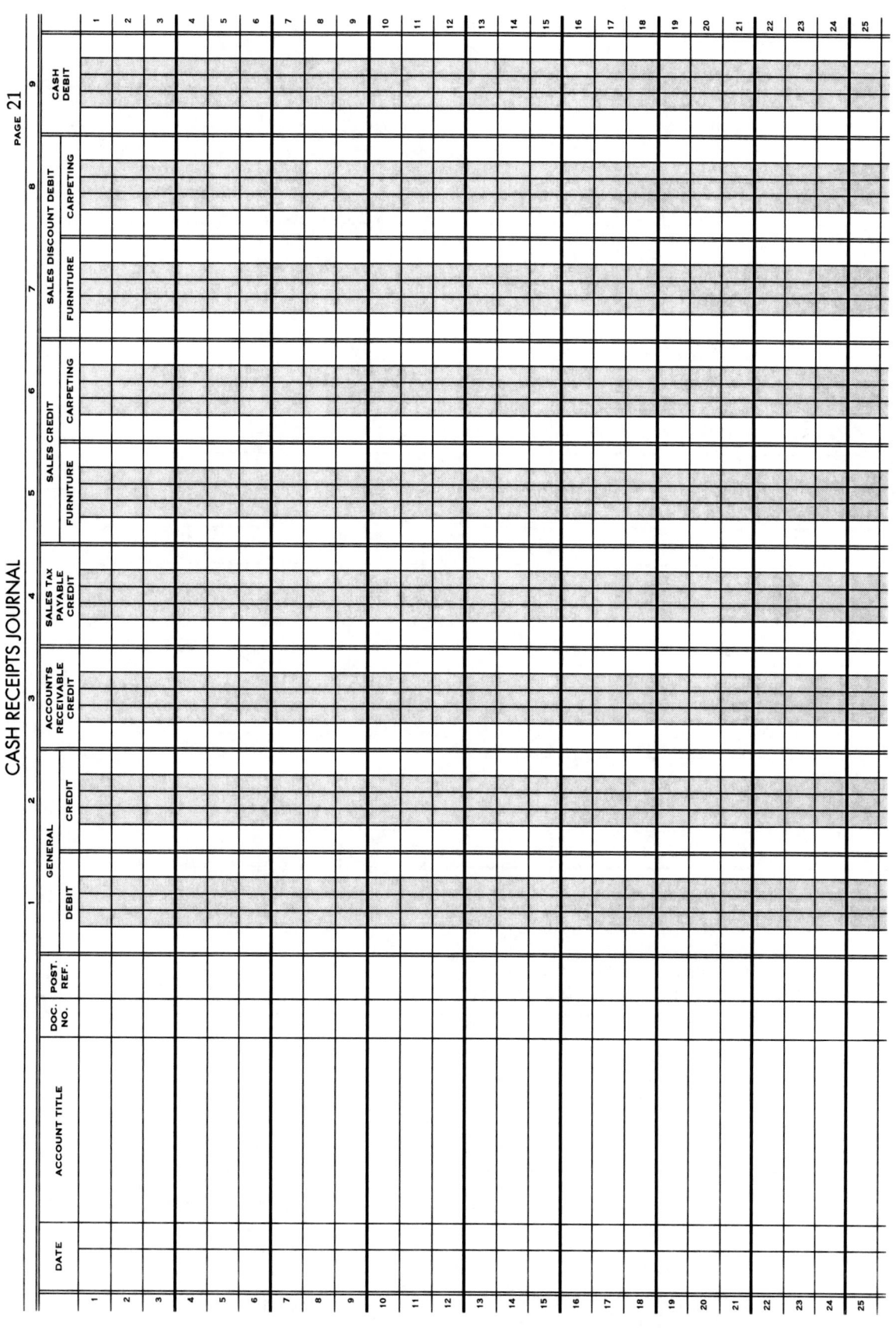

CASH RECEIPTS JOURNAL

PAGE 21

GENERAL LEDGER

ACCOUNT Cash   ACCOUNT NO. 1105

DATE		ITEM	POST. REF.	DEBIT	CREDIT	BALANCE	
						DEBIT	CREDIT
Feb.	1	Balance	✔			43 3 4 0 00	

ACCOUNT Accounts Receivable   ACCOUNT NO. 1205

DATE		ITEM	POST. REF.	DEBIT	CREDIT	BALANCE	
						DEBIT	CREDIT
Feb.	1	Balance	✔			5 7 2 4 00	

ACCOUNT Sales Tax Payable   ACCOUNT NO. 2230

DATE		ITEM	POST. REF.	DEBIT	CREDIT	BALANCE	
						DEBIT	CREDIT
Feb.	1	Balance	✔				3 8 7 0 00

ACCOUNT Sales—Furniture   ACCOUNT NO. 4105

DATE		ITEM	POST. REF.	DEBIT	CREDIT	BALANCE	
						DEBIT	CREDIT

2-2 **WORK TOGETHER (continued)**

[1, 2]

GENERAL LEDGER

ACCOUNT Sales Discount—Furniture   ACCOUNT NO. 4110

DATE	ITEM	POST. REF.	DEBIT	CREDIT	BALANCE DEBIT	BALANCE CREDIT

ACCOUNT Sales—Carpeting   ACCOUNT NO. 4205

DATE	ITEM	POST. REF.	DEBIT	CREDIT	BALANCE DEBIT	BALANCE CREDIT

ACCOUNT Sales Discount—Carpeting   ACCOUNT NO. 4210

DATE	ITEM	POST. REF.	DEBIT	CREDIT	BALANCE DEBIT	BALANCE CREDIT

ACCOUNTS RECEIVABLE LEDGER

CUSTOMER Melinda Ashworth   CUSTOMER NO. 110

DATE		ITEM	POST. REF.	DEBIT	CREDIT	DEBIT BALANCE
20-- Feb.	1	Balance	✔			3 2 8 6 00

CUSTOMER Carlee Hanks   CUSTOMER NO. 120

DATE		ITEM	POST. REF.	DEBIT	CREDIT	DEBIT BALANCE
20-- Feb.	1	Balance	✔			8 4 8 00

CUSTOMER Filo Raines   CUSTOMER NO. 130

DATE		ITEM	POST. REF.	DEBIT	CREDIT	DEBIT BALANCE
20-- Feb.	1	Balance	✔			1 5 9 0 00

2-2 ON YOUR OWN, p. 50

Journalizing and posting departmental cash receipts [1, 2]

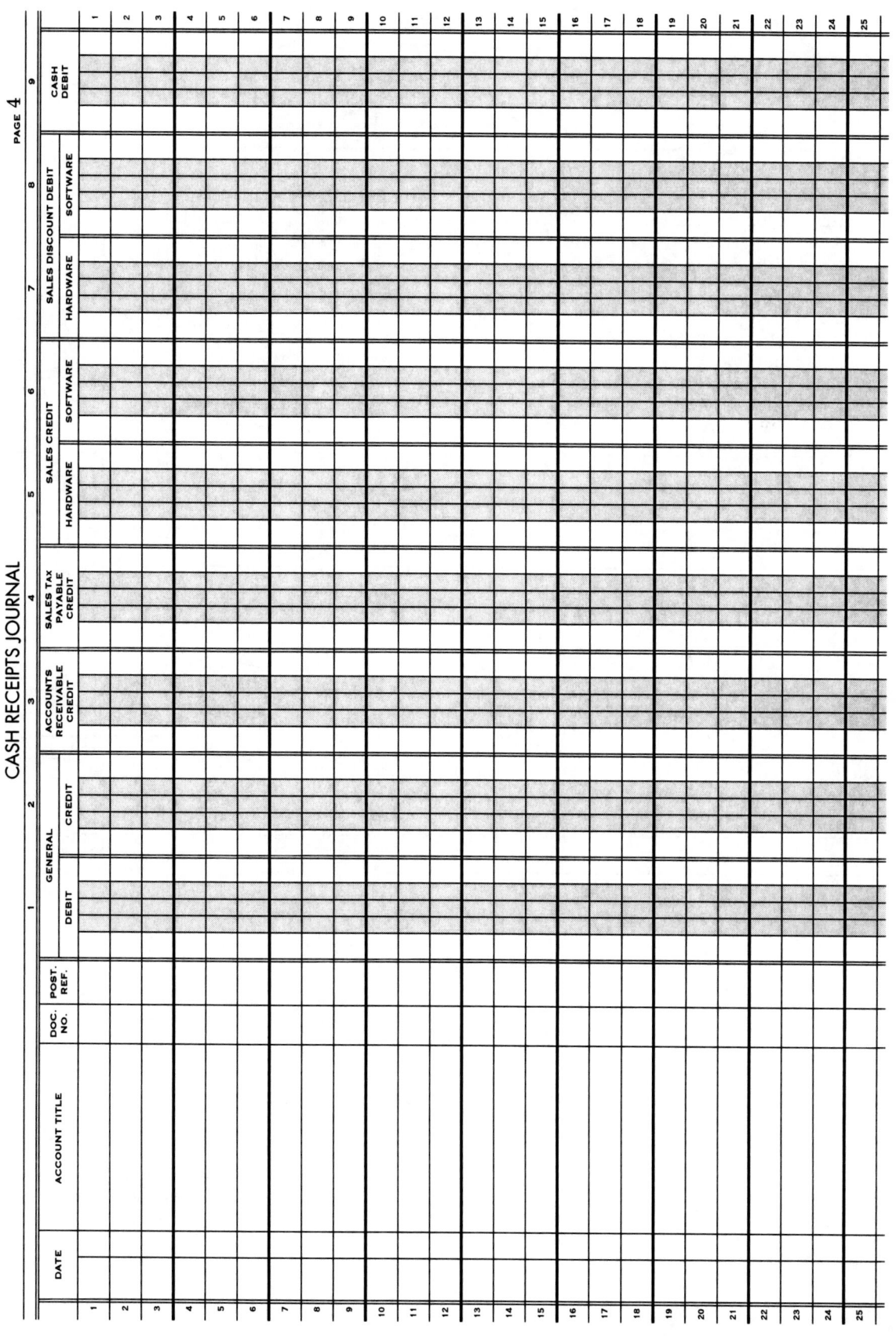

CASH RECEIPTS JOURNAL   PAGE 4

GENERAL LEDGER

ACCOUNT Cash   ACCOUNT NO. 1105

DATE		ITEM	POST. REF.	DEBIT	CREDIT	BALANCE DEBIT	BALANCE CREDIT
Feb.	1	Balance	✔			43 3 4 0 00	

ACCOUNT Accounts Receivable   ACCOUNT NO. 1205

DATE		ITEM	POST. REF.	DEBIT	CREDIT	BALANCE DEBIT	BALANCE CREDIT
Feb.	1	Balance	✔			7 5 5 6 90	

ACCOUNT Sales Tax Payable   ACCOUNT NO. 2230

DATE		ITEM	POST. REF.	DEBIT	CREDIT	BALANCE DEBIT	BALANCE CREDIT
Feb.	1	Balance	✔				1 8 7 0 00

ACCOUNT Sales—Hardware   ACCOUNT NO. 4105

DATE	ITEM	POST. REF.	DEBIT	CREDIT	BALANCE DEBIT	BALANCE CREDIT

GENERAL LEDGER

ACCOUNT Sales Discount—Hardware   ACCOUNT NO. 4110

DATE	ITEM	POST. REF.	DEBIT	CREDIT	BALANCE DEBIT	BALANCE CREDIT

ACCOUNT Sales—Software   ACCOUNT NO. 4205

DATE	ITEM	POST. REF.	DEBIT	CREDIT	BALANCE DEBIT	BALANCE CREDIT

ACCOUNT Sales Discount—Software   ACCOUNT NO. 4210

DATE	ITEM	POST. REF.	DEBIT	CREDIT	BALANCE DEBIT	BALANCE CREDIT

ACCOUNTS RECEIVABLE LEDGER

CUSTOMER Data Systems, Inc.   CUSTOMER NO. 110

DATE		ITEM	POST. REF.	DEBIT	CREDIT	DEBIT BALANCE
20-- Feb.	1	Balance	✔			2 1 4 3 15

CUSTOMER Gear Web Design Co.   CUSTOMER NO. 120

DATE		ITEM	POST. REF.	DEBIT	CREDIT	DEBIT BALANCE
20-- Feb.	1	Balance	✔			1 2 0 3 75

CUSTOMER QuikPrint Co.   CUSTOMER NO. 130

DATE		ITEM	POST. REF.	DEBIT	CREDIT	DEBIT BALANCE
20-- Feb.	1	Balance	✔			4 2 1 0 00

2-1 APPLICATION PROBLEM, p. 52

**Journalizing and posting departmental sales on account and
sales returns and allowances**

[1, 2]

SALES JOURNAL

PAGE 4

	DATE	ACCOUNT DEBITED	SALE NO.	POST. REF.	ACCOUNTS RECEIVABLE DEBIT 1	SALES TAX PAYABLE CREDIT 2	SALES CREDIT CLOTHING 3	SALES CREDIT SHOES 4	
1									1
2									2
3									3
4									4
5									5
6									6
7									7
8									8
9									9
10									10
11									11
12									12

[1]

GENERAL JOURNAL

PAGE 6

	DATE	ACCOUNT TITLE	DOC. NO.	POST. REF.	DEBIT	CREDIT	
1							1
2							2
3							3
4							4
5							5
6							6
7							7
8							8
9							9
10							10
11							11
12							12
13							13
14							14

GENERAL LEDGER

ACCOUNT Accounts Receivable   ACCOUNT NO. 1205

DATE	ITEM	POST. REF.	DEBIT	CREDIT	BALANCE DEBIT	BALANCE CREDIT
20-- Apr. 1	Balance	✔			1 6 5 8 75	

ACCOUNT Sales Tax Payable   ACCOUNT NO. 2230

DATE	ITEM	POST. REF.	DEBIT	CREDIT	BALANCE DEBIT	BALANCE CREDIT
20-- Apr. 1	Balance	✔				1 5 8 70

ACCOUNT Sales—Clothing   ACCOUNT NO. 4105

DATE	ITEM	POST. REF.	DEBIT	CREDIT	BALANCE DEBIT	BALANCE CREDIT

ACCOUNT Sales Returns and Allowances—Clothing   ACCOUNT NO. 4115

DATE	ITEM	POST. REF.	DEBIT	CREDIT	BALANCE DEBIT	BALANCE CREDIT

ACCOUNT Sales—Shoes   ACCOUNT NO. 4205

DATE	ITEM	POST. REF.	DEBIT	CREDIT	BALANCE DEBIT	BALANCE CREDIT

ACCOUNT Sales Returns and Allowances—Shoes   ACCOUNT NO. 4215

DATE	ITEM	POST. REF.	DEBIT	CREDIT	BALANCE DEBIT	BALANCE CREDIT

2-1 **APPLICATION PROBLEM (continued)**

ACCOUNTS RECEIVABLE LEDGER

CUSTOMER Andersen Vocational Center   CUSTOMER NO. 110

DATE		ITEM	POST. REF.	DEBIT	CREDIT	DEBIT BALANCE
Apr.	1	Balance	✔			425 00

CUSTOMER Elias Carrasco   CUSTOMER NO. 120

DATE		ITEM	POST. REF.	DEBIT	CREDIT	DEBIT BALANCE
Apr.	1	Balance	✔			472 50

CUSTOMER Sridhar Duggirala   CUSTOMER NO. 130

DATE		ITEM	POST. REF.	DEBIT	CREDIT	DEBIT BALANCE
Apr.	1	Balance	✔			199 25

CUSTOMER Dean Fujiwara   CUSTOMER NO. 140

DATE		ITEM	POST. REF.	DEBIT	CREDIT	DEBIT BALANCE

CUSTOMER Tianshu Jian   CUSTOMER NO. 150

DATE		ITEM	POST. REF.	DEBIT	CREDIT	DEBIT BALANCE
Apr.	1	Balance	✔			373 00

ACCOUNTS RECEIVABLE LEDGER

CUSTOMER Gail Mahr   CUSTOMER NO. 160

DATE	ITEM	POST. REF.	DEBIT	CREDIT	DEBIT BALANCE

CUSTOMER Jeffrey O'Connell   CUSTOMER NO. 170

DATE	ITEM	POST. REF.	DEBIT	CREDIT	DEBIT BALANCE
20-- Apr. 1	Balance	✔			1 8 9 00

CUSTOMER Thuc Quan   CUSTOMER NO. 180

DATE	ITEM	POST. REF.	DEBIT	CREDIT	DEBIT BALANCE

2-2 APPLICATION PROBLEM, p. 52

Journalizing and posting departmental cash receipts   [1, 2]

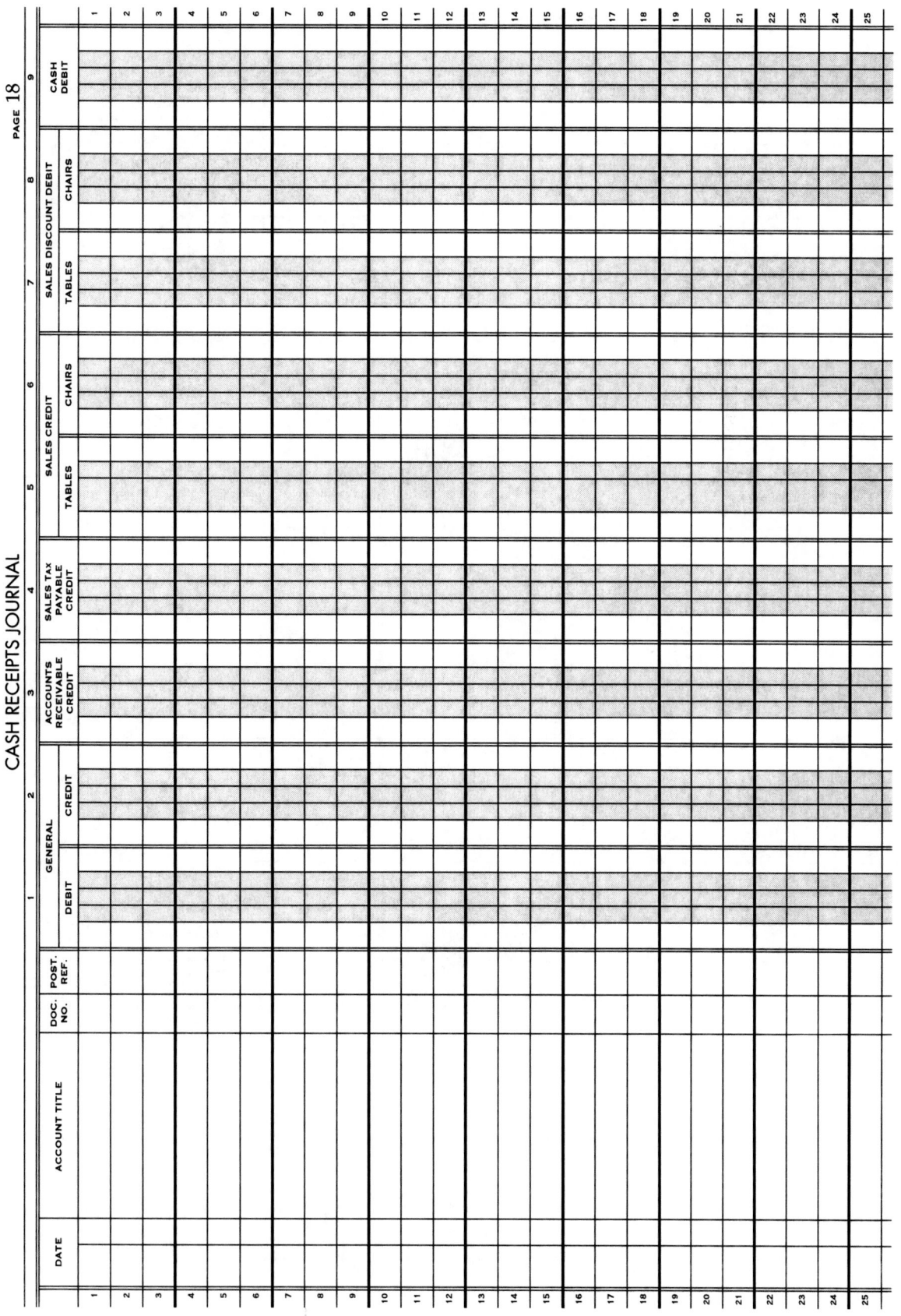

CASH RECEIPTS JOURNAL

PAGE 18

GENERAL LEDGER

ACCOUNT Cash   ACCOUNT NO. 1105

DATE		ITEM	POST. REF.	DEBIT	CREDIT	BALANCE	
						DEBIT	CREDIT
June	1	Balance	✔			59 9 1 3 00	

ACCOUNT Accounts Receivable   ACCOUNT NO. 1205

DATE		ITEM	POST. REF.	DEBIT	CREDIT	BALANCE	
						DEBIT	CREDIT
June	1	Balance	✔			3 5 4 1 20	

ACCOUNT Sales Tax Payable   ACCOUNT NO. 2230

DATE		ITEM	POST. REF.	DEBIT	CREDIT	BALANCE	
						DEBIT	CREDIT
June	1	Balance	✔				4 4 6 00

ACCOUNT Sales—Tables   ACCOUNT NO. 4105

DATE		ITEM	POST. REF.	DEBIT	CREDIT	BALANCE	
						DEBIT	CREDIT

ACCOUNT Sales Discount—Tables   ACCOUNT NO. 4110

DATE		ITEM	POST. REF.	DEBIT	CREDIT	BALANCE	
						DEBIT	CREDIT

2-2 APPLICATION PROBLEM (continued)

[1, 2]

GENERAL LEDGER

ACCOUNT Sales—Chairs   ACCOUNT NO. 4205

DATE	ITEM	POST. REF.	DEBIT	CREDIT	BALANCE DEBIT	BALANCE CREDIT

ACCOUNT Sales Discount—Chairs   ACCOUNT NO. 4210

DATE	ITEM	POST. REF.	DEBIT	CREDIT	BALANCE DEBIT	BALANCE CREDIT

[1]

ACCOUNTS RECEIVABLE LEDGER

CUSTOMER Amy Cannon   CUSTOMER NO. 110

DATE	ITEM	POST. REF.	DEBIT	CREDIT	DEBIT BALANCE
20-- June 1	Balance	✔			8 2 3 70

CUSTOMER Wayne Miller   CUSTOMER NO. 120

DATE	ITEM	POST. REF.	DEBIT	CREDIT	DEBIT BALANCE
20-- June 1	Balance	✔			2 0 0 00

ACCOUNTS RECEIVABLE LEDGER

CUSTOMER Joe Ricardo   CUSTOMER NO. 130

DATE		ITEM	POST. REF.	DEBIT	CREDIT	DEBIT BALANCE
20-- June	1	Balance	✔			1 0 5 9 90

CUSTOMER David Ring   CUSTOMER NO. 140

DATE		ITEM	POST. REF.	DEBIT	CREDIT	DEBIT BALANCE
20-- June	1	Balance	✔			4 5 1 50

CUSTOMER Dawn Sanzone   CUSTOMER NO. 150

DATE		ITEM	POST. REF.	DEBIT	CREDIT	DEBIT BALANCE
20-- June	1	Balance	✔			5 2 5 00

CUSTOMER Bob Witt   CUSTOMER NO. 160

DATE		ITEM	POST. REF.	DEBIT	CREDIT	DEBIT BALANCE
20-- June	1	Balance	✔			4 8 1 10

2-3 MASTERY PROBLEM, p. 53

Journalizing departmental sales, sales returns and allowances, and cash receipts [1, 2]

SALES JOURNAL
PAGE 9

	DATE	ACCOUNT DEBITED	SALE NO.	POST. REF.	ACCOUNTS RECEIVABLE DEBIT (1)	SALES TAX PAYABLE CREDIT (2)	SALES CREDIT	
							JEWELRY (3)	WATCHES (4)
1								
2								
3								
4								
5								
6								
7								
8								
9								
10								
11								

[1]

GENERAL JOURNAL
PAGE 9

	DATE	ACCOUNT TITLE	DOC. NO.	POST. REF.	DEBIT	CREDIT
1						
2						
3						
4						
5						
6						
7						
8						
9						
10						
11						
12						
13						
14						
15						

CASH RECEIPTS JOURNAL

PAGE 12

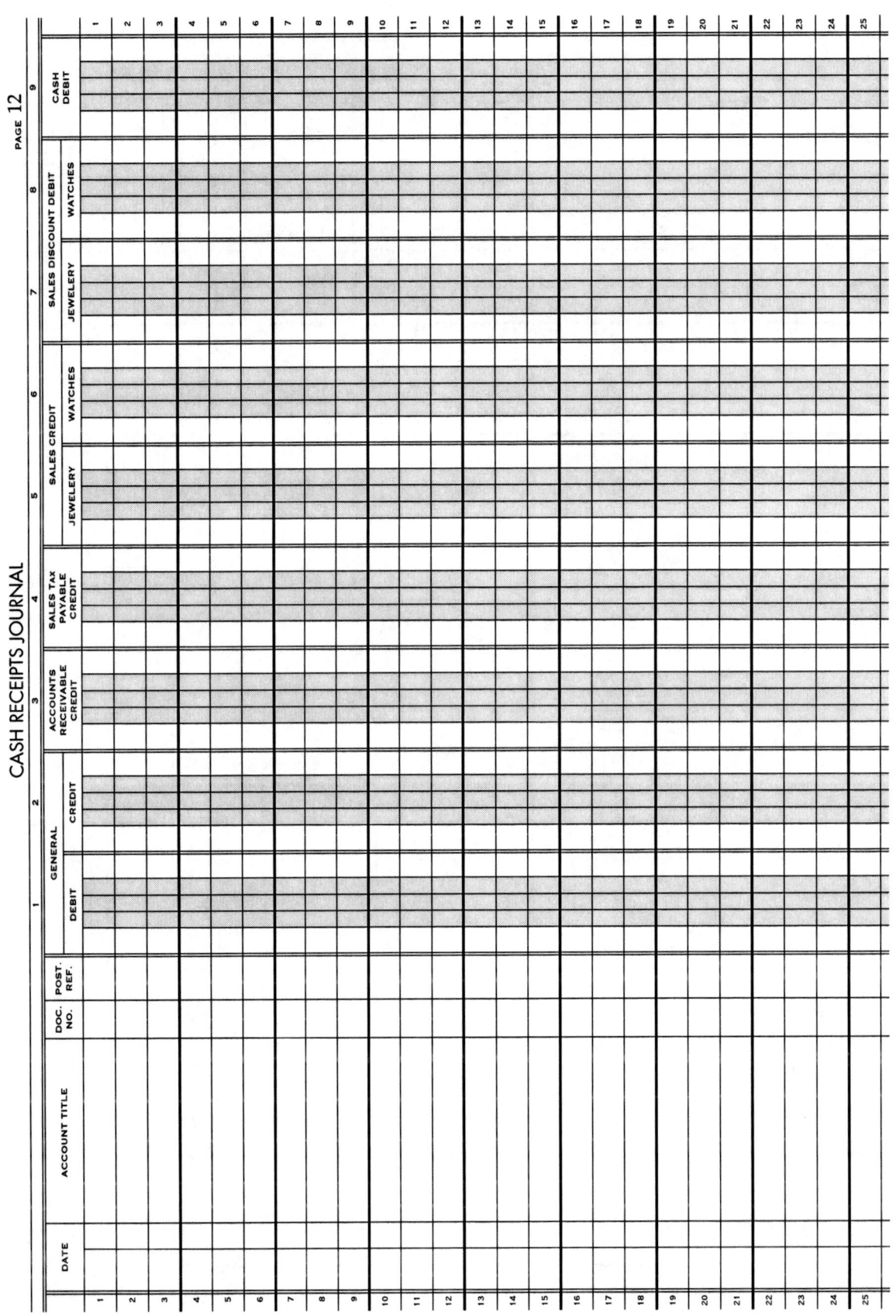

	DATE	ACCOUNT TITLE	DOC. NO.	POST. REF.	GENERAL DEBIT	GENERAL CREDIT	ACCOUNTS RECEIVABLE CREDIT	SALES TAX PAYABLE CREDIT	SALES CREDIT JEWELERY	SALES CREDIT WATCHES	SALES DISCOUNT DEBIT JEWELERY	SALES DISCOUNT DEBIT WATCHES	CASH DEBIT
					1	2	3	4	5	6	7	8	9
1													
2													
3													
4													
5													
6													
7													
8													
9													
10													
11													
12													
13													
14													
15													
16													
17													
18													
19													
20													
21													
22													
23													
24													
25													

2-4 CHALLENGE PROBLEM, p. 54

Journalizing departmental sales, sales returns and allowances, and cash receipts   [1, 2]

SALES JOURNAL

PAGE 9

	DATE	ACCOUNT DEBITED	SALE NO.	POST. REF.	ACCOUNTS RECEIVABLE DEBIT (1)	SALES CREDIT JEWELRY (2)	SALES CREDIT WATCHES (3)	
1								1
2								2
3								3
4								4
5								5
6								6
7								7
8								8
9								9
10								10
11								11

[1]

GENERAL JOURNAL

PAGE 15

	DATE	ACCOUNT TITLE	DOC. NO.	POST. REF.	DEBIT	CREDIT	
1							1
2							2
3							3
4							4
5							5
6							6
7							7
8							8
9							9
10							10
11							11
12							12
13							13
14							14
15							15

CASH RECEIPTS JOURNAL

PAGE 12

| | | | | GENERAL | | ACCOUNTS RECEIVABLE CREDIT | SALES CREDIT | | SALES DISCOUNT DEBIT | | CASH DEBIT |
DATE	ACCOUNT TITLE	DOC. NO.	POST. REF.	DEBIT	CREDIT		JEWELRY	WATCHES	JEWELRY	WATCHES	

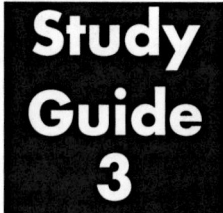

Name	Perfect Score	Your Score
Analyzing Departmental Payroll Procedures	25 Pts.	
Identifying Accounting Terms	10 Pts.	
Analyzing Payroll Accounting	10 Pts.	
Total	45 Pts.	

Part One—Analyzing Departmental Payroll Procedures

Directions: Place a *T* for True or an *F* for False in the Answers column to show whether each of the following statements is true or false.

Answers

1. Federal, state, and local laws require employers to keep records of the payroll information and other payments related to employee services. (p. 60) 1. _____

2. One payroll system is used by all employers in the United States. (p. 60) 2. _____

3. Employers are required by law to withhold certain payroll taxes from employee salaries each pay period. (p. 60) 3. _____

4. Employers pay government agencies all payroll taxes withheld from employee salaries on an annual basis. (p. 60) 4. _____

5. By January 31, businesses must report to employees the earnings and amounts withheld for the previous calendar year. (p. 60) 5. _____

6. Payroll records must show an employee's earnings, amounts withheld, net amount paid, and the total amount of payroll taxes that a business must pay. (p. 60) 6. _____

7. Income and two FICA taxes are the federal taxes deducted from earnings of each employee. (p. 61) 7. _____

8. The amount of federal income tax to be withheld is determined solely by the number of withholding allowances. (p. 61) 8. _____

9. Congress sets the tax base and the tax rates for social security tax. (p. 61) 9. _____

10. Like social security, Medicare has a tax base. (p. 61) 10. _____

11. Laws for handling state, city, and county taxes vary. (p. 61) 11. _____

12. Other deductions from employee earnings include health insurance, life insurance, pension plans, and savings deposits. (p. 61) 12. _____

13. All time worked in excess of 40 hours in any one week is considered overtime. (p. 62) 13. _____

14. Employees are paid two times the regular rate for overtime hours. (p. 62) 14. _____

15. Commissions, cost-of-living adjustments, a share of profits, and a bonus are included in an employee's earnings. (p. 63) 15. _____

16. In proving a payroll register's accuracy, the total of the Net Pay column is subtracted from the Total Deductions column. (p. 65) 16. _____

17. An employee's total earnings and deductions for the quarter are summarized on one line of the employee earnings record. (p. 67) 17. _____

18. After a biweekly payroll register has been completed, a check for the total earnings indicated on the payroll register is written for each employee. (p. 70) 18. _____

19. Transferring payroll amounts electronically from the employer's account to the employee's bank account is known as electronic funds transfer. (p. 70) 19. _____

20. Unemployment taxes are used to pay qualified workers cash benefits for limited periods of unemployment. (p. 70)

21. Both employers and employees are required to pay a federal unemployment tax. (p. 72)

22. The frequency of payments for federal, state, and local government taxes is determined by the amount of tax paid each year. (p. 74)

23. If a business is classified as a monthly schedule depositor, the business must pay the total amount due by the 15th day of the following month. (p. 74)

24. Businesses that paid more than $50,000 in taxes during the previous four quarters are classified as semiweekly schedule depositors. (p. 74)

25. Businesses with a quarterly federal unemployment tax of more than $500.00 must make quarterly payments in the month following the end of the quarter. (p. 75)

Part Two—Identifying Accounting Terms

Directions: Select the one term in Column I that best fits each definition in Column II. Print the letter identifying your choice in the Answers column.

Column I	Column II	Answers
A. automatic check deposit	**1.** The money paid for employee services. (p. 60)	**1.** _____
B. electronic funds transfer (EFT)	**2.** The period covered by a salary payment. (p. 60)	**2.** _____
C. employee earnings record	**3.** The total amount earned by all employees for a pay period. (p. 60)	**3.** _____
	4. Taxes based on the payroll of a business. (p. 60)	**4.** _____
D. pay period	**5.** A deduction from total earnings for each person legally supported by a taxpayer. (p. 61)	**5.** _____
E. payroll	**6.** The maximum amount of earnings on which a tax is calculated. (p. 61)	**6.** _____
F. payroll register	**7.** A business form used to record payroll information. (p. 64)	**7.** _____
G. payroll taxes	**8.** A business form used to record details affecting payments made to an employee. (p. 67)	**8.** _____
H. salary	**9.** Depositing payroll checks directly to an employee's checking or savings account in a specified bank. (p. 70)	**9.** _____
I. tax base	**10.** A computerized cash payments system that transfers funds without the use of checks, currency, or other paper documents. (p. 70)	**10.** _____
J. withholding allowance		

Part Three—Analyzing Payroll Accounting

Directions: For each item below, select the choice that best completes the sentence. Print the letter identifying your choice in the Answers column.

1. The social security tax provides insurance for (A) old-age (B) survivors (C) disability (D) all of the above. (p. 61)

1. _____

2. In a biweekly payroll system employees are paid (A) once a week (B) twice a week (C) every two weeks (D) twice a month. (p. 62)

2. _____

3. When employees are paid a percentage of sales in addition to their regular salary, the earnings are often referred to as (A) salary (B) pensions (C) commissions (D) wages. (p. 63)

3. _____

4. The amount due an individual for a pay period after deductions is referred to as (A) regular earnings (B) overtime (C) total earnings (D) none of these. (p. 65)

4. _____

5. When all employees have cashed their payroll checks, the balance of the payroll bank account (A) equals zero (B) equals the net pay for the period (C) equals total earnings for the period (D) none of these. (p. 70)

5. _____

6. A payroll tax which the employer does not pay is (A) social security tax (B) Medicare tax (C) federal income tax (D) federal unemployment tax. (p. 70)

6. _____

7. Social security and Medicare taxes are paid by (A) the employees (B) the employer (C) both A and B (D) none of these. (p. 72)

7. _____

8. A tax which is not deducted from employees' pay is (A) Medicare tax (B) state income tax (C) federal unemployment tax (D) federal income tax. (p. 72)

8. _____

9. The frequency of employer payments of payroll taxes is determined by (A) the amount owed (B) the employer's geographic location (C) the type of business (D) none of these. (p. 74)

9. _____

10. If the quarterly federal unemployment tax for a business is $500.00 or more, the business must (A) make quarterly payments in the month following the end of the quarter (B) make the tax in one payment by January 31 of the following year (C) make the payment at the end of each month (D) make the payment at the end of each quarter. (p. 75)

10. _____

3-1 WORK TOGETHER, p. 68

Completing payroll records

[1]

COMMISSIONS RECORD

Employee No._____ Employee Name_____

Commission Rate_____ Month_____ Year_____

Department_____ Regular Biweekly Salary_____

Sales on Account $ _____
Cash and Credit Card Sales   _____
equals Total Sales for the Month $ _____

Less:
Sales Discounts $
Sales Returns and Allowances   _____

Equals:
Net Sales $ _____
times Commission Rate   _____
equals: Commission on Net Sales $ _____

---

[2]

PAY PERIOD ENDED 7/3/20--					PAYROLL REGISTER			
	1	2	3	4	5	6	7	8	9

	EMPL. NO.	EMPLOYEE NAME	MARI- TAL STATUS	NO. OF ALLOW- ANCES	TOTAL HOURS	EARNINGS			
						REGULAR	OVERTIME	COMMISSION	TOTAL	
1										1
2										2
3										3
4										4
5										5
6										6
7										7
8										8
9										9
10										10
11										11
12										12
13										13
14										14
15						14 1 8 0 00	7 7 6 40	5 8 2 00	15 5 3 8 40	15

[3]

EARNINGS RECORD FOR QUARTER ENDED Sept. 30, 20--

EMPLOYEE NO. 4   NAME Lee, James   SOCIAL SECURITY NO. 555-72-5782

MARITAL STATUS S   WITHHOLDING ALLOWANCES 1   HOURLY RATE $10.00   SALARY

DEPARTMENT Hardware   POSITION Salesclerk

	1	2	3	4	5	6	7	8	9	10	11
PAY PERIOD		TOTAL EARNINGS	DEDUCTIONS						NET PAY	ACCUMULATED EARNINGS
NO.	ENDED		FEDERAL INCOME TAX	STATE INCOME TAX	SOC. SEC. TAX	MEDICARE TAX	OTHER	TOTAL		
1										
2										
3										
4										
5										
6										
7										
8										
9										
10										

3-1 WORK TOGETHER (concluded)

[2]

DATE OF PAYMENT 7/10/20 – –						PAYROLL REGISTER					
10	11	12	13	14	15	16	17	18	19	20	
DEPARTMENT		ADMIN. SALARIES	DEDUCTIONS						PAID		
HARDWARE	PAINT		FEDERAL INCOME TAX	STATE INCOME TAX	SOC. SEC. TAX	MEDICARE TAX	OTHER	TOTAL	NET PAY	CHECK NO.	
											1
											2
											3
											4
											5
											6
											7
											8
											9
											10
											11
											12
											13
											14
7 6 0 5 80	5 0 7 0 60	2 8 6 2 00	1 3 0 5 00	7 7 6 92	9 6 3 38	2 2 5 31	H 5 8 8 00 / L 1 0 2 40	3 9 6 1 01	11 5 7 7 39		15

[This page left blank intentionally.]

Name _____ Date _____ Class _____

Completing payroll records [1]

COMMISSIONS RECORD

Employee No._____   Employee Name_____

Commission Rate_____   Month_____   Year_____

Department_____   Regular Biweekly Salary_____

Sales on Account $_____
Cash and Credit Card Sales   _____
equals Total Sales for the Month $_____

Less:
Sales Discounts $_____
Sales Returns and Allowances   _____

Equals:
Net Sales $_____
times Commission Rate   _____
equals: Commission on Net Sales $_____

Completing payroll records [2]

PAY PERIOD ENDED 10/2/20--		PAYROLL REGISTER								
	1	2	3	4	5	6	7	8	9	
	EMPL. NO.	EMPLOYEE NAME	MARITAL STATUS	NO. OF ALLOW-ANCES	TOTAL HOURS	EARNINGS				
						REGULAR	OVERTIME	COMMISSION	TOTAL	
1										1
2										2
3										3
4										4
5										5
6										6
7										7
8										8
9										9
10										10
11										11
12										12
13										13
14										14
15						14 9 0 0 00	8 1 5 00	6 1 1 00	16 3 2 6 00	15

[3]

EARNINGS RECORD FOR QUARTER ENDED							Dec. 31, 20--			
EMPLOYEE NO. 12 NAME Sutphin, Aaron						SOCIAL SECURITY NO. 555-75-1782				
MARITAL STATUS S	WITHHOLDING ALLOWANCES 1			HOURLY RATE $9.50			SALARY			
DEPARTMENT Paint				POSITION Salesclerk						
1	2	3	4	5	6	7	8	9	10	11
PAY PERIOD		TOTAL EARNINGS	DEDUCTIONS						NET PAY	ACCUMULATED EARNINGS
NO.	ENDED		FEDERAL INCOME TAX	STATE INCOME TAX	SOC. SEC. TAX	MEDICARE TAX	OTHER	TOTAL		
1										
2										
3										
4										
5										
6										
7										
8										
9										
10										

3-1 ON YOUR OWN (concluded)

[2]

DATE OF PAYMENT 10/9/20 – –   PAYROLL REGISTER

	10	11	12	13	14	15	16	17	18	19	20
	DEPARTMENT		ADMIN. SALARIES	DEDUCTIONS						PAID	
	HARDWARE	PAINT		FEDERAL INCOME TAX	STATE INCOME TAX	SOC. SEC. TAX	MEDICARE TAX	OTHER	TOTAL	NET PAY	CHECK NO.
1											
2											
3											
4											
5											
6											
7											
8											
9											
10											
11											
12											
13											
14											
15	7 2 6 6 00	5 9 4 5 00	3 1 1 5 00	1 3 8 8 00	8 1 6 30	1 0 1 2 21	2 3 6 73	H 5 8 8 00 L 1 0 2 40	4 1 4 3 64	12 1 8 2 36	

[This page left blank intentionally.]

3-2 WORK TOGETHER, p. 76

Journalizing and paying payroll and payroll taxes

[1]

Department	FICA Taxable Salaries	Unemployment Taxable Salaries	Social Security 6.2%	Medicare 1.45%	Federal Unemployment 0.8%	State Unemployment 5.4%	Total
Hardware	$ 7,605.80	$2,132.00					
Paint	5,070.60	1,983.00					
Administrative	2,862.00	985.00					
Total	$15,538.40	$5,100.00					

[2]

CASH PAYMENTS JOURNAL

PAGE 15

DATE	ACCOUNT TITLE	CK. NO.	POST. REF.	GENERAL DEBIT	GENERAL CREDIT	ACCOUNTS PAYABLE DEBIT	PURCH. DISCOUNT CR. HARDWARE	PURCH. DISCOUNT CR. PAINT	CASH CREDIT

GENERAL JOURNAL   PAGE 7

	DATE		ACCOUNT TITLE	DOC. NO.	POST. REF.	DEBIT	CREDIT	
1								1
2								2
3								3
4								4
5								5
6								6
7								7
8								8
9								9
10								10
11								11
12								12
13								13
14								14
15								15
16								16
17								17
18								18
19								19
20								20
21								21
22								22
23								23
24								24
25								25
26								26
27								27
28								28
29								29
30								30
31								31
32								32

3-2 ON YOUR OWN, p. 76

Journalizing and paying payroll and payroll taxes

[1]

Department	FICA Taxable Salaries	Unemployment Taxable Salaries	Social Security 6.2%	Medicare 1.45%	Federal Unemployment 0.8%	State Unemployment 5.4%	Total
Hardware	$ 7,266.00	$2,050.00					
Paint	5,945.00	1,850.00					
Administrative	3,115.00	1,010.00					
Total	$16,326.00	$4,910.00					

[2]

CASH PAYMENTS JOURNAL

PAGE 18

				1	2	3	4	5	6	
DATE	ACCOUNT TITLE	CK. NO.	POST. REF.	GENERAL DEBIT	GENERAL CREDIT	ACCOUNTS PAYABLE DEBIT	PURCH. DISCOUNT CR. HARDWARE	PURCH. DISCOUNT CR. PAINT	CASH CREDIT	
										1
										2
										3
										4
										5
										6
										7
										8
										9
										10
										11
										12
										13
										14
										15

GENERAL JOURNAL   PAGE 10

	DATE		ACCOUNT TITLE	DOC. NO.	POST. REF.	DEBIT	CREDIT	
1								1
2								2
3								3
4								4
5								5
6								6
7								7
8								8
9								9
10								10
11								11
12								12
13								13
14								14
15								15
16								16
17								17
18								18
19								19
20								20
21								21
22								22
23								23
24								24
25								25
26								26
27								27
28								28
29								29
30								30
31								31
32								32

3-1 **APPLICATION PROBLEM, p. 78**

Preparing departmental commissions records
[The commissions records prepared in this problem are needed to complete Application Problem 3-2.]

COMMISSIONS RECORD

Employee No._____   Employee Name_____

Commission Rate_____   Month_____   Year_____

Department_____   Regular Biweekly Salary_____

Sales on Account $_____
Cash and Credit Card Sales   _____
equals Total Sales for the Month $_____

Less:
Sales Discounts $
Sales Returns and Allowances   _____

Equals:
Net Sales $_____
times Commission Rate   _____
equals: Commission on Net Sales $_____

COMMISSIONS RECORD

Employee No._____   Employee Name_____

Commission Rate_____   Month_____   Year_____

Department_____   Regular Biweekly Salary_____

Sales on Account $_____
Cash and Credit Card Sales   _____
equals Total Sales for the Month $_____

Less:
Sales Discounts $
Sales Returns and Allowances   _____

Equals:
Net Sales $_____
times Commission Rate   _____
equals: Commission on Net Sales $_____

3-2 APPLICATION PROBLEM, p. 78

Completing a payroll register

[The commissions records prepared in Application Problem 3-1 are needed to complete this problem. The payroll register prepared in Application Problem 3-2 is needed to complete Application Problems 3-3 and 3-4.]

	EMPL. NO.	EMPLOYEE NAME	MARI-TAL STATUS	NO. OF ALLOW-ANCES	TOTAL HOURS	EARNINGS				
						REGULAR	OVERTIME	COMMISSION	TOTAL	
1	7	Bodade, Nilesh	M	3						1
2	10	Logan, Sarah	S	1						2
3	16	Paniaqua, Ryan	M	2						3
4	9	Quinn, Benjamin	M	2						4
5	15	Ragasa, Corazan	S	2						5
13		Totals				7 0 9 0 00	1 9 4 10	6 7 4 30	7 9 5 8 40	13
14										14

PAY PERIOD ENDED 3/12/20-- PAYROLL REGISTER

3-3 APPLICATION PROBLEM, p. 79

Completing an employee earnings record

[The payroll register prepared in Application Problem 3-2 is needed to complete this problem.]

EARNINGS RECORD FOR QUARTER ENDED March 31, 20--

EMPLOYEE NO. 7 NAME Bodade, Nilesh SOCIAL SECURITY NO. _____

MARITAL STATUS M WITHHOLDING ALLOWANCES 3 HOURLY RATE $7.00 SALARY _____

DEPARTMENT Carpet POSITION Salesclerk

PAY PERIOD		TOTAL EARNINGS	DEDUCTIONS						NET PAY	ACCUMULATED EARNINGS
NO.	ENDED		FEDERAL INCOME TAX	STATE INCOME TAX	SOC. SEC. TAX	MEDICARE TAX	OTHER	TOTAL		
5	2/27	5 6 0 00	0 00	1 1 20	3 4 72	8 12	DH 9 40 13 20	7 6 64	4 8 3 36	2 9 6 8 00
6										
QUARTERLY TOTALS										

3-2 APPLICATION PROBLEM (concluded)

DATE OF PAYMENT 3/19/20 – – PAYROLL REGISTER

		10	11	12	13	14	15	16	17	18	19	20	
		DEPARTMENT		ADMIN. SALARIES	DEDUCTIONS						PAID		
		CARPET	DRAPERY		FEDERAL INCOME TAX	STATE INCOME TAX	SOC. SEC. TAX	MEDICARE TAX	OTHER	TOTAL	NET PAY	CHECK NO.	
1													1
2													2
3													3
4													4
5													5
13		3 6 9 5 04	2 7 4 2 86	1 5 2 0 50	4 2 4 00	1 5 9 17	4 9 3 42	1 1 5 40	D 1 1 2 80 / H 1 5 8 40	1 4 6 3 19	6 4 9 5 21		13
14													14

3-3 APPLICATION PROBLEM (continued)

EARNINGS RECORD FOR QUARTER ENDED   March 31, 20--

EMPLOYEE NO. 10   NAME Logan, Sarah   SOCIAL SECURITY NO. _____

MARITAL STATUS S   WITHHOLDING ALLOWANCES 1   HOURLY RATE —   SALARY $540.00

DEPARTMENT Carpet   POSITION Manager

1	2	3	4	5	6	7	8	9	10	11
PAY PERIOD		TOTAL EARNINGS	DEDUCTIONS						NET PAY	ACCUMULATED EARNINGS
NO.	ENDED		FEDERAL INCOME TAX	STATE INCOME TAX	SOC. SEC. TAX	MEDICARE TAX	OTHER	TOTAL		
5	2/27	5 4 0 00	3 6 00	1 0 80	3 3 48	7 83	D 9 40 / H 1 3 20	1 1 0 71	4 2 9 29	3 1 5 0 00
6										
QUARTERLY TOTALS										

EARNINGS RECORD FOR QUARTER ENDED March 31, 20--

EMPLOYEE NO. 16 NAME Paniaqua, Ryan SOCIAL SECURITY NO.

MARITAL STATUS M WITHHOLDING ALLOWANCES 2 HOURLY RATE SALARY $520.00

DEPARTMENT Drapery POSITION Manager

PAY PERIOD		TOTAL EARNINGS	DEDUCTIONS						NET PAY	ACCUMULATED EARNINGS
NO.	ENDED		FEDERAL INCOME TAX	STATE INCOME TAX	SOC. SEC. TAX	MEDICARE TAX	OTHER	TOTAL		
5	2/27	560 00	0 00	11 20	34 72	8 12	DH 1 3 9 40 20	76 64	483 36	3350 00
6										
QUARTERLY TOTALS										

EARNINGS RECORD FOR QUARTER ENDED March 31, 20--

EMPLOYEE NO. 9 NAME Quinn, Benjamin SOCIAL SECURITY NO.

MARITAL STATUS M WITHHOLDING ALLOWANCES 2 HOURLY RATE $6.50 SALARY

DEPARTMENT Administrative POSITION Clerk

PAY PERIOD		TOTAL EARNINGS	DEDUCTIONS						NET PAY	ACCUMULATED EARNINGS
NO.	ENDED		FEDERAL INCOME TAX	STATE INCOME TAX	SOC. SEC. TAX	MEDICARE TAX	OTHER	TOTAL		
5	2/27	529 75	0 00	10 60	32 84	7 68	DH 1 3 9 40 20	73 72	456 03	2756 00
6										
QUARTERLY TOTALS										

EARNINGS RECORD FOR QUARTER ENDED March 31, 20--

EMPLOYEE NO. 15 NAME Ragasa, Corazan SOCIAL SECURITY NO.

MARITAL STATUS S WITHHOLDING ALLOWANCES 2 HOURLY RATE $8.00 SALARY

DEPARTMENT Drapery POSITION Salesclerk

PAY PERIOD		TOTAL EARNINGS	DEDUCTIONS						NET PAY	ACCUMULATED EARNINGS
NO.	ENDED		FEDERAL INCOME TAX	STATE INCOME TAX	SOC. SEC. TAX	MEDICARE TAX	OTHER	TOTAL		
5	2/27	560 00	0 00	11 20	34 72	8 12	DH 1 3 9 40 20	76 64	483 36	3404 00
6										
QUARTERLY TOTALS										

3-4 APPLICATION PROBLEM, p. 79

Journalizing payment of a departmental payroll
[The payroll register from Application Problem 3-2 is needed to complete this problem.]

[2]

Department	Taxable Earnings	Social Security 6.2%	Medicare 1.45%	Federal Unemployment 0.8%	State Unemployment 5.4%	Total
Carpet	$3,695.04					
Drapery	2,742.86					
Administrative	1,520.50					
Total	$7,958.40					

[3]

GENERAL JOURNAL   PAGE 6

	DATE	ACCOUNT TITLE	DOC. NO.	POST. REF.	DEBIT	CREDIT	
1							1
2							2
3							3
4							4
5							5
6							6
7							7
8							8
9							9
10							10
11							11
12							12
13							13
14							14
15							15
16							16
17							17
18							18
19							19
20							20
21							21

[1]

CASH PAYMENTS JOURNAL

PAGE 6

	DATE	ACCOUNT TITLE	CK. NO.	POST. REF.	GENERAL DEBIT	GENERAL CREDIT	ACCOUNTS PAYABLE DEBIT	PURCH. DISCOUNT CR. CARPET	PURCH. DISCOUNT CR. DRAPERY	CASH CREDIT	
1											1
2											2
3											3
4											4
5											5
6											6
7											7
8											8
9											9
10											10
11											11
12											12
13											13
14											14
15											15
16											16
17											17
18											18
19											19
20											20
21											21
22											22
23											23

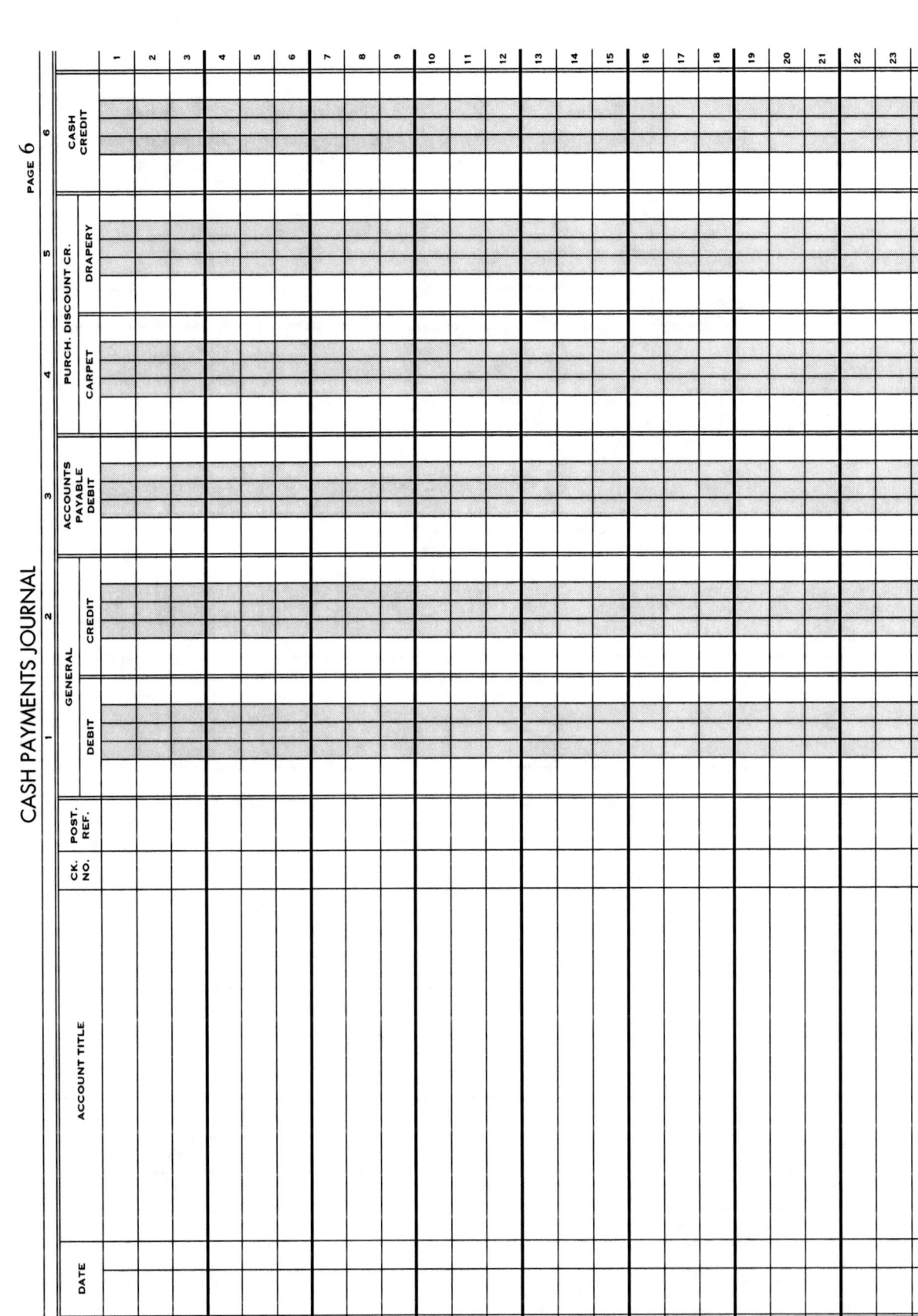

3-5 APPLICATION PROBLEM, p. 79

Calculating and journalizing payment of payroll tax liabilities

[1]

CASH PAYMENTS JOURNAL

PAGE 7

| | | | | GENERAL | | ACCOUNTS PAYABLE DEBIT | PURCH. DISCOUNT CR. | CASH CREDIT |
				DEBIT	CREDIT			
DATE	ACCOUNT TITLE	CK. NO.	POST. REF.	1	2	3	4 5	6

(rows 1 through 12)

[2, 3]

CASH PAYMENTS JOURNAL

PAGE 8

| | | | | GENERAL | | ACCOUNTS PAYABLE DEBIT | PURCH. DISCOUNT CR. | CASH CREDIT |
				DEBIT	CREDIT			
DATE	ACCOUNT TITLE	CK. NO.	POST. REF.	1	2	3	4 5	6

(rows 1 through 6)

[This page left blank intentionally.]

3-6 MASTERY PROBLEM, p. 80

Completing payroll records, journalizing payment of a payroll, and journalizing payroll taxes   [1]

COMMISSIONS RECORD

Employee No._____   Employee Name_____

Commission Rate_____   Month_____ Year_____

Department_____   Regular Biweekly Salary_____

Sales on Account $_____
Cash and Credit Card Sales   _____
equals Total Sales for the Month $_____

Less:
Sales Discounts $
Sales Returns and Allowances   _____

Equals:
Net Sales $_____
times Commission Rate   _____
equals: Commission on Net Sales $_____

COMMISSIONS RECORD

Employee No. _____   Employee Name_____

Commission Rate_____   Month_____ Year_____

Department_____   Regular Biweekly Salary_____

Sales on Account $_____
Cash and Credit Card Sales   _____
equals Total Sales for the Month $_____

Less:
Sales Discounts $
Sales Returns and Allowances   _____

Equals:
Net Sales $_____
times Commission Rate   _____
equals: Commission on Net Sales $_____

PAY PERIOD ENDED 3/14/20-- **PAYROLL REGISTER**

	EMPL. NO.	EMPLOYEE NAME	MARI-TAL STATUS	NO. OF ALLOW-ANCES	TOTAL HOURS	EARNINGS				
						REGULAR	OVERTIME	COMMISSION	TOTAL	
1	2	Bullock, Andrea E.	M	3						1
2	3	Demars, Scott R.	S	2						2
3	1	Kabic, Zora E.	S	1						3
4	4	Mondero, Teodora C.	M	2						4
5	5	Purdy, Julie M.	M	2						5
6	6	Trang, Phuong M.	S	1						6
7		Totals								7
8										8

EARNINGS RECORD FOR QUARTER ENDED March 31, 20--

EMPLOYEE NO. 2   NAME Bullock, Andrea E.   SOCIAL SECURITY NO. ___

MARITAL STATUS M   WITHHOLDING ALLOWANCES 3   HOURLY RATE —   SALARY $600.00

DEPARTMENT Windows   POSITION Manager

PAY PERIOD		TOTAL EARNINGS	DEDUCTIONS						NET PAY	ACCUMULATED EARNINGS
NO.	ENDED		FEDERAL INCOME TAX	STATE INCOME TAX	SOC. SEC. TAX	MEDICARE TAX	OTHER	TOTAL		
4	2/28	600 00	27 00	18 00	37 20	8 70	M D 14 80 8 20	113 90	486 10	2904 00
5										
QUARTERLY TOTALS										

3-6 MASTERY PROBLEM (continued)

[2]

DATE OF PAYMENT 3/21/20 – –   PAYROLL REGISTER

| | DEPARTMENT | | ADMIN. SALARIES | DEDUCTIONS | | | | | | PAID | |
	DOORS	WINDOWS		FEDERAL INCOME TAX	STATE INCOME TAX	SOC. SEC. TAX	MEDICARE TAX	OTHER	TOTAL	NET PAY	CHECK NO.
1											1
2											2
3											3
4											4
5											5
6											6
7											7
8											8

[3]

EARNINGS RECORD FOR QUARTER ENDED   March 31, 20--

EMPLOYEE NO. __3__   NAME __Demars, Scott R.__   SOCIAL SECURITY NO. _____

MARITAL STATUS __S__   WITHHOLDING ALLOWANCES __2__   HOURLY RATE __$7.50__   SALARY _____

DEPARTMENT __Doors__   POSITION __Salesclerk__

| PAY PERIOD | | TOTAL EARNINGS | DEDUCTIONS | | | | | | NET PAY | ACCUMULATED EARNINGS |
NO.	ENDED		FEDERAL INCOME TAX	STATE INCOME TAX	SOC. SEC. TAX	MEDICARE TAX	OTHER	TOTAL		
4	2/28	645 00	33 00	19 35	39 99	9 35	MD 14 80 8 20	124 69	520 31	2568 75
5										
QUARTERLY TOTALS										

EARNINGS RECORD FOR QUARTER ENDED March 31, 20--

EMPLOYEE NO. 1 NAME Kabic, Zora E. SOCIAL SECURITY NO.

MARITAL STATUS S WITHHOLDING ALLOWANCES 1 HOURLY RATE $7.40 SALARY

DEPARTMENT Windows POSITION Salesclerk

1	2	3	4	5	6	7	8	9	10	11
PAY PERIOD		TOTAL EARNINGS	DEDUCTIONS						NET PAY	ACCUMULATED EARNINGS
NO.	ENDED		FEDERAL INCOME TAX	STATE INCOME TAX	SOC. SEC. TAX	MEDICARE TAX	OTHER	TOTAL		
4	2/28	600 00	45 00	18 00	37 20	8 70	MD 14 80 8 20	131 90	468 10	2904 00
5										
QUARTERLY TOTALS										

EARNINGS RECORD FOR QUARTER ENDED March 31, 20--

EMPLOYEE NO. 4 NAME Mondero, Teodora C. SOCIAL SECURITY NO.

MARITAL STATUS M WITHHOLDING ALLOWANCES 2 HOURLY RATE SALARY $620.00

DEPARTMENT Doors POSITION Manager

1	2	3	4	5	6	7	8	9	10	11
PAY PERIOD		TOTAL EARNINGS	DEDUCTIONS						NET PAY	ACCUMULATED EARNINGS
NO.	ENDED		FEDERAL INCOME TAX	STATE INCOME TAX	SOC. SEC. TAX	MEDICARE TAX	OTHER	TOTAL		
5	2/28	600 00	6 00	18 00	37 20	8 70	MD 14 80 8 20	92 90	507 10	2990 00
6										
QUARTERLY TOTALS										

3-6 MASTERY PROBLEM (continued)

[3]

EARNINGS RECORD FOR QUARTER ENDED	March 31, 20--

EMPLOYEE NO. 5 NAME Purdy, Julie M. SOCIAL SECURITY NO. _____

MARITAL STATUS M WITHHOLDING ALLOWANCES 2 HOURLY RATE $6.60 SALARY _____

DEPARTMENT Windows POSITION Salesclerk

					DEDUCTIONS						
1	2	3	4	5	6	7	8	9	10	11	
PAY PERIOD		TOTAL EARNINGS	FEDERAL INCOME TAX	STATE INCOME TAX	SOC. SEC. TAX	MEDICARE TAX	OTHER	TOTAL	NET PAY	ACCUMULATED EARNINGS	
NO.	ENDED										
4	2/28	567 60	2 00	17 03	35 19	8 23	MD 14 80 8 20	85 45	482 15	2 904 00	
5											
QUARTERLY TOTALS											

EARNINGS RECORD FOR QUARTER ENDED	March 31, 20--

EMPLOYEE NO. 6 NAME Trang, Phuong M. SOCIAL SECURITY NO. _____

MARITAL STATUS S WITHHOLDING ALLOWANCES 1 HOURLY RATE $6.50 SALARY _____

DEPARTMENT Administrative POSITION Clerk

					DEDUCTIONS						
1	2	3	4	5	6	7	8	9	10	11	
PAY PERIOD		TOTAL EARNINGS	FEDERAL INCOME TAX	STATE INCOME TAX	SOC. SEC. TAX	MEDICARE TAX	OTHER	TOTAL	NET PAY	ACCUMULATED EARNINGS	
NO.	ENDED										
4	2/28	617 51	45 00	18 53	38 29	8 95	MD 14 80 8 20	133 77	483 73	3 102 00	
5											
QUARTERLY TOTALS											

[5]

Department	Taxable Salaries	Social Security 6.2%	Medicare 1.45%	Federal Unemployment 0.8%	State Unemployment 5.4%	Total
Doors						
Windows						
Administrative						
Total						

[4]

CASH PAYMENTS JOURNAL

PAGE 5

	DATE	ACCOUNT TITLE	CK. NO.	POST. REF.	GENERAL DEBIT	GENERAL CREDIT	ACCOUNTS PAYABLE DEBIT	PURCH. DISCOUNT CR. DOORS	PURCH. DISCOUNT CR. WINDOWS	CASH CREDIT	
1											1
2											2
3											3
4											4
5											5
6											6
7											7
8											8
9											9
10											10
11											11

[6]

GENERAL JOURNAL

PAGE 7

	DATE	ACCOUNT TITLE	DOC. NO.	POST. REF.	DEBIT	CREDIT	
1							1
2							2
3							3
4							4
5							5
6							6
7							7
8							8

3-7

CHALLENGE PROBLEM, p. 81

Completing a payroll register, journalizing payment of a payroll, and journalizing payroll taxes

[2]

CASH PAYMENTS JOURNAL

PAGE 5

				1	2		3	4	5	6
					GENERAL		ACCOUNTS PAYABLE DEBIT	PURCH. DISCOUNT CR.		CASH CREDIT
DATE	ACCOUNT TITLE	CK. NO.	POST. REF.	DEBIT	CREDIT			DOORS	WINDOWS	
1										
2										
3										
4										
5										
6										
7										
8										
9										
10										
11										

[4]

GENERAL JOURNAL

PAGE 7

DATE	ACCOUNT TITLE	DOC. NO.	POST. REF.	DEBIT		CREDIT	
1							
2							
3							
4							
5							
6							
7							
8							

[1]

		PAY PERIOD ENDED 3/14/20 - -				PAYROLL REGISTER							
	1	2	3	4	5	6		7		8		9	
	EMPL. NO.	EMPLOYEE NAME	MARI- TAL STATUS	NO. OF ALLOW- ANCES	TOTAL HOURS	EARNINGS							
						REGULAR		OVERTIME		COMMISSION		TOTAL	
1	2	Bullock, Andrea E.	M	3									1
2	3	Demars, Scott R.	S	2									2
3	1	Kabic, Zora E.	S	1									3
4	4	Mondero, Teodora C.	M	2									4
5	5	Purdy, Julie M.	M	2									5
6	6	Trang, Phuong M.	S	1									6
7		Totals											7
8													8

[3]

Department	Taxable Salaries	Social Security 7.1%	Medicare Tax 2.05%	Federal Unemployment 0.9%	State Unemployment 5.9%	Total
Doors						
Windows						
Administrative						
Total						

3-7 **CHALLENGE PROBLEM (continued)**

[1]

DATE OF PAYMENT 3/21/20 – –				PAYROLL REGISTER								
10	11	12	13	14	15	16	17	18	19	20
DEPARTMENT		ADMIN. SALARIES	DEDUCTIONS						PAID		
DOORS	WINDOWS		FEDERAL INCOME TAX	STATE INCOME TAX	SOC. SEC. TAX	MEDICARE TAX	OTHER	TOTAL	NET PAY	CHECK NO.	
1											1
2											2
3											3
4											4
5											5
6											6
7											7
8											8

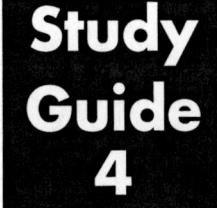

Study Guide 4

Name		Perfect Score	Your Score
	Identifying Accounting Terms	29 Pts.	
	Analyzing Departmental Adjusting and Closing Entries	20 Pts.	
	Analyzing Financial Reporting Procedures for a Departmentalized Business	8 Pts.	
	Total	57 Pts.	

Part One—Identifying Accounting Terms

Directions: Select the one term in Column I that best fits each definition in
Column II. Print the letter identifying your choice in the Answers column.

Column I	Column II	Answers
A. accounting cycle	**1.** The length of time for which a business summarizes and reports financial information. (p. 88)	1. _____
B. adjusting entries	**2.** Assigning control of business revenues, costs, and expenses as a responsibility of a specific manager. (p. 89)	2. _____
C. balance sheet	**3.** An operating expense identifiable with and chargeable to the operation of a specific department. (p. 89)	3. _____
D. capital stock	**4.** An operating expense chargeable to overall business operations and not identifiable with a specific department. (p. 89)	4. _____
E. closing entries	**5.** The revenue earned by a department less its cost of merchandise sold and less its direct expenses. (p. 89)	5. _____
F. component percentage	**6.** A statement that reports departmental margin for a specific department. (p. 89)	6. _____
G. departmental margin	**7.** The amount of revenue from sales less the cost of goods sold. (p. 93)	7. _____
H. departmental margin statement	**8.** A statement showing the gross profit for each department. (p. 93)	8. _____
I. departmental statement of gross profit	**9.** A merchandise inventory determined by counting, weighing, or measuring items of merchandise on hand. (p. 93)	9. _____
J. depreciation expense	**10.** Merchandise inventory determined by keeping a continuous record of increases, decreases, and balance on hand. (p. 93)	10. _____
K. direct expense	**11.** Estimating inventory by using the previous year's percentage of gross profit on operations. (p. 93)	11. _____
L. dividends	**12.** The percentage relationship between one financial statement item and the total that includes that item. (p. 95)	12. _____
M. fiscal period	**13.** A list of customer accounts, account balances, and total amount due from all customers. (p. 99)	13. _____
N. gross profit	**14.** A list of vendor accounts, account balances, and total amount due all vendors. (p. 99)	14. _____
O. gross profit method of estimating an inventory	**15.** A columnar accounting form used to summarize the general ledger information needed to prepare financial statements. (p. 100)	15. _____
P. income statement	**16.** A proof of the equality of debits and credits in a general ledger. (p. 100)	16. _____

Column I	Column II	Answers
Q. indirect expense	**17.** Assets that will be used for a number of years in the operation of a business. (p. 106)	**17.** _____
R. periodic inventory		
S. perpetual inventory	**18.** The portion of a plant asset's cost that is transferred to an expense account in each fiscal period during a plant asset's useful life. (p. 106)	**18.** _____
T. plant assets		
U. post-closing trial balance	**19.** Financial statements reporting revenue, costs, and direct expenses under a specific department's control. (p. 111)	**19.** _____
V. responsibility accounting	**20.** A financial statement showing the revenue and expenses for a fiscal period. (p. 114)	**20.** _____
W. responsibility statements	**21.** A financial statement that shows changes in a corporation's ownership for a fiscal period. (p. 115)	**21.** _____
	22. The total shares of ownership in a corporation. (p. 115)	**22.** _____
X. retained earnings		
Y. schedule of accounts payable	**23.** An amount earned by a corporation and not yet distributed to stockholders. (p. 115)	**23.** _____
Z. schedule of accounts receivable	**24.** Earnings distributed to stockholders. (p. 115)	**24.** _____
	25. A financial statement that reports assets, liabilities, and owners' equity on a specific date. (p. 116)	**25.** _____
AA. statement of stockholders' equity	**26.** Journal entries recorded to update general ledger accounts at the end of a fiscal period. (p. 118)	**26.** _____
BB. trial balance	**27.** Journal entries used to prepare temporary accounts for a new fiscal period. (p. 119)	**27.** _____
CC. work sheet	**28.** A trial balance prepared after closing entries are posted. (p. 122)	**28.** _____
	29. The series of accounting activities included in recording financial information for a fiscal period. (p. 123)	**29.** _____

Part Two—Analyzing Departmental Adjusting and Closing Entries

Directions: For each transaction below, print in the proper Answers column the identifying letters of the accounts to be debited and credited.

Accounts	Transaction	Answers Debit	Credit
A. Accum. Depr.—Equipment	1. Adjust Uncollectible Accounts Expense. (p. 104)	1. _____	2. _____
B. Allow. for Uncoll. Accounts	2. Adjust ending merchandise inventory (increase). (p. 105)	3. _____	4. _____
C. departmental contra cost accounts	3. Adjust ending merchandise inventory (decrease). (p. 105)	5. _____	6. _____
D. departmental contra sales accounts	4. Adjust Supplies. (p. 106)	7. _____	8. _____
E. departmental cost accounts	5. Adjust Prepaid Insurance. (p. 106)	9. _____	10. _____
F. departmental income summary	6. Adjust Depr. Expense—Equipment. (p. 107)	11. _____	12. _____
G. departmental merchandise inventory accounts	7. Close departmental income statement accounts (credit balances), sales, and contra cost accounts. (p. 120)	13. _____	14. _____
H. departmental sales accounts	8. Close departmental income statement accounts (debit balances), contra sales, cost, and expense accounts. (p. 121)	15. _____	16. _____
I. Depr. Expense—Equipment	9. Close Income Summary—General account. (p. 121)	17. _____	18. _____
J. expense accounts	10. Close Income Summary—General account (net loss). (p. 121)	19. _____	20. _____
K. Income Summary—General			
L. Insurance Expense			
M. Prepaid Insurance			
N. Retained Earnings			
O. Supplies			
P. Supplies Expense			
Q. Uncollectible Accounts Expense			

Directions: Place a *T* for True or an *F* for False in the Answers column to show whether each of the following statements is true or false.

Answers

1. A common length of time for a fiscal period is one year. (p. 88)

    1. _____

2. A departmental statement of gross profit provides a manager with information about revenue and costs for each department. (p. 93)

    2. _____

3. Component percentages in a departmentalized business are used to analyze the financial results for each department. (p. 95)

    3. _____

4. Allowance for Uncollectible Accounts is debited in the adjustment for uncollectible accounts expense. (p. 104)

    4. _____

5. Income Summary—General is used for adjusting the merchandise inventory account balances for a departmentalized business. (p. 105)

    5. _____

6. The income summary—general account balance is equal to the net income (or net loss) for a fiscal period. (p. 121)

    6. _____

7. A departmentalized business does not prepare a post-closing trial balance. (p. 122)

    7. _____

8. Completing end-of-fiscal-period work is an application of the Accounting Period Cycle concept. (p. 123)

    8. _____

4-1 WORK TOGETHER, p. 91

Identifying direct and indirect expenses

Trans. No.	Direct Expense or Indirect Expense	Expense Account Title
1	Indirect	Utilities Expense
2		
3		
4		
5		
6		
7		
8		
9		
10		

4-1 ON YOUR OWN, p. 92

Identifying direct and indirect expenses

Trans. No.	Direct Expense or Indirect Expense	Expense Account Title
1		
2		
3		
4		
5		
6		
7		
8		
9		
10		

Preparing an interim departmental statement of gross profit [1]

ESTIMATED MERCHANDISE INVENTORY SHEET
Gross Profit Method

DEPARTMENT _____   DATE _____

1	Beginning inventory, January 1		$ _____
2	Net purchases to date		_____
3	Merchandise available for sale		$ _____
4	Net sales to date	$ _____	
5	Less estimated gross profit	_____	
	(Net sales × Estimated gross profit 48.0%)		
6	Estimated cost of merchandise sold		_____
7	Estimated ending inventory		$ _____

ESTIMATED MERCHANDISE INVENTORY SHEET
Gross Profit Method

DEPARTMENT _____   DATE _____

1	Beginning inventory, January 1		$ _____
2	Net purchases to date		_____
3	Merchandise available for sale		$ _____
4	Net sales to date	$ _____	
5	Less estimated gross profit	_____	
	(Net sales × Estimated gross profit 45.0%)		
6	Estimated cost of merchandise sold		_____
7	Estimated ending inventory		$ _____

4-2 WORK TOGETHER (concluded)

[2]

Willow Glen Interior Design
Interim Departmental Statement of Gross Profit
For Month Ended May 31, 20 – –

	KITCHEN	*% OF NET SALES	BATH	*% OF NET SALES	TOTAL	*% OF NET SALES
Operating Revenue:						
Net Sales						
Cost of Merchandise Sold:						
Est. Mdse. Inv., May 1						
Net Purchases						
Mdse. Available for Sale						
Less Est. End. Inv., May 31						
Cost of Merchandise Sold						
Gross Profit on Operations						
*Rounded to nearest 0.1%						

Preparing an interim departmental statement of gross profit [1]

ESTIMATED MERCHANDISE INVENTORY SHEET
Gross Profit Method

DEPARTMENT _____   DATE _____

1	Beginning inventory, January 1	$ _____
2	Net purchases to date	_____
3	Merchandise available for sale	$ _____
4	Net sales to date . . . . $ _____	
5	Less estimated gross profit . . . . _____	
	(Net sales × Estimated gross profit 42.0%)	
6	Estimated cost of merchandise sold	_____
7	Estimated ending inventory	$ _____

ESTIMATED MERCHANDISE INVENTORY SHEET
Gross Profit Method

DEPARTMENT _____   DATE _____

1	Beginning inventory, January 1	$ _____
2	Net purchases to date	_____
3	Merchandise available for sale	$ _____
4	Net sales to date . . . . $ _____	
5	Less estimated gross profit . . . . _____	
	(Net sales × Estimated gross profit 48.0%)	
6	Estimated cost of merchandise sold	_____
7	Estimated ending inventory	$ _____

4-2 **ON YOUR OWN (concluded)**

[2]

Lassen Heating and Air Conditioning, Inc.

Interim Departmental Statement of Gross Profit

For Month Ended April 30, 20 – –

	COMMERCIAL	*% OF NET SALES	RESIDENTIAL	*% OF NET SALES	TOTAL	*% OF NET SALES
Operating Revenue:						
Net Sales						
Cost of Merchandise Sold:						
Est. Mdse. Inv., April 1						
Net Purchases						
Mdse. Available for Sale						
Less Est. End. Inv., April 30						
Cost of Merchandise Sold						
Gross Profit on Operations						
*Rounded to nearest 0.1%						

Preparing a work sheet with departmental margins [1]

The adjustment information below is used to complete the work sheet for Work Together 4-3.

Uncollectible Accounts Expense, estimated at 2.5% of sales on account

Sales on account for the quarter	$130,200.00
Merchandise Inventory—Books	85,200.80
Merchandise Inventory—Music	129,903.20
Supplies Used—Books	824.00
Supplies Used—Music	697.00
Supplies Used—Administrative	2,922.00
Insurance Expired	2,700.00
Depreciation Expense—Office Equipment	2,400.00
Depreciation Expense—Store Equipment, Books	3,450.00
Depreciation Expense—Store Equipment, Music	3,780.00
Federal Income Tax for the Year	10,316.18

Preparing a work sheet with departmental margins [1]

The adjustment information below is used to complete the work sheet for On Your Own 4-3.

Uncollectible Accounts Expense, estimated at 1.0% of sales on account

Sales on account for the quarter	$148,000.00
Merchandise Inventory—Accessories	114,860.00
Merchandise Inventory—Spas	137,744.00
Supplies Used—Accessories	1,925.00
Supplies Used—Spas	1,403.00
Supplies Used—Administrative	3,241.00
Insurance Expired	2,100.00
Depreciation Expense—Office Equipment	2,700.00
Depreciation Expense—Store Equipment, Accessories	3,720.00
Depreciation Expense—Store Equipment, Spas	3,540.00
Federal Income Tax for the Year	9,336.20

[This page left blank intentionally.]

The work sheet completed in this problem is needed to complete Work Together 4-4 and 4-5.   **[1, 2]**

Callostay
Work
For the Year

	ACCOUNT TITLE	TRIAL BALANCE		ADJUSTMENTS	
		DEBIT	CREDIT	DEBIT	CREDIT
1	Cash	42 6 1 3 30			
2	Accounts Receivable	30 8 7 2 00			
3	Allow. for Uncoll. Accts.		1 3 3 90		
4	Merchandise Inventory—Books	92 3 6 0 80			
5	Merchandise Inventory—Music	138 9 2 1 20			
6	Supplies—Administrative	5 4 0 0 00			
7	Supplies—Books	2 6 5 0 00			
8	Supplies—Music	2 4 8 5 00			
9	Prepaid Insurance	3 6 0 0 00			
10	Office Equipment	22 5 0 0 00			
11	Acc. Depr.—Office Equipment		2 8 0 0 00		
12	Store Equipment—Books	31 5 8 0 20			
13	Acc. Depr.—Store Equipment, Books		4 9 2 5 40		
14	Store Equipment—Music	27 6 0 2 80			
15	Acc. Depr.—Store Equipment, Music		5 6 1 2 30		
16	Accounts Payable		27 8 2 3 50		
17	Employee Income Tax Payable—Federal		1 1 1 0 90		
18	Employee Income Tax Payable—State		1 1 1 8 19		
19	Federal Income Tax Payable				
20	Social Security Tax Payable		1 6 0 3 14		
21	Medicare Tax Payable		3 6 9 96		
22	Sales Tax Payable		2 5 2 0 00		
23	Unemployment Tax Payable—Federal		4 9 00		
24	Unemployment Tax Payable—State		3 3 0 75		
25	Health Insurance Premiums Payable		1 6 2 5 00		
26	Life Insurance Premiums Payable		3 1 8 00		
27	Dividends Payable		5 0 0 0 00		
28	Capital Stock		200 0 0 0 00		
29	Retained Earnings		62 3 7 4 55		
30	Dividends	5 0 0 0 00			
31	Income Summary—Books				
32	Income Summary—Music				
33	Income Summary—General				
34	Sales—Books		235 2 5 3 40		
35	Sales Discount—Books	1 2 0 1 52			
36	Sales Returns and Allowances—Books	1 4 2 08			
37	Sales—Music		226 9 5 2 50		
38	Sales Discount—Music	1 1 8 6 92			
39	Sales Returns and Allowances—Music	1 0 9 4 18			

(Note: Work Sheet continues on p. 114.)

4-3 WORK TOGETHER (continued)

Co.

Sheet

Ended December 31, 20 – –

	5	6	7	8	9	10	11	12	
	DEPARTMENTAL MARGINS STATEMENTS				INCOME STATEMENT		BALANCE SHEET		
	BOOKS		MUSIC						
	DEBIT	CREDIT	DEBIT	CREDIT	DEBIT	CREDIT	DEBIT	CREDIT	

(Note: Work Sheet continues on p. 115.)

	ACCOUNT TITLE	TRIAL BALANCE		ADJUSTMENTS	
		DEBIT	CREDIT	DEBIT	CREDIT
40	Purchases—Books	85 2 1 8 20			
41	Purchases Discount—Books		1 1 5 8 30		
42	Purch. Returns and Allowances—Books		2 2 1 4 60		
43	Purchases—Music	98 8 4 4 50			
44	Purchases Discount—Music		1 2 5 5 38		
45	Purch. Returns and Allowances—Music		2 0 3 6 92		
46	Advertising Expense—Books	2 3 1 0 10			
47	Depr. Exp.—Store Equipment, Books				
48	Payroll Taxes Expense—Books	4 5 8 3 97			
49	Salary Expense—Books	54 2 4 8 00			
50	Supplies Expense—Books				
51	Advertising Expense—Music	1 5 3 8 20			
52	Depr. Exp.—Store Equipment, Music				
53	Payroll Taxes Expense—Music	4 0 8 3 35			
54	Salary Expense—Music	47 7 0 4 00			
55	Supplies Expense—Music				
56	Credit Card Fee Expense	4 5 8 6 30			
57	Depr. Exp.—Office Equipment				
58	Insurance Expense				
59	Miscellaneous Expense	1 2 4 5 20			
60	Payroll Taxes Expense—Administrative	3 2 0 0 57			
61	Rent Expense	24 0 0 0 00			
62	Salary Expense—Administrative	31 3 8 0 00			
63	Supplies Expense—Administrative				
64	Uncollectible Accounts Expense				
65	Utilities Expense	4 8 3 3 30			
66					
67	Department Margin—Books				
68	Department Margin—Music				
69					
70	Federal Income Tax Expense	9 6 0 0 00			
71		786 5 8 5 69	786 5 8 5 69		
72	Net Income after Federal Income Tax				
73					
74					

4-3 WORK TOGETHER (continued)

	5	6	7	8	9	10	11	12	
	DEPARTMENTAL MARGIN STATEMENTS				INCOME STATEMENT		BALANCE SHEET		
	BOOKS		MUSIC						
	DEBIT	CREDIT	DEBIT	CREDIT	DEBIT	CREDIT	DEBIT	CREDIT	
									40
									41
									42
									43
									44
									45
									46
									47
									48
									49
									50
									51
									52
									53
									54
									55
									56
									57
									58
									59
									60
									61
									62
									63
									64
									65
									66
									67
									68
									69
									70
									71
									72
									73
									74

The work sheet completed in this problem is needed to complete On Your Own 4-4 and 4-5.　　　　[1, 2]

Saratoga

Work

For the Year

	ACCOUNT TITLE	TRIAL BALANCE		ADJUSTMENTS	
		DEBIT	CREDIT	DEBIT	CREDIT
1	Cash	31 1 1 7 50			
2	Accounts Receivable	32 4 6 3 00			
3	Allow. for Uncoll. Accts.		3 8 9 00		
4	Merchandise Inventory—Accessories	121 4 5 0 00			
5	Merchandise Inventory—Spas	152 9 8 7 00			
6	Supplies—Administrative	4 7 0 0 00			
7	Supplies—Accessories	3 1 1 0 00			
8	Supplies—Spas	2 8 5 4 00			
9	Prepaid Insurance	2 8 0 0 00			
10	Office Equipment	19 8 5 0 00			
11	Acc. Depr.—Office Equipment		3 1 0 0 00		
12	Store Equipment—Accessories	15 2 4 7 00			
13	Acc. Depr.—Store Equipment, Accessories		5 5 4 0 00		
14	Store Equipment—Spas	22 4 1 9 00			
15	Acc. Depr.—Store Equipment, Spas		6 6 4 3 00		
16	Accounts Payable		35 9 8 0 00		
17	Employee Income Tax Payable—Federal		1 2 5 3 30		
18	Employee Income Tax Payable—State		10 0 7 8 00		
19	Federal Income Tax Payable				
20	Social Security Tax Payable		1 7 2 0 65		
21	Medicare Tax Payable		4 0 2 41		
22	Sales Tax Payable		3 1 1 0 00		
23	Unemployment Tax Payable—Federal		3 9 00		
24	Unemployment Tax Payable—State		2 8 5 00		
25	Health Insurance Premiums Payable		1 1 5 0 00		
26	Life Insurance Premiums Payable		4 2 5 00		
27	Dividends Payable		25 0 0 0 00		
28	Capital Stock		159 0 0 0 00		
29	Retained Earnings		73 9 9 5 35		
30	Dividends	10 0 0 0 00			
31	Income Summary—Accessories				
32	Income Summary—Spas				
33	Income Summary—General				
34	Sales—Accessories		228 5 6 2 00		
35	Sales Discount—Accessories	2 2 5 1 00			
36	Sales Returns and Allowances—Accessories	3 7 8 9 00			
37	Sales—Spas		250 5 4 1 00		
38	Sales Discount—Spas	4 3 2 5 00			
39	Sales Returns and Allowances—Spas	10 9 8 7 00			

(Note: Work Sheet continues on p. 118.)

4-3 **ON YOUR OWN (continued)**

Spas _____

Sheet _____

Ended December 31, 20 – –

5		**6**		**7**		**8**		**9**		**10**	
DEPARTMENTAL MARGIN STATEMENTS								INCOME STATEMENT			
ACCESSORIES				SPAS							
DEBIT		CREDIT		DEBIT		CREDIT		DEBIT		CREDIT	

(Note: Work Sheet continues on p. 119.)

	ACCOUNT TITLE	TRIAL BALANCE		ADJUSTMENTS	
		DEBIT	CREDIT	DEBIT	CREDIT
40	Purchases—Accessories	99 8 5 2 00			
41	Purchases Discount—Accessories		3 8 5 3 00		
42	Purch. Returns and Allowances—Accessories		5 2 6 4 00		
43	Purchases—Spas	108 8 4 4 50			
44	Purchases Discount—Spas		5 5 4 1 00		
45	Purch. Returns and Allowances—Spas		8 9 7 3 00		
46	Advertising Expense—Accessories	3 1 2 6 00			
47	Depr. Exp.—Store Equipment, Accessories				
48	Payroll Taxes Expense—Accessories	4 3 4 1 97			
49	Salary Expense—Accessories	48 2 4 8 00			
50	Supplies Expense—Accessories				
51	Advertising Expense—Spas	4 9 8 5 00			
52	Depr. Exp.—Store Equipment, Spas				
53	Payroll Taxes Expense—Spas	3 5 7 1 36			
54	Salary Expense—Spas	39 7 0 4 00			
55	Supplies Expense—Spas				
56	Credit Card Fee Expense	4 8 5 5 70			
57	Depr. Exp.—Office Equipment				
58	Insurance Expense				
59	Miscellaneous Expense	1 1 5 4 00			
60	Payroll Taxes Expense—Administrative	2 7 1 7 68			
61	Rent Expense	24 0 0 0 00			
62	Salary Expense—Administrative	29 8 5 2 00			
63	Supplies Expense—Administrative				
64	Uncollectible Accounts Expense				
65	Utilities Expense	6 8 4 3 00			
66					
67	Department Margin—Accessories				
68	Department Margin—Spas				
69					
70	Federal Income Tax Expense	8 4 0 0 00			
71		830 8 4 4 71	830 8 4 4 71		
72	Net Income after Federal Income Tax				
73					
74					
75					

4-3 **ON YOUR OWN (continued)**

	5	6	7	8	9	10	11	12	
	DEPARTMENTAL MARGIN STATEMENTS				INCOME STATEMENT		BALANCE SHEET		
	ACCESSORIES		SPAS						
	DEBIT	CREDIT	DEBIT	CREDIT	DEBIT	CREDIT	DEBIT	CREDIT	
									40
									41
									42
									43
									44
									45
									46
									47
									48
									49
									50
									51
									52
									53
									54
									55
									56
									57
									58
									59
									60
									61
									62
									63
									64
									65
									66
									67
									68
									69
									70
									71
									72
									73
									74
									75

Preparing financial statements

[1]

					*% OF NET SALES
*Rounded to the nearest 0.1%					

4-4 **WORK TOGETHER (continued)**

[1]

																*% OF NET SALES
*Rounded to the nearest 0.1%																

		DEPARTMENTAL		COMPANY		
		BOOKS	MUSIC		AMOUNTS	*% OF NET SALES
*Rounded to the nearest 0.1%						

4-4 **WORK TOGETHER (continued)**

[3]

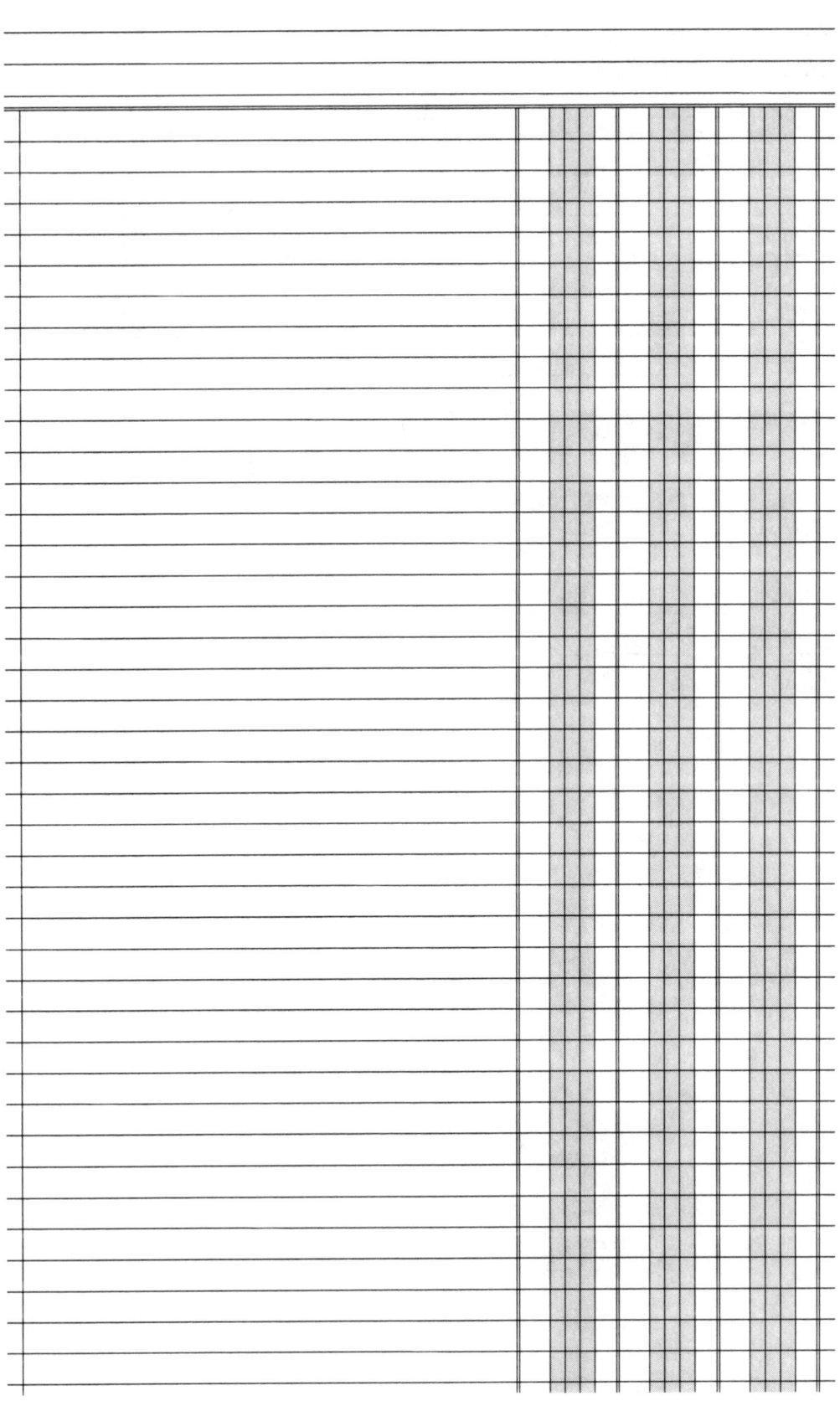

4-4 ON YOUR OWN, p. 117

Preparing financial statements [1]

							*% OF NET SALES
*Rounded to the nearest 0.1%							

[1]

					*% OF NET SALES
*Rounded to the nearest 0.1%					

4-4 **ON YOUR OWN (continued)**

[2]

		DEPARTMENTAL			COMPANY					
		ACCESSORIES		SPAS			AMOUNTS			*% OF NET SALES
*Rounded to the nearest 0.1%										

4-4 ON YOUR OWN (concluded)

[4]

Journalizing adjusting and closing entries

[1]

GENERAL JOURNAL

PAGE 13

	DATE		ACCOUNT TITLE	DOC. NO.	POST. REF.	DEBIT	CREDIT	
1								1
2								2
3								3
4								4
5								5
6								6
7								7
8								8
9								9
10								10
11								11
12								12
13								13
14								14
15								15
16								16
17								17
18								18
19								19
20								20
21								21
22								22
23								23
24								24
25								25
26								26
27								27
28								28
29								29
30								30
31								31
32								32
33								33
34								34
35								35
36								36
37								37
38								38
39								39
40								40

4-5 WORK TOGETHER (continued)

[2]

GENERAL JOURNAL   PAGE 14

	DATE	ACCOUNT TITLE	DOC. NO.	POST. REF.	DEBIT	CREDIT	
1							1
2							2
3							3
4							4
5							5
6							6
7							7
8							8
9							9
10							10
11							11
12							12
13							13
14							14
15							15
16							16
17							17
18							18
19							19
20							20
21							21
22							22
23							23
24							24
25							25
26							26
27							27
28							28
29							29
30							30
31							31
32							32
33							33
34							34
35							35
36							36
37							37
38							38
39							39
40							40

GENERAL JOURNAL   PAGE 15

	DATE		ACCOUNT TITLE	DOC. NO.	POST. REF.	DEBIT	CREDIT	
1								1
2								2
3								3
4								4
5								5
6								6
7								7
8								8
9								9
10								10
11								11
12								12
13								13
14								14
15								15
16								16
17								17
18								18
19								19
20								20
21								21
22								22
23								23
24								24
25								25
26								26
27								27
28								28
29								29
30								30
31								31
32								32
33								33
34								34
35								35
36								36
37								37
38								38
39								39
40								40

4-5 ON YOUR OWN, p. 124

Journalizing adjusting and closing entries　　　　　　　　　　　　　　　**[1]**

GENERAL JOURNAL　　　　　　　　　　PAGE 13

	DATE	ACCOUNT TITLE	DOC. NO.	POST. REF.	DEBIT	CREDIT	
1							1
2							2
3							3
4							4
5							5
6							6
7							7
8							8
9							9
10							10
11							11
12							12
13							13
14							14
15							15
16							16
17							17
18							18
19							19
20							20
21							21
22							22
23							23
24							24
25							25
26							26
27							27
28							28
29							29
30							30
31							31
32							32
33							33
34							34
35							35
36							36
37							37
38							38
39							39
40							40

GENERAL JOURNAL   PAGE 14

	DATE		ACCOUNT TITLE	DOC. NO.	POST. REF.	DEBIT	CREDIT	
1								1
2								2
3								3
4								4
5								5
6								6
7								7
8								8
9								9
10								10
11								11
12								12
13								13
14								14
15								15
16								16
17								17
18								18
19								19
20								20
21								21
22								22
23								23
24								24
25								25
26								26
27								27
28								28
29								29
30								30
31								31
32								32
33								33
34								34
35								35
36								36
37								37
38								38
39								39
40								40

4-5 **ON YOUR OWN (concluded)**

[2]

GENERAL JOURNAL PAGE 15

	DATE	ACCOUNT TITLE	DOC. NO.	POST. REF.	DEBIT	CREDIT	
1							1
2							2
3							3
4							4
5							5
6							6
7							7
8							8
9							9
10							10
11							11
12							12
13							13
14							14
15							15
16							16
17							17
18							18
19							19
20							20
21							21
22							22
23							23
24							24
25							25
26							26
27							27
28							28
29							29
30							30
31							31
32							32
33							33
34							34
35							35
36							36
37							37
38							38
39							39
40							40

Identifying direct and indirect expenses

Trans. No.	Direct Expense or Indirect Expense	Expense Account Title
1		
2		
3		
4		
5		
6		
7		
8		
9		
10		

Name _____ Date _____ Class _____

Preparing an interim departmental statement of gross profit; calculating component percentages [1]

ESTIMATED MERCHANDISE INVENTORY SHEET
Gross Profit Method

DEPARTMENT _____ DATE _____

1	Beginning inventory, January 1		$ _____
2	Net purchases to date		_____
3	Merchandise available for sale		$ _____
4	Net sales to date	$ _____	
5	Less estimated gross profit	_____	
	(Net sales × Estimated gross profit 40.0%)		
6	Estimated cost of merchandise sold		_____
7	Estimated ending inventory		$ _____

ESTIMATED MERCHANDISE INVENTORY SHEET
Gross Profit Method

DEPARTMENT _____ DATE _____

1	Beginning inventory, January 1		$ _____
2	Net purchases to date		_____
3	Merchandise available for sale		$ _____
4	Net sales to date	$ _____	
5	Less estimated gross profit	_____	
	(Net sales × Estimated gross profit 50.0%)		
6	Estimated cost of merchandise sold		_____
7	Estimated ending inventory		$ _____

---

[2]

LightSource

Interim Departmental Statement of Gross Profit

For Month Ended March 31, 20 – –

	OFFICE	*% OF NET SALES	RESIDENTIAL	*% OF NET SALES	TOTAL	*% OF NET SALES
Operating Revenue:						
Net Sales						
Cost of Merchandise Sold:						
Est. Mdse. Inv., March 1						
Net Purchases						
Mdse. Available for Sale						
Less Est. End. Inv., March 31						
Cost of Merchandise Sold						
Gross Profit on Operations						
*Rounded to nearest 0.1%						

[This page left blank intentionally.]

Preparing a work sheet with departmental margins [1, 2]

The work sheet completed in this problem is needed to complete Application Problems 4-4 and 4-5.

AllSports

Work

For Year Ended

	ACCOUNT TITLE	TRIAL BALANCE DEBIT	TRIAL BALANCE CREDIT	ADJUSTMENTS DEBIT	ADJUSTMENTS CREDIT
1	Cash	38 2 1 3 00			
2	Accounts Receivable	36 9 3 5 00			
3	Allowances for Uncoll. Accounts		5 3 3 70		
4	Merchandise Inventory—Clothing	82 3 6 0 00			
5	Merchandise Inventory—Equipment	108 9 2 1 00			
6	Supplies—Administrative	1 6 4 9 00			
7	Supplies—Clothing	2 4 8 0 00			
8	Supplies—Equipment	3 1 2 2 00			
9	Prepaid Insurance	8 4 0 0 00			
10	Office Equipment	8 4 2 6 00			
11	Accum. Depr.—Office Equipment		3 1 5 0 00		
12	Store Equipment—Clothing	14 5 8 0 00			
13	Accum. Depr.—Store Equipment, Clothing		7 2 1 4 00		
14	Store Equipment—Equipment	12 0 1 0 00			
15	Accum. Depr.—Store Equipment, Equipment		7 6 5 0 00		
16	Accounts Payable		24 8 2 3 00		
17	Employee Income Tax Payable—Federal		1 2 5 3 30		
18	Employee Income Tax Payable—State		2 0 7 8 00		
19	Federal Income Tax Payable				
20	Social Security Tax Payable		1 4 8 8 00		
21	Medicare Tax Payable		3 4 8 00		
22	Sales Tax Payable		2 6 5 3 00		
23	Unemployment Tax Payable—Federal		4 4 00		
24	Unemployment Tax Payable—State		1 5 1 00		
25	Health Insurance Premiums Payable		1 2 4 0 00		
26	U.S. Savings Bonds Payable		2 1 5 00		
27	Dividends Payable		12 0 0 0 00		
28	Capital Stock		100 0 0 0 00		
29	Retained Earnings		68 3 7 2 00		
30	Dividends	12 0 0 0 00			
31	Income Summary—Clothing				
32	Income Summary—Equipment				
33	Income Summary—General				
34	Sales—Clothing		244 2 5 3 00		
35	Sales Discount—Clothing	3 6 5 4 00			
36	Sales Returns and Allowances—Clothing	3 4 7 8 00			
37	Sales—Equipment		281 4 9 5 00		
38	Sales Discount—Equipment	2 1 5 3 00			
39	Sales Returns and Allowances—Equipment	5 1 1 0 00			
40	Purchases—Clothing	102 8 5 2 00			
41	Purchases Discount—Clothing		1 7 6 5 00		

(Note: Work Sheet continues on p. 142.)

Center

Sheet

December 31, 20--

	5		6		7		8		9		10		11		12	
	DEPARTMENTAL MARGIN STATEMENTS							INCOME STATEMENT				BALANCE SHEET			
	CLOTHING				EQUIPMENT										
	DEBIT		CREDIT		DEBIT		CREDIT		DEBIT		CREDIT		DEBIT		CREDIT	

(Note: Work Sheet continues on p. 143.)

	ACCOUNT TITLE	TRIAL BALANCE		ADJUSTMENTS	
		DEBIT	CREDIT	DEBIT	CREDIT
42	Purch. Returns and Allowances—Clothing		3 5 8 1 00		
43	Purchases—Equipment	145 2 7 7 00			
44	Purchases Discount—Equipment		1 8 6 2 00		
45	Purch. Returns and Allowances—Equipment		4 9 7 3 00		
46	Advertising Expense—Clothing	2 5 5 1 00			
47	Depr. Expense—Store Equipment, Clothing				
48	Payroll Taxes Expense—Clothing	5 1 9 2 00			
49	Salary Expense—Clothing	36 5 6 2 00			
50	Supplies Expense—Clothing				
51	Advertising Expense—Equipment	2 5 9 0 00			
52	Depr. Expense—Store Equipment, Equipment				
53	Payroll Taxes Expense—Equipment	5 7 5 8 00			
54	Salary Expense—Equipment	43 9 2 6 00			
55	Supplies Expense—Equipment				
56	Credit Card Fee Expense	2 7 8 6 00			
57	Depr. Expense—Office Equipment				
58	Insurance Expense				
59	Miscellaneous Expense	1 4 9 8 00			
60	Payroll Taxes Expense—Administrative	2 3 6 4 00			
61	Rent Expense	28 0 0 0 00			
62	Salary Expense—Administrative	24 8 4 5 00			
63	Supplies Expense—Administrative				
64	Uncollectible Accounts Expense				
65	Utilities Expense	8 4 5 0 00			
66					
67	Department Margin—Clothing				
68	Department Margin—Equipment				
69					
70	Federal Income Tax Expense	15 0 0 0 00			
71		771 1 4 2 00	771 1 4 2 00		
72	Net Income after Federal Income Tax				
73					

4-3 **APPLICATION PROBLEM (continued)**

	5	6	7	8	9	10	11	12	
	DEPARTMENTAL MARGIN STATEMENTS				INCOME STATEMENT		BALANCE SHEET		
	CLOTHING		EQUIPMENT						
	DEBIT	CREDIT	DEBIT	CREDIT	DEBIT	CREDIT	DEBIT	CREDIT	
									42
									43
									44
									45
									46
									47
									48
									49
									50
									51
									52
									53
									54
									55
									56
									57
									58
									59
									60
									61
									62
									63
									64
									65
									66
									67
									68
									69
									70
									71
									72
									73

Preparing financial statements

[1]

					*% OF NET SALES
*Rounded to the nearest 0.1%					

4-4 **APPLICATION PROBLEM (continued)**

[1]

					*% OF NET SALES
*Rounded to the nearest 0.1%					

| | DEPARTMENTAL | | COMPANY | | |
	CLOTHING	EQUIPMENT		AMOUNTS	*% OF NET SALES
*Rounded to the nearest 0.1%					

4-4 **APPLICATION PROBLEM (continued)**

[3]

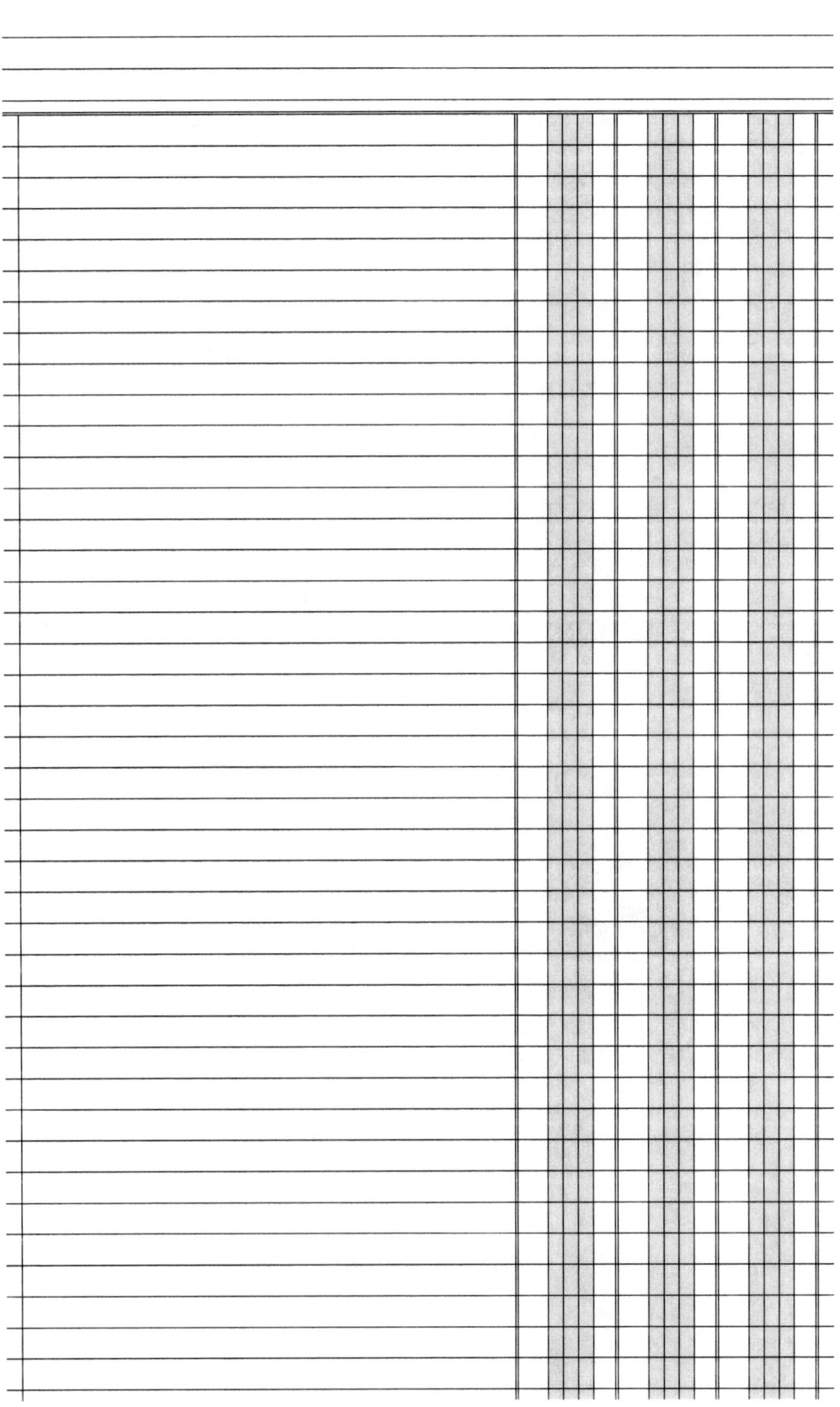

4-5 APPLICATION PROBLEM, p. 128

Journalizing adjusting and closing entries for a departmentalized business [1]

GENERAL JOURNAL   PAGE 13

	DATE		ACCOUNT TITLE	DOC. NO.	POST. REF.	DEBIT	CREDIT	
1								1
2								2
3								3
4								4
5								5
6								6
7								7
8								8
9								9
10								10
11								11
12								12
13								13
14								14
15								15
16								16
17								17
18								18
19								19
20								20
21								21
22								22
23								23
24								24
25								25
26								26
27								27
28								28
29								29
30								30
31								31
32								32
33								33
34								34
35								35
36								36
37								37
38								38
39								39
40								40

GENERAL JOURNAL   PAGE 14

	DATE		ACCOUNT TITLE	DOC. NO.	POST. REF.	DEBIT	CREDIT	
1								1
2								2
3								3
4								4
5								5
6								6
7								7
8								8
9								9
10								10
11								11
12								12
13								13
14								14
15								15
16								16
17								17
18								18
19								19
20								20
21								21
22								22
23								23
24								24
25								25
26								26
27								27
28								28
29								29
30								30
31								31
32								32
33								33
34								34
35								35
36								36
37								37
38								38
39								39
40								40

4-5 **APPLICATION PROBLEM (concluded)**

[2]

GENERAL JOURNAL   PAGE 15

	DATE	ACCOUNT TITLE	DOC. NO.	POST. REF.	DEBIT	CREDIT	
1							1
2							2
3							3
4							4
5							5
6							6
7							7
8							8
9							9
10							10
11							11
12							12
13							13
14							14
15							15
16							16
17							17
18							18
19							19
20							20
21							21
22							22
23							23
24							24
25							25
26							26
27							27
28							28
29							29
30							30
31							31
32							32
33							33
34							34
35							35
36							36
37							37
38							38
39							39
40							40

Completing end-of-fiscal-period work for a merchandising business using departmental margins

[1, 2]

Klein Sporting

Work

For Year Ended

	ACCOUNT TITLE	TRIAL BALANCE		ADJUSTMENTS	
		DEBIT	CREDIT	DEBIT	CREDIT
1	Cash	98 4 3 1 00			
2	Accounts Receivable	30 1 6 0 80			
3	Allowance for Uncollectible Accounts		1 3 9 5 00		
4	Merchandise Inventory—Golf	127 7 4 0 00			
5	Merchandise Inventory—Tennis	156 4 3 0 00			
6	Supplies—Administrative	2 6 4 9 00			
7	Supplies—Golf	3 1 8 0 00			
8	Supplies—Tennis	3 3 7 1 00			
9	Prepaid Insurance	8 7 0 0 00			
10	Office Equipment	12 7 0 0 00			
11	Accum. Depr.—Office Equipment		3 0 5 0 00		
12	Store Equipment—Golf	24 6 0 0 00			
13	Accum. Depr.—Store Equipment, Golf		5 4 0 0 00		
14	Store Equipment—Tennis	17 8 1 0 00			
15	Accum. Depr.—Store Equipment, Tennis		7 8 0 0 00		
16	Accounts Payable		21 6 2 0 00		
17	Employee Income Tax Payable—Federal		2 2 4 5 00		
18	Employee Income Tax Payable—State		1 0 0 5 00		
19	Federal Income Tax Payable				
20	Social Security Tax Payable		1 0 3 7 00		
21	Medicare Tax Payable		2 4 3 00		
22	Sales Tax Payable		2 8 7 2 00		
23	Unemployment Tax Payable—Federal		4 1 20		
24	Unemployment Tax Payable—State		2 7 8 00		
25	Health Insurance Premiums Payable		2 2 6 0 00		
26	U.S. Savings Bonds Payable		2 1 5 00		
27	Dividends Payable		10 0 0 0 00		
28	Capital Stock		270 0 0 0 00		
29	Retained Earnings		66 8 5 1 25		
30	Dividends	10 0 0 0 00			
31	Income Summary—Golf				
32	Income Summary—Tennis				
33	Income Summary—General				
34	Sales—Golf		441 2 1 9 05		
35	Sales Discount—Golf	1 8 2 5 70			
36	Sales Returns and Allowances—Golf	3 9 5 4 00			
37	Sales—Tennis		360 6 4 1 00		
38	Sales Discount—Tennis	2 1 6 0 00			
39	Sales Returns and Allowances—Tennis	6 4 3 3 00			
40	Purchases—Golf	210 7 8 8 00			
41	Purchases Discount—Golf		4 3 2 5 00		
42	Purchases Returns and Allowances—Golf		7 9 8 4 00		
43	Purchases—Tennis	221 4 5 5 00			

(Note: Work Sheet continues on p. 154.)

Goods _____

Sheet _____

December 31, 20 – –

	5	6	7	8	9	10	11	12	
	DEPARTMENTAL MARGIN STATEMENTS				INCOME STATEMENT		BALANCE SHEET		
	GOLF		TENNIS						
	DEBIT	CREDIT	DEBIT	CREDIT	DEBIT	CREDIT	DEBIT	CREDIT	
1									1
2									2
3									3
4									4
5									5
6									6
7									7
8									8
9									9
10									10
11									11
12									12
13									13
14									14
15									15
16									16
17									17
18									18
19									19
20									20
21									21
22									22
23									23
24									24
25									25
26									26
27									27
28									28
29									29
30									30
31									31
32									32
33									33
34									34
35									35
36									36
37									37
38									38
39									39
40									40
41									41
42									42
43									43

(Note: Work Sheet continues on p. 155.)

	ACCOUNT TITLE	TRIAL BALANCE		ADJUSTMENTS	
		DEBIT	CREDIT	DEBIT	CREDIT
44	Purchases Discount—Tennis		4 4 5 6 00		
45	Purch. Returns and Allowances—Tennis		8 7 5 6 00		
46	Advertising Expense—Golf	2 3 7 5 00			
47	Depr. Expense—Store Equipment, Golf				
48	Payroll Taxes Expense—Golf	6 9 9 6 00			
49	Salary Expense—Golf	91 4 5 0 00			
50	Supplies Expense—Golf				
51	Advertising Expense—Tennis	3 2 3 0 00			
52	Depr. Expense—Store Equipment, Tennis				
53	Payroll Taxes Expense—Tennis	5 3 1 8 00			
54	Salary Expense—Tennis	69 5 1 2 00			
55	Supplies Expense—Tennis				
56	Credit Card Fee Expense	4 7 8 0 00			
57	Depr. Expense—Office Equipment				
58	Insurance Expense				
59	Miscellaneous Expense	6 0 0 5 00			
60	Payroll Taxes Expense—Administrative	3 0 4 3 00			
61	Rent Expense	39 7 8 0 00			
62	Salary Expense—Administrative	24 8 4 5 00			
63	Supplies Expense—Administrative				
64	Uncollectible Accounts Expense				
65	Utilities Expense	4 1 7 2 00			
66					
67	Department Margin—Golf				
68	Department Margin—Equipment				
69					
70	Federal Income Tax Expense	19 8 0 0 00			
71		1223 6 9 3 50	1223 6 9 3 50		
72	Net Income after Federal Income Tax				
73					

4-6 **MASTERY PROBLEM (continued)**

5	6	7	8	9	10	11	12	
DEPARTMENTAL MARGIN STATEMENTS				INCOME STATEMENT		BALANCE SHEET		
GOLF		TENNIS						
DEBIT	CREDIT	DEBIT	CREDIT	DEBIT	CREDIT	DEBIT	CREDIT	
								44
								45
								46
								47
								48
								49
								50
								51
								52
								53
								54
								55
								56
								57
								58
								59
								60
								61
								62
								63
								64
								65
								66
								67
								68
								69
								70
								71
								72
								73

									*% OF NET SALES
*Rounded to the nearest 0.1%									

4-6 MASTERY PROBLEM (continued)

[3]

							*% OF NET SALES
*Rounded to the nearest 0.1%							

	DEPARTMENTAL		COMPANY	
	GOLF	TENNIS	AMOUNTS	*% OF NET SALES
*Rounded to the nearest 0.1%				

4-6 **MASTERY PROBLEM (continued)**

[5]

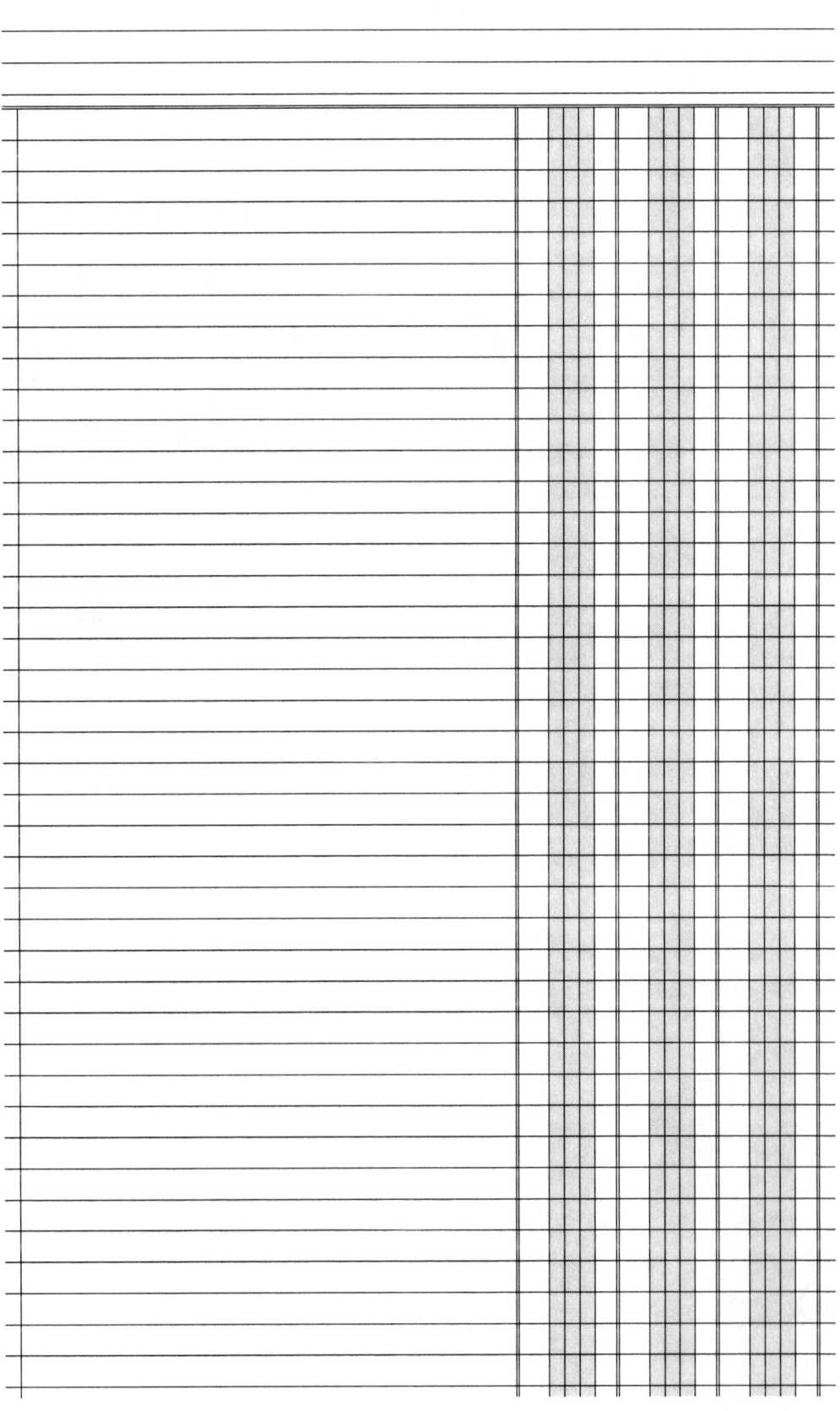

4-6 **MASTERY PROBLEM (continued)**

[7]

GENERAL JOURNAL   PAGE 13

	DATE	ACCOUNT TITLE	DOC. NO.	POST. REF.	DEBIT	CREDIT	
1							1
2							2
3							3
4							4
5							5
6							6
7							7
8							8
9							9
10							10
11							11
12							12
13							13
14							14
15							15
16							16
17							17
18							18
19							19
20							20
21							21
22							22
23							23
24							24
25							25
26							26
27							27
28							28
29							29
30							30
31							31
32							32
33							33
34							34
35							35
36							36
37							37
38							38
39							39
40							40

GENERAL JOURNAL   PAGE 14

	DATE	ACCOUNT TITLE	DOC. NO.	POST. REF.	DEBIT	CREDIT	
1							1
2							2
3							3
4							4
5							5
6							6
7							7
8							8
9							9
10							10
11							11
12							12
13							13
14							14
15							15
16							16
17							17
18							18
19							19
20							20
21							21
22							22
23							23
24							24
25							25
26							26
27							27
28							28
29							29
30							30
31							31
32							32
33							33
34							34
35							35
36							36
37							37
38							38
39							39
40							40

4-6 **MASTERY PROBLEM (concluded)**

[8]

GENERAL JOURNAL   PAGE 15

	DATE	ACCOUNT TITLE	DOC. NO.	POST. REF.	DEBIT	CREDIT	
1							1
2							2
3							3
4							4
5							5
6							6
7							7
8							8
9							9
10							10
11							11
12							12
13							13
14							14
15							15
16							16
17							17
18							18
19							19
20							20
21							21
22							22
23							23
24							24
25							25
26							26
27							27
28							28
29							29
30							30
31							31
32							32
33							33
34							34
35							35
36							36
37							37
38							38

Analyzing a departmental margin statement [1]

DigitalHelp, Inc.

Departmental Margin Statement—Personal Digital Assistant

For Years Ended December 31, 20X9 and 20X8

	20X9 AMOUNTS	20X9 % OF NET SALES	20X8 AMOUNTS	20X8 % OF NET SALES
Operating Revenue:				
Sales	432 611 90		384 805 90	100.4
Less Sales Returns and Allowances	1 718 80		1 533 10	0.4
Net Sales		430 893 10	383 272 80	100.0
Cost of Merchandise Sold:				
Mdse. Inventory, January 1, 20 – –	46 166 80		41 010 20	10.7
Purchases	237 204 90		203 901 10	53.2
Total Cost of Mdse. Available for Sale	283 371 70		244 911 30	63.9
Less Mdse. Inventory, Dec. 31, 20 – –	42 048 50		45 609 50	11.9
Cost of Merchandise Sold		241 323 20	199 301 80	52.0
Gross Profit on Operations		189 569 90	183 971 00	48.0
Direct Expenses:				
Advertising Expense	4 320 90		3 449 50	0.9
Delivery Expense	10 237 20		8 432 00	2.2
Depr. Expense—Delivery Equipment	5 960 10		4 599 30	1.2
Depr. Expense—Store Equipment	3 901 60		3 432 60	0.9
Insurance Expense	3 398 20		3 023 70	0.8
Payroll Taxes Expense	5 265 30		4 360 40	1.1
Salary Expense	50 243 70		42 960 00	11.2
Supplies Expense	3 922 80		2 981 90	0.8
Uncollectible Accounts Expense	4 899 60		3 827 90	1.0
Total Direct Expenses		92 149 40	77 067 30	20.1
Departmental Margin		97 420 50	106 903 70	27.9

Name _____ Date _____ Class _____

4-7 CHALLENGE PROBLEM (concluded)

[2]

Change in % of Net Sales	
a. Cost of Merchandise Sold	
b. Gross Profit	
c. Total Direct Departmental Expenses	
d. Departmental Margin	

[3]

a. Is the departmental margin for the PDA Department at a satisfactory percentage of sales? Explain why it is or is not satisfactory.

_____

_____

_____

_____

_____

_____

b. Is the trend of the cost of merchandise sold percentage favorable or unfavorable? Explain why it is or is not favorable. Suggest some possible reasons for the change in cost of merchandise sold from 20X8 to 20X9.

_____

_____

_____

_____

_____

c. Is the trend of the total direct departmental expenses percentage favorable or unfavorable? Explain why the trend is or is not favorable.

_____

_____

_____

_____

_____

_____

REINFORCEMENT ACTIVITY 1, p. 134

Processing and reporting departmentalized accounting data [1]

ESTIMATED MERCHANDISE INVENTORY SHEET
Gross Profit Method

DEPARTMENT _____ DATE _____

1	Beginning inventory, January 1	$ _____
2	Net purchases to date	_____
3	Merchandise available for sale	$ _____
4	Net sales to date . . . . $ _____	
5	Less estimated gross profit . . . . _____	
	(Net sales × Estimated gross profit 45.0%)	
6	Estimated cost of merchandise sold	_____
7	Estimated ending inventory	$ _____

ESTIMATED MERCHANDISE INVENTORY SHEET
Gross Profit Method

DEPARTMENT _____ DATE _____

1	Beginning inventory, January 1	$ _____
2	Net purchases to date	_____
3	Merchandise available for sale	$ _____
4	Net sales to date . . . . $ _____	
5	Less estimated gross profit . . . . _____	
	(Net sales × Estimated gross profit 47.0%)	
6	Estimated cost of merchandise sold	_____
7	Estimated ending inventory	$ _____

BooksPlus, Inc.

Interim Departmental Statement of Gross Profit

For Month Ended November 30, 20 – –

	BOOKS	*% OF NET SALES	MAGAZINES	*% OF NET SALES	TOTAL	*% OF NET SALES
Operating Revenue:						
Net Sales						
Cost of Merchandise Sold:						
Est. Mdse. Inv., November 1						
Net Purchases						
Mdse. Available for Sale						
Less Est. End. Inv., November 30						
Cost of Merchandise Sold						
Gross Profit on Operations						
*Rounded to nearest 0.1%						

REINFORCEMENT ACTIVITY 1 (continued)

[3–9, 11, 17–19]

GENERAL LEDGER

ACCOUNT Cash   ACCOUNT NO. 1105

DATE		ITEM	POST. REF.	DEBIT	CREDIT	BALANCE DEBIT	BALANCE CREDIT
20-- Dec.	1	Balance	✓			35 1 9 3 79	

ACCOUNT Petty Cash   ACCOUNT NO. 1110

DATE		ITEM	POST. REF.	DEBIT	CREDIT	BALANCE DEBIT	BALANCE CREDIT
20-- Dec.	1	Balance	✓			5 0 0 00	

ACCOUNT Accounts Receivable   ACCOUNT NO. 1205

DATE		ITEM	POST. REF.	DEBIT	CREDIT	BALANCE DEBIT	BALANCE CREDIT
20-- Dec.	1	Balance	✓			16 5 8 8 20	

ACCOUNT Allowance for Uncollectible Accounts   ACCOUNT NO. 1210

DATE		ITEM	POST. REF.	DEBIT	CREDIT	BALANCE DEBIT	BALANCE CREDIT
20-- Dec.	1	Balance	✓				3 4 1 00

ACCOUNT Merchandise Inventory—Books   ACCOUNT NO. 1305

DATE		ITEM	POST. REF.	DEBIT	CREDIT	BALANCE DEBIT	BALANCE CREDIT
20-- Dec.	1	Balance	✓			164 1 6 4 20	

ACCOUNT Merchandise Inventory—Magazines   ACCOUNT NO. 1310

DATE		ITEM	POST. REF.	DEBIT	CREDIT	BALANCE DEBIT	BALANCE CREDIT
20-- Dec.	1	Balance	✓			147 8 4 0 30	

GENERAL LEDGER

ACCOUNT Supplies—Administrative   ACCOUNT NO. 1315

DATE	ITEM	POST. REF.	DEBIT	CREDIT	BALANCE DEBIT	BALANCE CREDIT
Dec. 1	Balance	✔			4 0 4 1 00	

ACCOUNT Supplies—Books   ACCOUNT NO. 1320

DATE	ITEM	POST. REF.	DEBIT	CREDIT	BALANCE DEBIT	BALANCE CREDIT
Dec. 1	Balance	✔			3 6 2 0 00	

ACCOUNT Supplies—Magazines   ACCOUNT NO. 1325

DATE	ITEM	POST. REF.	DEBIT	CREDIT	BALANCE DEBIT	BALANCE CREDIT
Dec. 1	Balance	✔			4 4 6 0 00	

ACCOUNT Prepaid Insurance   ACCOUNT NO. 1405

DATE	ITEM	POST. REF.	DEBIT	CREDIT	BALANCE DEBIT	BALANCE CREDIT
Dec. 1	Balance	✔			5 2 8 0 00	

ACCOUNT Display Equipment—Books   ACCOUNT NO. 1505

DATE	ITEM	POST. REF.	DEBIT	CREDIT	BALANCE DEBIT	BALANCE CREDIT
Dec. 1	Balance	✔			10 0 8 0 00	

ACCOUNT Accumulated Depreciation—Display Equipment, Books   ACCOUNT NO. 1510

DATE	ITEM	POST. REF.	DEBIT	CREDIT	BALANCE DEBIT	BALANCE CREDIT
Dec. 1	Balance	✔				7 0 2 0 00

ACCOUNT Display Equipment—Magazines   ACCOUNT NO. 1515

DATE	ITEM	POST. REF.	DEBIT	CREDIT	BALANCE DEBIT	BALANCE CREDIT
Dec. 1	Balance	✔			11 1 0 0 00	

REINFORCEMENT ACTIVITY 1 (continued)

[3–9, 11, 17–19]

GENERAL LEDGER

ACCOUNT Accumulated Depreciation—Display Equipment, Magazines   ACCOUNT NO. 1520

DATE		ITEM	POST. REF.	DEBIT	CREDIT	BALANCE DEBIT	BALANCE CREDIT
Dec.	1	Balance	✔				6 6 0 0 00

ACCOUNT Office Equipment   ACCOUNT NO. 1605

DATE		ITEM	POST. REF.	DEBIT	CREDIT	BALANCE DEBIT	BALANCE CREDIT
Dec.	1	Balance	✔			20 9 3 6 45	

ACCOUNT Accumulated Depreciation—Office Equipment   ACCOUNT NO. 1610

DATE		ITEM	POST. REF.	DEBIT	CREDIT	BALANCE DEBIT	BALANCE CREDIT
Dec.	1	Balance	✔				8 7 6 0 00

ACCOUNT Accounts Payable   ACCOUNT NO. 2105

DATE		ITEM	POST. REF.	DEBIT	CREDIT	BALANCE DEBIT	BALANCE CREDIT
Dec.	1	Balance	✔				13 1 4 5 85

ACCOUNT Employee Income Tax Payable—Federal   ACCOUNT NO. 2205

DATE		ITEM	POST. REF.	DEBIT	CREDIT	BALANCE DEBIT	BALANCE CREDIT
Dec.	1	Balance	✔				1 2 4 0 00

ACCOUNT Employee Income Tax Payable—State   ACCOUNT NO. 2210

DATE		ITEM	POST. REF.	DEBIT	CREDIT	BALANCE DEBIT	BALANCE CREDIT
Dec.	1	Balance	✔				5 6 5 40

ACCOUNT Federal Income Tax Payable   ACCOUNT NO. 2215

DATE		ITEM	POST. REF.	DEBIT	CREDIT	BALANCE DEBIT	BALANCE CREDIT

GENERAL LEDGER

ACCOUNT Social Security Tax Payable   ACCOUNT NO. 2220

DATE		ITEM	POST. REF.	DEBIT	CREDIT	BALANCE	
						DEBIT	CREDIT
20-- Dec.	1	Balance	✔				1 2 8 6 11

ACCOUNT Medicare Tax Payable   ACCOUNT NO. 2225

DATE		ITEM	POST. REF.	DEBIT	CREDIT	BALANCE	
						DEBIT	CREDIT
20-- Dec.	1	Balance	✔				3 0 0 78

ACCOUNT Sales Tax Payable   ACCOUNT NO. 2230

DATE		ITEM	POST. REF.	DEBIT	CREDIT	BALANCE	
						DEBIT	CREDIT
20-- Dec.	1	Balance	✔				2 5 6 6 31

ACCOUNT Unemployment Tax Payable—Federal   ACCOUNT NO. 2235

DATE		ITEM	POST. REF.	DEBIT	CREDIT	BALANCE	
						DEBIT	CREDIT
20-- Dec.	1	Balance	✔				3 2 80

REINFORCEMENT ACTIVITY 1 (continued)

[3–9, 11, 17–19]

GENERAL LEDGER

ACCOUNT Unemployment Tax Payable—State   ACCOUNT NO. 2240

DATE		ITEM	POST. REF.	DEBIT	CREDIT	BALANCE DEBIT	BALANCE CREDIT
20-- Dec.	1	Balance	✔				2 2 1 40

ACCOUNT Health Insurance Premiums Payable   ACCOUNT NO. 2245

DATE		ITEM	POST. REF.	DEBIT	CREDIT	BALANCE DEBIT	BALANCE CREDIT
20-- Dec.	1	Balance	✔				1 8 8 8 00

ACCOUNT Dividends Payable   ACCOUNT NO. 2305

DATE		ITEM	POST. REF.	DEBIT	CREDIT	BALANCE DEBIT	BALANCE CREDIT

ACCOUNT Capital Stock   ACCOUNT NO. 3105

DATE		ITEM	POST. REF.	DEBIT	CREDIT	BALANCE DEBIT	BALANCE CREDIT
20-- Dec.	1	Balance	✔				300 0 0 0 00

ACCOUNT Retained Earnings   ACCOUNT NO. 3110

DATE		ITEM	POST. REF.	DEBIT	CREDIT	BALANCE DEBIT	BALANCE CREDIT
20-- Dec.	1	Balance	✔				97 5 2 5 70

ACCOUNT Dividends   ACCOUNT NO. 3115

DATE		ITEM	POST. REF.	DEBIT	CREDIT	BALANCE DEBIT	BALANCE CREDIT
20-- Dec.	1	Balance	✔			20 0 0 0 00	

GENERAL LEDGER

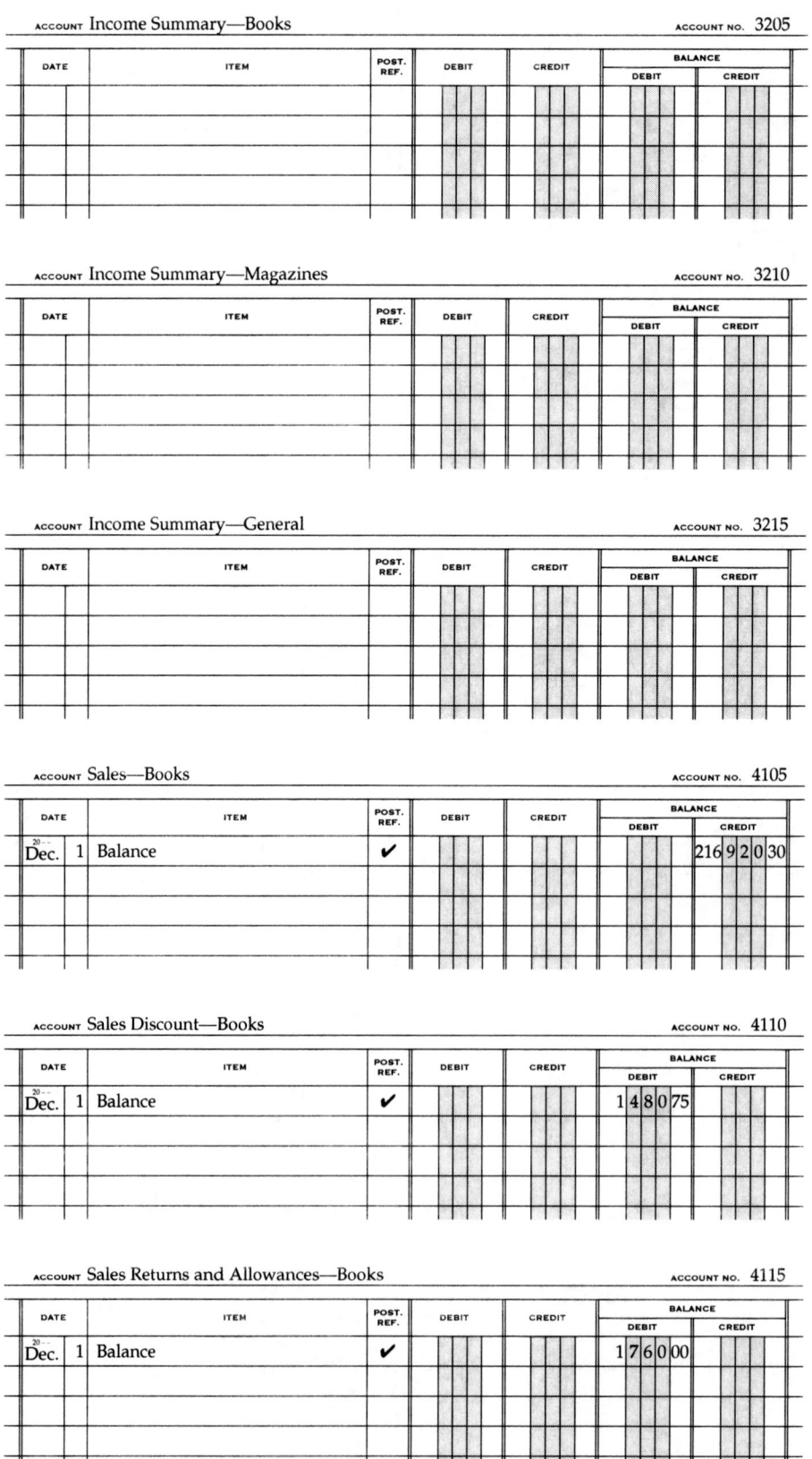

ACCOUNT Income Summary—Books   **ACCOUNT NO.** 3205

DATE	ITEM	POST. REF.	DEBIT	CREDIT	BALANCE DEBIT	BALANCE CREDIT

ACCOUNT Income Summary—Magazines   **ACCOUNT NO.** 3210

DATE	ITEM	POST. REF.	DEBIT	CREDIT	BALANCE DEBIT	BALANCE CREDIT

ACCOUNT Income Summary—General   **ACCOUNT NO.** 3215

DATE	ITEM	POST. REF.	DEBIT	CREDIT	BALANCE DEBIT	BALANCE CREDIT

ACCOUNT Sales—Books   **ACCOUNT NO.** 4105

DATE	ITEM	POST. REF.	DEBIT	CREDIT	BALANCE DEBIT	BALANCE CREDIT
Dec. 1	Balance	✔				216 920 30

ACCOUNT Sales Discount—Books   **ACCOUNT NO.** 4110

DATE	ITEM	POST. REF.	DEBIT	CREDIT	BALANCE DEBIT	BALANCE CREDIT
Dec. 1	Balance	✔			1 480 75	

ACCOUNT Sales Returns and Allowances—Books   **ACCOUNT NO.** 4115

DATE	ITEM	POST. REF.	DEBIT	CREDIT	BALANCE DEBIT	BALANCE CREDIT
Dec. 1	Balance	✔			1 760 00	

REINFORCEMENT ACTIVITY 1 (continued)

GENERAL LEDGER

ACCOUNT Sales—Magazines   ACCOUNT NO. 4205

DATE		ITEM	POST. REF.	DEBIT	CREDIT	BALANCE DEBIT	BALANCE CREDIT
20-- Dec.	1	Balance	✔				229 0 2 9 74

ACCOUNT Sales Discount—Magazines   ACCOUNT NO. 4210

DATE		ITEM	POST. REF.	DEBIT	CREDIT	BALANCE DEBIT	BALANCE CREDIT
20-- Dec.	1	Balance	✔			1 8 1 0 30	

ACCOUNT Sales Returns and Allowances—Magazines   ACCOUNT NO. 4215

DATE		ITEM	POST. REF.	DEBIT	CREDIT	BALANCE DEBIT	BALANCE CREDIT
20-- Dec.	1	Balance	✔			2 1 3 0 20	

ACCOUNT Purchases—Books   ACCOUNT NO. 5105

DATE		ITEM	POST. REF.	DEBIT	CREDIT	BALANCE DEBIT	BALANCE CREDIT
20-- Dec.	1	Balance	✔			140 3 1 0 40	

ACCOUNT Purchases Discount—Books   ACCOUNT NO. 5110

DATE		ITEM	POST. REF.	DEBIT	CREDIT	BALANCE DEBIT	BALANCE CREDIT
20-- Dec.	1	Balance	✔				3 1 6 0 80

ACCOUNT Purchases Returns and Allowances—Books   ACCOUNT NO. 5115

DATE		ITEM	POST. REF.	DEBIT	CREDIT	BALANCE DEBIT	BALANCE CREDIT
20-- Dec.	1	Balance	✔				3 8 1 0 00

GENERAL LEDGER

ACCOUNT Purchases—Magazines   ACCOUNT NO. 5205

DATE		ITEM	POST. REF.	DEBIT	CREDIT	BALANCE	
						DEBIT	CREDIT
Dec.	1	Balance	✔			140 09 9 40	

ACCOUNT Purchases Discount—Magazines   ACCOUNT NO. 5210

DATE		ITEM	POST. REF.	DEBIT	CREDIT	BALANCE	
						DEBIT	CREDIT
Dec.	1	Balance	✔				3 4 2 0 30

ACCOUNT Purchases Returns and Allowances—Magazines   ACCOUNT NO. 5215

DATE		ITEM	POST. REF.	DEBIT	CREDIT	BALANCE	
						DEBIT	CREDIT
Dec.	1	Balance	✔				4 1 2 0 70

ACCOUNT Advertising Expense—Books   ACCOUNT NO. 6105

DATE		ITEM	POST. REF.	DEBIT	CREDIT	BALANCE	
						DEBIT	CREDIT
Dec.	1	Balance	✔			2 0 7 0 00	

ACCOUNT Depreciation Expense—Display Equipment, Books   ACCOUNT NO. 6110

DATE		ITEM	POST. REF.	DEBIT	CREDIT	BALANCE	
						DEBIT	CREDIT

ACCOUNT Payroll Taxes Expense—Books   ACCOUNT NO. 6115

DATE		ITEM	POST. REF.	DEBIT	CREDIT	BALANCE	
						DEBIT	CREDIT
Dec.	1	Balance	✔			5 7 3 0 65	

REINFORCEMENT ACTIVITY 1 (continued)

[3–9, 11, 17–19]

GENERAL LEDGER

ACCOUNT Salary Expense—Books   ACCOUNT NO. 6120

DATE		ITEM	POST. REF.	DEBIT	CREDIT	BALANCE DEBIT	BALANCE CREDIT
Dec.	1	Balance	✔			49 5 0 0 00	

ACCOUNT Supplies Expense—Books   ACCOUNT NO. 6125

DATE		ITEM	POST. REF.	DEBIT	CREDIT	BALANCE DEBIT	BALANCE CREDIT

ACCOUNT Advertising Expense—Magazines   ACCOUNT NO. 6205

DATE		ITEM	POST. REF.	DEBIT	CREDIT	BALANCE DEBIT	BALANCE CREDIT
Dec.	1	Balance	✔			2 9 0 0 20	

ACCOUNT Depreciation Expense—Display Equipment, Magazines   ACCOUNT NO. 6210

DATE		ITEM	POST. REF.	DEBIT	CREDIT	BALANCE DEBIT	BALANCE CREDIT

ACCOUNT Payroll Taxes Expense—Magazines   ACCOUNT NO. 6215

DATE		ITEM	POST. REF.	DEBIT	CREDIT	BALANCE DEBIT	BALANCE CREDIT
Dec.	1	Balance	✔			5 3 4 9 55	

ACCOUNT Salary Expense—Magazines   ACCOUNT NO. 6220

DATE		ITEM	POST. REF.	DEBIT	CREDIT	BALANCE DEBIT	BALANCE CREDIT
Dec.	1	Balance	✔			46 2 0 0 00	

GENERAL LEDGER

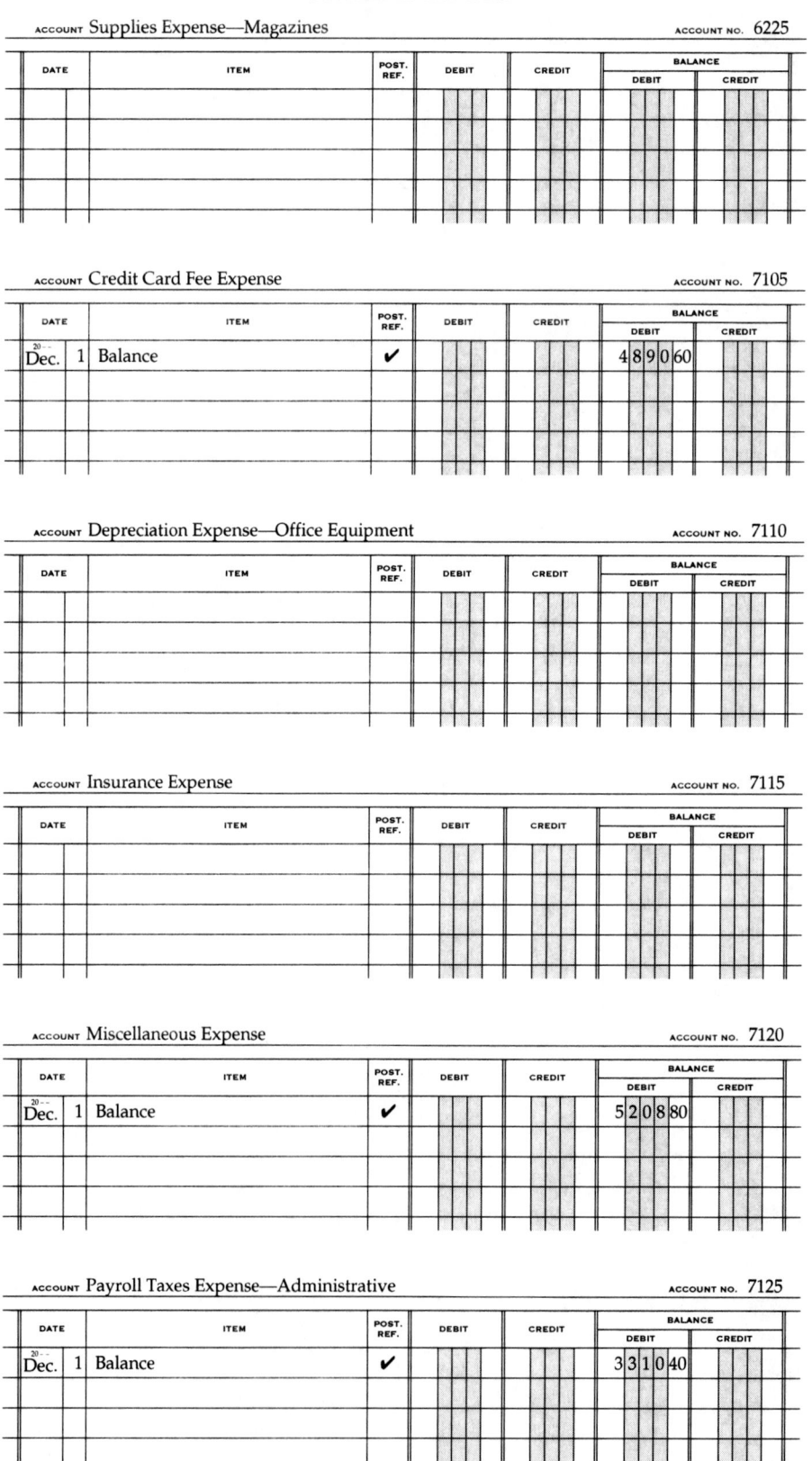

ACCOUNT Supplies Expense—Magazines   ACCOUNT NO. 6225

DATE	ITEM	POST. REF.	DEBIT	CREDIT	BALANCE DEBIT	BALANCE CREDIT

ACCOUNT Credit Card Fee Expense   ACCOUNT NO. 7105

DATE	ITEM	POST. REF.	DEBIT	CREDIT	BALANCE DEBIT	BALANCE CREDIT
Dec. 1	Balance	✔			4 8 9 0 60	

ACCOUNT Depreciation Expense—Office Equipment   ACCOUNT NO. 7110

DATE	ITEM	POST. REF.	DEBIT	CREDIT	BALANCE DEBIT	BALANCE CREDIT

ACCOUNT Insurance Expense   ACCOUNT NO. 7115

DATE	ITEM	POST. REF.	DEBIT	CREDIT	BALANCE DEBIT	BALANCE CREDIT

ACCOUNT Miscellaneous Expense   ACCOUNT NO. 7120

DATE	ITEM	POST. REF.	DEBIT	CREDIT	BALANCE DEBIT	BALANCE CREDIT
Dec. 1	Balance	✔			5 2 0 8 80	

ACCOUNT Payroll Taxes Expense—Administrative   ACCOUNT NO. 7125

DATE	ITEM	POST. REF.	DEBIT	CREDIT	BALANCE DEBIT	BALANCE CREDIT
Dec. 1	Balance	✔			3 3 1 0 40	

REINFORCEMENT ACTIVITY 1 (continued)

[3-9, 11, 17-19]

GENERAL LEDGER

ACCOUNT Rent Expense   ACCOUNT NO. 7130

DATE		ITEM	POST. REF.	DEBIT	CREDIT	BALANCE DEBIT	BALANCE CREDIT
20-- Dec.	1	Balance	✔			13 2 0 0 00	

ACCOUNT Salary Expense—Administrative   ACCOUNT NO. 7135

DATE		ITEM	POST. REF.	DEBIT	CREDIT	BALANCE DEBIT	BALANCE CREDIT
20-- Dec.	1	Balance	✔			28 6 0 0 00	

ACCOUNT Supplies Expense—Administrative   ACCOUNT NO. 7140

DATE		ITEM	POST. REF.	DEBIT	CREDIT	BALANCE DEBIT	BALANCE CREDIT

ACCOUNT Uncollectible Accounts Expense   ACCOUNT NO. 7145

DATE		ITEM	POST. REF.	DEBIT	CREDIT	BALANCE DEBIT	BALANCE CREDIT

ACCOUNT Federal Income Tax Expense   ACCOUNT NO. 8105

DATE		ITEM	POST. REF.	DEBIT	CREDIT	BALANCE DEBIT	BALANCE CREDIT
20-- Dec.	1	Balance	✔			3 6 0 0 00	

ACCOUNTS RECEIVABLE LEDGER

customer Marcella Amco   customer no. 110

DATE	ITEM	POST. REF.	DEBIT	CREDIT	DEBIT BALANCE

customer Matthew Barasso   customer no. 120

DATE	ITEM	POST. REF.	DEBIT	CREDIT	DEBIT BALANCE

customer Tanya Dockman   customer no. 130

DATE	ITEM	POST. REF.	DEBIT	CREDIT	DEBIT BALANCE
Dec. 1	Balance	✔			5 0 4 00

customer Brian Fadstad   customer no. 140

DATE	ITEM	POST. REF.	DEBIT	CREDIT	DEBIT BALANCE

customer Gilmore Public Schools   customer no. 150

DATE	ITEM	POST. REF.	DEBIT	CREDIT	DEBIT BALANCE
Dec. 1	Balance	✔			6 2 4 0 20

REINFORCEMENT ACTIVITY 1 (continued)

ACCOUNTS RECEIVABLE LEDGER

CUSTOMER Belinda Judd   CUSTOMER NO. 160

DATE		ITEM	POST. REF.	DEBIT	CREDIT	DEBIT BALANCE
20-- Dec.	1	Balance	✔			2 6 2 50

CUSTOMER Janelle Kamschorr   CUSTOMER NO. 170

DATE		ITEM	POST. REF.	DEBIT	CREDIT	DEBIT BALANCE

CUSTOMER Donald Lindgren   CUSTOMER NO. 180

DATE		ITEM	POST. REF.	DEBIT	CREDIT	DEBIT BALANCE

CUSTOMER Renville Public Schools   CUSTOMER NO. 190

DATE		ITEM	POST. REF.	DEBIT	CREDIT	DEBIT BALANCE
20-- Dec.	1	Balance	✔			9 5 8 1 50

ACCOUNTS PAYABLE LEDGER

VENDOR A-1 Publishing   VENDOR NO. 210

DATE	ITEM	POST. REF.	DEBIT	CREDIT	CREDIT BALANCE

VENDOR CBG Distributors   VENDOR NO. 220

DATE	ITEM	POST. REF.	DEBIT	CREDIT	CREDIT BALANCE
Dec. 1	Balance	✔			2 2 3 0 10

VENDOR Grandway Products   VENDOR NO. 230

DATE	ITEM	POST. REF.	DEBIT	CREDIT	CREDIT BALANCE

VENDOR H & B Books   VENDOR NO. 240

DATE	ITEM	POST. REF.	DEBIT	CREDIT	CREDIT BALANCE
Dec. 1	Balance	✔			5 4 3 0 15

REINFORCEMENT ACTIVITY 1 (continued)

ACCOUNTS PAYABLE LEDGER

VENDOR Maryland Books & Magazines   VENDOR NO. 250

DATE		ITEM	POST. REF.	DEBIT	CREDIT	CREDIT BALANCE
20-- Dec.	1	Balance	✔			5 6 5 40

VENDOR Oliver Books, Inc.   VENDOR NO. 260

DATE		ITEM	POST. REF.	DEBIT	CREDIT	CREDIT BALANCE
20-- Dec.	1	Balance	✔			4 9 2 0 20

VENDOR Strup Publishers, Inc.   VENDOR NO. 270

DATE		ITEM	POST. REF.	DEBIT	CREDIT	CREDIT BALANCE

GENERAL JOURNAL

PAGE 12

	DATE	ACCOUNT TITLE	DOC. NO.	POST. REF.	DEBIT	CREDIT	
1							1
2							2
3							3
4							4
5							5
6							6
7							7
8							8
9							9
10							10
11							11
12							12
13							13
14							14
15							15
16							16
17							17
18							18
19							19
20							20
21							21
22							22
23							23
24							24
25							25
26							26
27							27
28							28
29							29
30							30
31							31
32							32

REINFORCEMENT ACTIVITY 1 (continued)

[3, 6, 7, 9]

CASH PAYMENTS JOURNAL

PAGE 23

	DATE	ACCOUNT TITLE	CK. NO.	POST. REF.	GENERAL DEBIT 1	GENERAL CREDIT 2	ACCOUNTS PAYABLE DEBIT 3	PURCH. DISCOUNT CR. BOOKS 4	PURCH. DISCOUNT CR. MAGAZINES 5	CASH CREDIT 6	
1											1
2											2
3											3
4											4
5											5
6											6
7											7
8											8
9											9
10											10
11											11
12											12
13											13
14											14
15											15
16											16
17											17
18											18
19											19
20											20
21											21
22											22
23											23
24											24
25											25

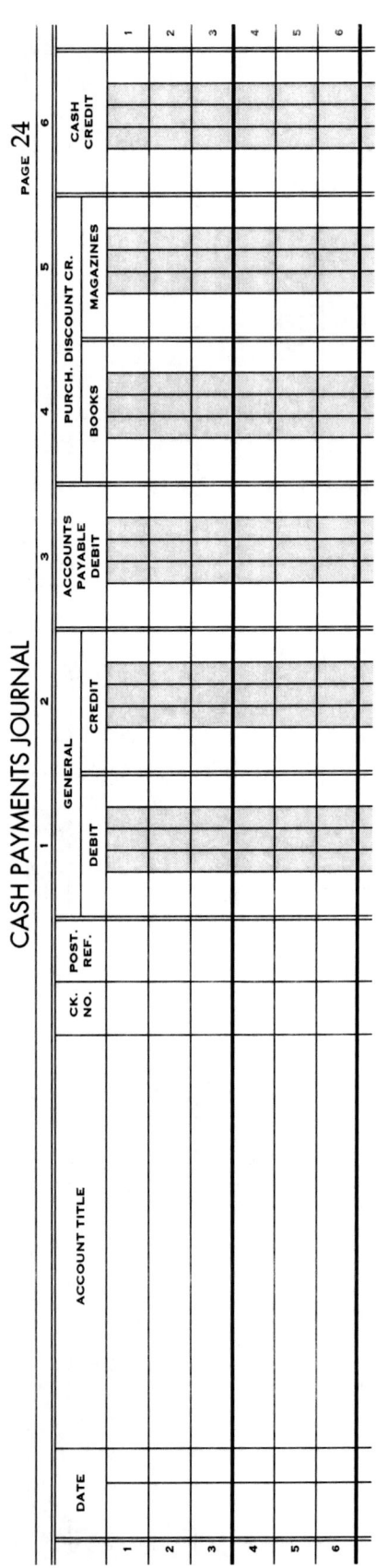

CASH PAYMENTS JOURNAL

PAGE 24

REINFORCEMENT ACTIVITY 1 (continued)

[3, 4]

SALES JOURNAL

	DATE	ACCOUNT DEBITED	SALE NO.	POST. REF.	ACCOUNTS RECEIVABLE DEBIT	SALES TAX PAYABLE CREDIT	SALES CREDIT BOOKS	SALES CREDIT MAGAZINES	
1									1
2									2
3									3
4									4
5									5
6									6
7									7
8									8
9									9
10									10
11									11
12									12
13									13
14									14
15									15
16									16
17									17
18									18

PURCHASES JOURNAL   PAGE 12

	DATE	ACCOUNT CREDITED	PURCH. NO.	POST. REF.	ACCOUNTS PAYABLE CREDIT 1	PURCHASES DEBIT BOOKS 2	PURCHASES DEBIT MAGAZINES 3	
1								1
2								2
3								3
4								4
5								5
6								6
7								7
8								8
9								9
10								10
11								11
12								12
13								13
14								14
15								15
16								16
17								17
18								18
19								19
20								20
21								21
22								22
23								23
24								24
25								25
26								26

REINFORCEMENT ACTIVITY 1 (continued)

[3, 6, 7, 8]

PAGE 12

CASH RECEIPTS JOURNAL

DATE	ACCOUNT TITLE	DOC. NO.	POST. REF.	GENERAL DEBIT	GENERAL CREDIT	ACCOUNTS RECEIVABLE CREDIT	SALES TAX PAYABLE CREDIT	SALES CREDIT BOOKS	SALES CREDIT MAGAZINES	SALES DISCOUNT DEBIT BOOKS	SALES DISCOUNT DEBIT MAGAZINES	CASH DEBIT
				1	2	3	4	5	6	7	8	9
1												
2												
3												
4												
5												
6												
7												
8												
9												
10												
11												
12												
13												
14												
15												
16												

[7]

Prove Cash:

Cash on hand at the beginning of the month . . . . $ _____

Plus total cash received during the month . . . . _____

Equals total . . . . _____

Less total cash paid during the month . . . . _____

Equals total cash on hand at the end of the month . . . . $ _____

[This page left blank intentionally.]

REINFORCEMENT ACTIVITY 1 (continued)

[10]

BooksPlus,

Work

For the Year Ended

| | TRIAL BALANCE | | ADJUSTMENTS | |
| | 1 | 2 | 3 | 4 |
ACCOUNT TITLE	DEBIT	CREDIT	DEBIT	CREDIT
1 Cash				
2 Petty Cash				
3 Accounts Receivable				
4 Allowance for Uncollectible Accounts				
5 Merchandise Inventory—Books				
6 Merchandise Inventory—Magazines				
7 Supplies—Administrative				
8 Supplies—Books				
9 Supplies—Magazines				
10 Prepaid Insurance				
11 Display Equipment—Books				
12 Acc. Depr.—Display Equipment, Books				
13 Display Equipment—Magazines				
14 Acc. Depr.—Display Equipment, Magazines				
15 Office Equipment				
16 Acc. Depr.—Office Equipment				
17 Accounts Payable				
18 Employee Income Tax Payable—Federal				
19 Employee Income Tax Payable—State				
20 Federal Income Tax Payable				
21 Social Security Tax Payable				
22 Medicare Tax Payable				
23 Sales Tax Payable				
24 Unemployment Tax Payable—Federal				
25 Unemployment Tax Payable—State				
26 Health Insurance Premiums Payable				
27 Dividends Payable				
28 Capital Stock				
29 Retained Earnings				
30 Dividends				
31 Income Summary—Books				
32 Income Summary—Magazines				
33 Income Summary—General				
34 Sales—Books				
35 Sales Discount—Books				
36 Sales Returns and Allowances—Books				

(Note: Work Sheet continues on p. 194.)

REINFORCEMENT ACTIVITY 1 (continued)

[11–18]

Inc.

Sheet

December 31, 20– –

	5	6	7	8	9	10	11	12	
	DEPARTMENTAL MARGIN STATEMENTS				INCOME STATEMENT		BALANCE SHEET		
	BOOKS		MAGAZINES						
	DEBIT	CREDIT	DEBIT	CREDIT	DEBIT	CREDIT	DEBIT	CREDIT	
									1
									2
									3
									4
									5
									6
									7
									8
									9
									10
									11
									12
									13
									14
									15
									16
									17
									18
									19
									20
									21
									22
									23
									24
									25
									26
									27
									28
									29
									30
									31
									32
									33
									34
									35
									36

(Note: Work Sheet continues on p. 195.)

	ACCOUNT TITLE	TRIAL BALANCE		ADJUSTMENTS	
		1 DEBIT	**2** CREDIT	**3** DEBIT	**4** CREDIT
37	Sales—Magazines				
38	Sales Discount—Magazines				
39	Sales Returns and Allowances—Magazines				
40	Purchases—Books				
41	Purchases Discount—Books				
42	Purch. Returns and Allowances—Books				
43	Purchases—Magazines				
44	Purchases Discount—Magazines				
45	Purch. Returns and Allowances—Magazines				
46	Advertising Expense—Books				
47	Depr. Exp.—Display Equipment, Books				
48	Payroll Taxes Expense—Books				
49	Salary Expense—Books				
50	Supplies Expense—Books				
51	Advertising Expense—Magazines				
52	Depr. Exp.—Display Equipment, Magazines				
53	Payroll Taxes Expense—Magazines				
54	Salary Expense—Magazines				
55	Supplies Expense—Magazines				
56	Credit Card Fee Expense				
57	Depr. Exp.—Office Equipment				
58	Insurance Expense				
59	Miscellaneous Expense				
60	Payroll Taxes Expense—Administrative				
61	Rent Expense				
62	Salary Expense—Administrative				
63	Supplies Expense—Administrative				
64	Uncollectible Accounts Expense				
65					
66	Department Margin—Books				
67	Department Margin—Equipment				
68					
69	Federal Income Tax Expense				
70					
71	Net Income after Federal Income Tax				
72					

REINFORCEMENT ACTIVITY 1 (continued)

	5		6		7		8		9		10		11		12	
	DEPARTMENTAL MARGIN STATEMENTS								INCOME STATEMENT				BALANCE SHEET			
	BOOKS				MAGAZINES											
	DEBIT		CREDIT		DEBIT		CREDIT		DEBIT		CREDIT		DEBIT		CREDIT		
																37
																38
																39
																40
																41
																42
																43
																44
																45
																46
																47
																48
																49
																50
																51
																52
																53
																54
																55
																56
																57
																58
																59
																60
																61
																62
																63
																64
																65
																66
																67
																68
																69
																70
																71
																72

															*% OF NET SALES
*Rounded to the nearest 0.1%															

REINFORCEMENT ACTIVITY 1 (continued)

[13]

																								*% OF NET SALES
*Rounded to the nearest 0.1%																								

	DEPARTMENTAL		COMPANY	
	BOOKS	MAGAZINES	AMOUNTS	*% OF NET SALES
*Rounded to the nearest 0.1%				

REINFORCEMENT ACTIVITY 1 (continued)

[15]

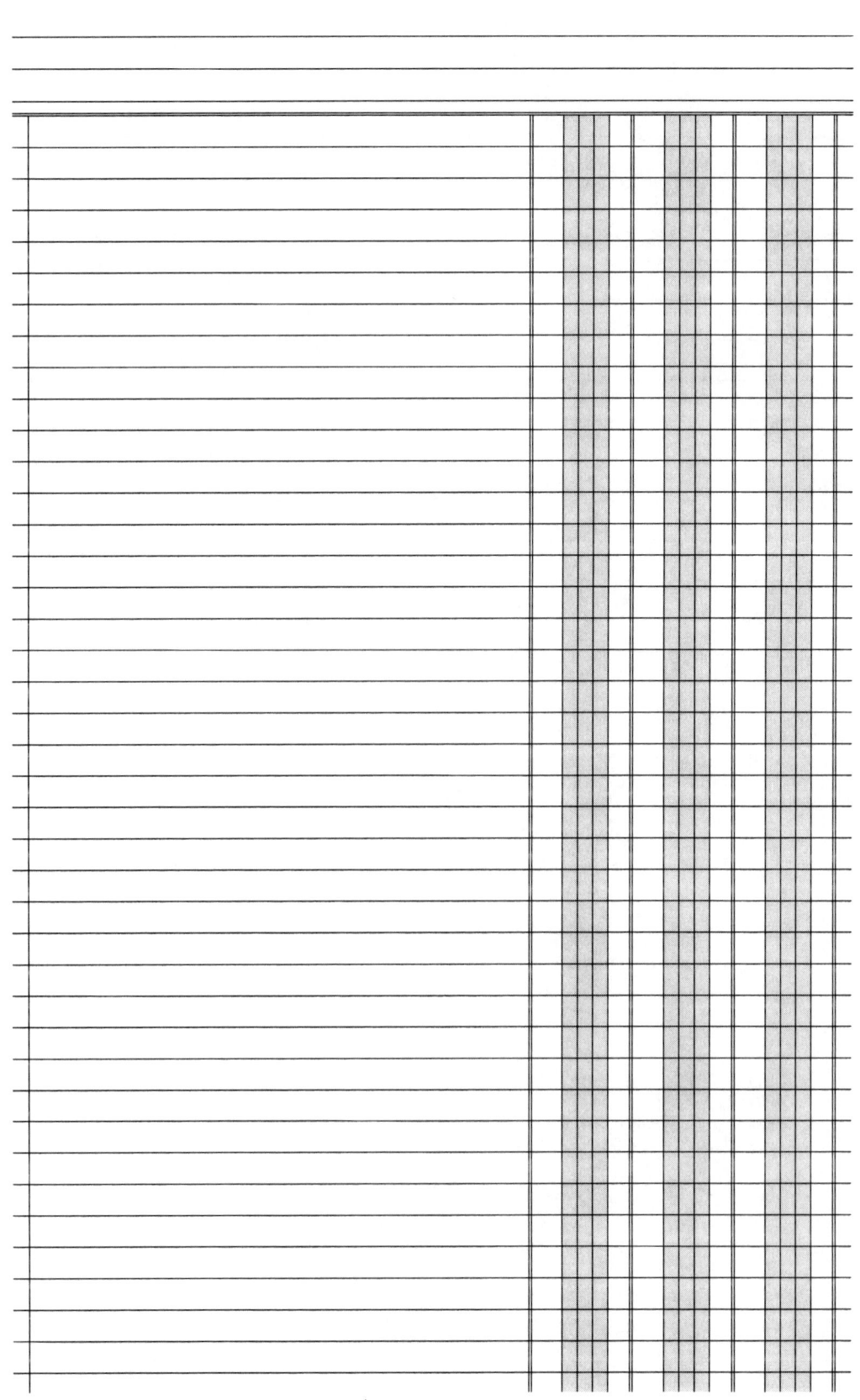

REINFORCEMENT ACTIVITY 1 (continued)

[17]

GENERAL JOURNAL   PAGE 13

	DATE		ACCOUNT TITLE	DOC. NO.	POST. REF.	DEBIT	CREDIT	
1								1
2								2
3								3
4								4
5								5
6								6
7								7
8								8
9								9
10								10
11								11
12								12
13								13
14								14
15								15
16								16
17								17
18								18
19								19
20								20
21								21
22								22
23								23
24								24
25								25
26								26
27								27
28								28
29								29
30								30
31								31
32								32
33								33
34								34
35								35
36								36

GENERAL JOURNAL   PAGE 14

	DATE		ACCOUNT TITLE	DOC. NO.	POST. REF.	DEBIT	CREDIT	
1								1
2								2
3								3
4								4
5								5
6								6
7								7
8								8
9								9
10								10
11								11
12								12
13								13
14								14
15								15
16								16
17								17
18								18
19								19
20								20
21								21
22								22
23								23
24								24
25								25
26								26
27								27
28								28
29								29
30								30
31								31
32								32
33								33
34								34
35								35
36								36

REINFORCEMENT ACTIVITY 1 (continued)

[18]

GENERAL JOURNAL

PAGE 15

	DATE		ACCOUNT TITLE	DOC. NO.	POST. REF.	DEBIT	CREDIT	
1								1
2								2
3								3
4								4
5								5
6								6
7								7
8								8
9								9
10								10
11								11
12								12
13								13
14								14
15								15
16								16
17								17
18								18
19								19
20								20
21								21
22								22
23								23
24								24
25								25
26								26
27								27
28								28
29								29
30								30
31								31
32								32
33								33
34								34
35								35
36								36

ACCOUNT TITLE	DEBIT	CREDIT

Name	Perfect Score	Your Score
Identifying Accounting Terms	5 Pts.	
Analyzing Concepts and Practices in a Voucher System	7 Pts.	
Analyzing Voucher Transactions	8 Pts.	
Analyzing Accounting Practices in a Voucher System	17 Pts.	
Total	37 Pts.	

Part One—Identifying Accounting Terms

Directions: Select the one term in Column I that best fits each definition in Column II. Print the letter identifying your choice in the Answers column.

Column I	**Column II**	**Answers**
A. check register	1. A check with space for writing details about a cash payment. (p. 150)	1. _____
B. voucher	2. A journal used to record vouchers. (p. 147)	2. _____
	3. A journal used in a voucher system to record cash payments. (p. 151)	3. _____
C. voucher check		
	4. A set of procedures for controlling cash payments by preparing and approving vouchers before payments are made. (p. 144)	4. _____
D. voucher register		
	5. A business form used to show an authorized person's approval for a cash payment. (p. 144)	5. _____
E. voucher system		

Part Two—Analyzing Concepts and Practices in a Voucher System

Directions: For each of the following items, select the choice that best completes the statement. Print the letter identifying your choice in the Answers column.

Answers

1. The source document for an entry in a voucher register is a(an) (p. 145)   1. _____
   (A) debit memorandum   (C) voucher
   (B) invoice   (D) none of these

2. The source document for an entry in a check register is a(an) (p. 151)   2. _____
   (A) check   (C) memorandum
   (B) voucher   (D) none of these

3. The liability account that is used in a voucher system in place of Accounts Payable is (p. 146)   3. _____
   (A) Notes Payable   (C) Vouchers Payable
   (B) Vouchers Receivable   (D) none of these

4. Vouchers to be paid are filed in the unpaid vouchers file according to the (p. 147)   4. _____
   (A) date of the invoice   (C) voucher number
   (B) date the voucher must be paid   (D) name of the vendor

5. When an account has no special columns in the voucher register, information is recorded in the (p. 148)   5. _____
   (A) Delivery Expense Debit column   (C) Purchases Debit column
   (B) General columns   (D) Vouchers Payable Credit column

6. A check register is similar to and replaces a (p. 151)   6. _____
   (A) purchases journal   (C) cash receipts journal
   (B) voucher register   (D) cash payments journal

7. Paid vouchers are filed by the (p. 150)   7. _____
   (A) voucher number   (C) name of the vendor
   (B) date of the voucher   (D) date of payment

Part Three—Analyzing Voucher Transactions

Directions: Decide in which register the following transactions will be recorded and analyze the transactions into their debit and credit parts. In Answers Column 1, print the abbreviation for the register in which each transaction is to be recorded. In Columns 2 and 3 print the letters identifying the accounts to be debited and credited for each transaction.

CR—check register   **VR—voucher register**   **Answers**

Account Title	Transaction	1 Reg.	2 Debit	3 Credit
A. Cash	1. Purchased merchandise on account. (p. 147)	1. _____	_____	_____
B. Delivery Expense	2. Received invoice for delivery expense. (p. 147)	2. _____	_____	_____
C. Purchases	3. Bought office equipment on account. (p. 148)	3. _____	_____	_____
D. Purchases Discount	4. Paid voucher for delivery expense. (p. 151)	4. _____	_____	_____
E. Purchases Returns and Allowances	5. Issued a debit memorandum. (p. 155)	5. _____	_____	_____
F. Office Equipment	6. Paid a voucher, no discount. (p. 151)	6. _____	_____	_____
G. Supplies	7. Bought supplies, no discount. (p. 148)	7. _____	_____	_____
H. Vouchers Payable	8. Paid voucher less a discount. (p. 151)	8. _____	_____	_____

Part Four—Analyzing Accounting Practices in a Voucher System

Directions: Place a *T* for True or *F* for False in the Answers column to show whether each of the following statements is true or false.

1. Invoices are verified before a voucher is prepared. (p. 144)   1. _____
2. Cash control procedures include storing cash in a safe place. (p. 144)   2. _____
3. Vouchers are prepared only for bills other than invoices. (p. 145)   3. _____
4. The source document for an entry in the voucher register is the approved invoice. (p. 145)   4. _____
5. In a voucher system, the account Vouchers Payable is used only for purchases of merchandise on account. (p. 145)   5. _____
6. Prenumbered vouchers are a control procedure in a voucher system. (p. 146)   6. _____
7. Vouchers must be approved before being recorded in the voucher register. (p. 146)   7. _____
8. When a voucher is recorded, a notation is made on the voucher. (p. 147)   8. _____
9. Vouchers are placed in the unpaid file according to the due date. (p. 147)   9. _____
10. When an amount is recorded in a special column in the voucher register, an account title must be written in the Account Title column. (p. 147)   10. _____
11. Separate amounts recorded in the General Debit column of a voucher register are posted individually during the month. (p. 148)   11. _____
12. Separate amounts recorded in special amount columns of a voucher register are posted individually during the month. (p. 148)   12. _____
13. Paid vouchers are filed according to the date paid. (p. 150)   13. _____
14. In addition to journalizing cash payments, a check register can also be used to maintain the checking account balance. (p. 151)   14. _____
15. Each check recorded in a check register includes a debit to Vouchers Payable and a credit to Cash. (p. 151)   15. _____
16. When a debit memo is issued for the return of merchandise purchased, the original voucher is discarded. (p. 155)   16. _____
17. The amount of net salaries is credited to Vouchers Payable to record the voucher for payroll. (p. 155)   17. _____

5-1 WORK TOGETHER, p. 149

Preparing a voucher and journalizing vouchers in a voucher register

[1]

Vchr. No.	**152**

Date_____ Due Date_____ Payment Date_____

To_____

Address_____
Street

_____
City   State   ZIP

ACCOUNTS DEBITED	AMOUNT
PURCHASES	
SUPPLIES—SALES	
SUPPLIES—ADMIN.	
MISCELLANEOUS EXPENSE—SALES	
MISCELLANEOUS EXPENSE—ADMIN.	
RENT EXPENSE	
SALARY EXPENSE—SALES	
SALARY EXPENSE—ADMIN.	
TOTAL DEBITS	

ACCOUNTS CREDITED	AMOUNT
VOUCHERS PAYABLE	
EMPLOYEE INC. TAX PAY.—FEDERAL	
EMPLOYEE INC. TAX PAY.—STATE	
SOCIAL SECURITY TAX PAYABLE	
MEDICARE TAX PAYABLE	
TOTAL CREDITS	

Voucher Approved by _____

Recorded in Voucher
Register Page _____ by _____

Paid { Date _____
Check No. _____ Amount $ _____
Approved by _____

This voucher register is needed to complete Work Together 5-2.

	DATE	PAYEE	VCHR. NO.	PAID DATE	PAID CK. NO.	VOUCHERS PAYABLE CREDIT	
1							1
2							2
3							3
4							4
5							5
6							6
7							7
8							8
9							9
10							10

PAGE 10 — WT 5-2 — VOUCHER 1

Extra form

	DATE	PAYEE	VCHR. NO.	PAID DATE	PAID CK. NO.	VOUCHERS PAYABLE CREDIT	
1							1
2							2
3							3
4							4
5							5
6							6
7							7
8							8
9							9
10							10

PAGE — VOUCHER 1

5-1 WORK TOGETHER (concluded)

[2, 3]

REGISTER
PAGE 10

		2		3		4	GENERAL			5		6		
		PURCHASES DEBIT		SUPPLIES— SALES DEBIT		SUPPLIES— ADMIN. DEBIT	ACCOUNT TITLE	POST. REF.	DEBIT		CREDIT			
1														1
2														2
3														3
4														4
5														5
6														6
7														7
8														8
9														9
10														10

Extra form

REGISTER
PAGE

		2		3		4	GENERAL			5		6		
		PURCHASES DEBIT		SUPPLIES— SALES DEBIT		SUPPLIES— ADMIN. DEBIT	ACCOUNT TITLE	POST. REF.	DEBIT		CREDIT			
1														1
2														2
3														3
4														4
5														5
6														6
7														7
8														8
9														9
10														10

[This page left blank intentionally.]

5-1 **ON YOUR OWN, p. 149**

Preparing a voucher and journalizing vouchers in a voucher register [1]

Vchr.
No. **89**

Due Payment
Date_____ Date_____ Date_____

To_____

Address_____
Street

_____
City   State   ZIP

ACCOUNTS DEBITED	AMOUNT	
PURCHASES		
SUPPLIES—SALES		
SUPPLIES—ADMIN.		
MISCELLANEOUS EXPENSE—SALES		
MISCELLANEOUS EXPENSE—ADMIN.		
RENT EXPENSE		
SALARY EXPENSE—SALES		
SALARY EXPENSE—ADMIN.		
TOTAL DEBITS		

ACCOUNTS CREDITED	AMOUNT	
VOUCHERS PAYABLE		
EMPLOYEE INC. TAX PAY.—FEDERAL		
EMPLOYEE INC. TAX PAY.—STATE		
SOCIAL SECURITY TAX PAYABLE		
MEDICARE TAX PAYABLE		
TOTAL CREDITS		

Voucher Approved by _____

Recorded in Voucher
Register Page _____ by _____

Paid {
Date _____
Check No. _____ Amount $ _____
Approved by _____

[2, 3]

This voucher register is needed to complete On Your Own 5-2.

PAGE 8   VOUCHER

| | DATE | PAYEE | VCHR. NO. | PAID | | VOUCHERS PAYABLE CREDIT | |
				DATE	CK. NO.		
1							1
2							2
3							3
4							4
5							5
6							6
7							7
8							8
9							9
10							10

Extra form

PAGE   VOUCHER

| | DATE | PAYEE | VCHR. NO. | PAID | | VOUCHERS PAYABLE CREDIT | |
				DATE	CK. NO.		
1							1
2							2
3							3
4							4
5							5
6							6
7							7
8							8
9							9
10							10

5-1 **ON YOUR OWN (concluded)**

[2, 3]

REGISTER

	2		3		4	GENERAL			5		6	
	PURCHASES DEBIT		SUPPLIES— SALES DEBIT		SUPPLIES— ADMIN. DEBIT	ACCOUNT TITLE	POST. REF.		DEBIT		CREDIT	
1												1
2												2
3												3
4												4
5												5
6												6
7												7
8												8
9												9
10												10

Extra form

REGISTER

PAGE

	2		3		4	GENERAL			5		6	
	PURCHASES DEBIT		SUPPLIES— SALES DEBIT		SUPPLIES— ADMIN. DEBIT	ACCOUNT TITLE	POST. REF.		DEBIT		CREDIT	
1												1
2												2
3												3
4												4
5												5
6												6
7												7
8												8
9												9
10												10

Journalizing cash payments and deposits in a check register [1–3]

The voucher register completed in Work Together 5-1 is needed to complete this Work Together.

CHECK REGISTER   PAGE 10

	DATE	PAYEE	CK. NO.	VCHR. NO.	VOUCHERS PAYABLE DEBIT	PURCHASES DISCOUNT CREDIT	CASH CREDIT	BANK DEPOSITS	BANK BALANCE	
1										1
2										2
3										3
4										4
5										5
6										6
7										7
8										8
9										9
10										10

Extra form

CHECK REGISTER   PAGE

	DATE	PAYEE	CK. NO.	VCHR. NO.	VOUCHERS PAYABLE DEBIT	PURCHASES DISCOUNT CREDIT	CASH CREDIT	BANK DEPOSITS	BANK BALANCE	
1										1
2										2
3										3
4										4
5										5
6										6
7										7
8										8
9										9
10										10

5-2 ON YOUR OWN, p. 154

Journalizing cash payments and deposits in a check register [1–3]

The voucher register completed in On Your Own 5-1 is needed to complete this On Your Own.

CHECK REGISTER PAGE 8

	DATE	PAYEE	CK. NO.	VCHR. NO.	VOUCHERS PAYABLE DEBIT	PURCHASES DISCOUNT CREDIT	CASH CREDIT	BANK DEPOSITS	BANK BALANCE	
					1	2	3	4	5	
1										1
2										2
3										3
4										4
5										5
6										6
7										7
8										8
9										9
10										10

Extra form

CHECK REGISTER PAGE

	DATE	PAYEE	CK. NO.	VCHR. NO.	VOUCHERS PAYABLE DEBIT	PURCHASES DISCOUNT CREDIT	CASH CREDIT	BANK DEPOSITS	BANK BALANCE	
					1	2	3	4	5	
1										1
2										2
3										3
4										4
5										5
6										6
7										7
8										8
9										9
10										10

Journalizing purchases returns and allowances and payroll in a voucher register [1]

PAGE 5

VOUCHER

	DATE	PAYEE	VCHR. NO.	PAID DATE	PAID CK. NO.	VOUCHERS PAYABLE CREDIT	
1							1
2							2
3							3
4							4
5							5
6							6
7							7
8							8
9							9
10							10

Extra form

PAGE

VOUCHER

	DATE	PAYEE	VCHR. NO.	PAID DATE	PAID CK. NO.	VOUCHERS PAYABLE CREDIT	
1							1
2							2
3							3
4							4
5							5
6							6
7							7
8							8
9							9
10							10

5-3 WORK TOGETHER (concluded)

[1]

REGISTER   PAGE 5

| | PURCHASES DEBIT | SUPPLIES—SALES DEBIT | SUPPLIES—ADMIN. DEBIT | GENERAL | | | |
				ACCOUNT TITLE	POST. REF.	DEBIT	CREDIT
1							
2							
3							
4							
5							
6							
7							
8							
9							
10							

Extra form

REGISTER   PAGE

| | PURCHASES DEBIT | SUPPLIES—SALES DEBIT | SUPPLIES—ADMIN. DEBIT | GENERAL | | | |
				ACCOUNT TITLE	POST. REF.	DEBIT	CREDIT
1							
2							
3							
4							
5							
6							
7							
8							
9							
10							

Journalizing purchases returns and allowances and payroll in a voucher register [1]

PAGE 6   VOUCHER

	DATE		PAYEE	VCHR. NO.	PAID DATE	CK. NO.	VOUCHERS PAYABLE CREDIT	
1								1
2								2
3								3
4								4
5								5
6								6
7								7
8								8
9								9
10								10

Extra form

PAGE   VOUCHER

	DATE		PAYEE	VCHR. NO.	PAID DATE	CK. NO.	VOUCHERS PAYABLE CREDIT	
1								1
2								2
3								3
4								4
5								5
6								6
7								7
8								8
9								9
10								10

5-3 ON YOUR OWN (concluded)

[1]

REGISTER   PAGE 6

		PURCHASES DEBIT		SUPPLIES—SALES DEBIT		SUPPLIES—ADMIN. DEBIT		GENERAL							
		2		3		4		ACCOUNT TITLE	POST. REF.	5 DEBIT		6 CREDIT			
1															1
2															2
3															3
4															4
5															5
6															6
7															7
8															8
9															9
10															10

Extra form

REGISTER   PAGE

		PURCHASES DEBIT		SUPPLIES—SALES DEBIT		SUPPLIES—ADMIN. DEBIT		GENERAL							
		2		3		4		ACCOUNT TITLE	POST. REF.	5 DEBIT		6 CREDIT			
1															1
2															2
3															3
4															4
5															5
6															6
7															7
8															8
9															9
10															10

[This page left blank intentionally.]

5-1 **APPLICATION PROBLEM, p. 161**

Preparing a voucher and journalizing vouchers in a voucher register **[1]**

Vchr. No. **87**		

Date _____ Due Date _____ Payment Date _____

To _____

Address _____
Street

_____
City   State   ZIP

ACCOUNTS DEBITED	AMOUNT	
PURCHASES		
SUPPLIES—SALES		
SUPPLIES—ADMIN.		
MISCELLANEOUS EXPENSE—SALES		
MISCELLANEOUS EXPENSE—ADMIN.		
RENT EXPENSE		
SALARY EXPENSE—SALES		
SALARY EXPENSE—ADMIN.		
TOTAL DEBITS		

ACCOUNTS CREDITED	AMOUNT	
VOUCHERS PAYABLE		
EMPLOYEE INC. TAX PAY.—FEDERAL		
EMPLOYEE INC. TAX PAY.—STATE		
SOCIAL SECURITY TAX PAYABLE		
MEDICARE TAX PAYABLE		
TOTAL CREDITS		

Voucher Approved by _____

Recorded in Voucher
Register Page _____ by _____

Paid {
Date _____
Check No. _____ Amount $ _____
Approved by _____
}

The voucher register prepared in Application Problem 5-1 is needed to complete Application Problem 5-2.

PAGE 9   VOUCHER

	DATE	PAYEE	VCHR. NO.	PAID DATE	CK. NO.	VOUCHERS PAYABLE CREDIT	
1							1
2							2
3							3
4							4
5							5
6							6
7							7
8							8
9							9
10							10
11							11
12							12
13							13
14							14
15							15

Extra form

PAGE   VOUCHER

	DATE	PAYEE	VCHR. NO.	PAID DATE	CK. NO.	VOUCHERS PAYABLE CREDIT	
1							1
2							2
3							3
4							4
5							5
6							6

5-1   APPLICATION PROBLEM (concluded)

[2, 3]

The voucher register prepared in Application Problem 5-1 is needed to complete Application Problem 5-2.

REGISTER   PAGE 9

	2		3		4		GENERAL			5		6	
	PURCHASES DEBIT		SUPPLIES—SALES DEBIT		SUPPLIES—ADMIN. DEBIT		ACCOUNT TITLE	POST. REF.	DEBIT		CREDIT		
1													1
2													2
3													3
4													4
5													5
6													6
7													7
8													8
9													9
10													10
11													11
12													12
13													13
14													14
15													15

Extra form

REGISTER   PAGE

	2		3		4		GENERAL			5		6	
	PURCHASES DEBIT		SUPPLIES—SALES DEBIT		SUPPLIES—ADMIN. DEBIT		ACCOUNT TITLE	POST. REF.	DEBIT		CREDIT		
1													1
2													2
3													3
4													4
5													5
6													6

[This page left blank intentionally.]

5-2 APPLICATION PROBLEM, p. 161

Journalizing cash payments and deposits in a check register   [1–3]

The voucher register prepared in Application Problem 5-1 is needed to complete Application
Problem 5-2.

CHECK REGISTER   PAGE 9

	DATE	PAYEE	CK. NO.	VCHR. NO.	VOUCHERS PAYABLE DEBIT	PURCHASES DISCOUNT CREDIT	CASH CREDIT	BANK DEPOSITS	BANK BALANCE	
					1	2	3	4	5	
1										1
2										2
3										3
4										4
5										5
6										6
7										7
8										8
9										9
10										10
11										11
12										12
13										13
14										14
15										15
16										16
17										17
18										18
19										19
20										20
21										21
22										22
23										23
24										24
25										25
26										26
27										27
28										28
29										29

Journalizing purchases returns and allowances in a voucher register

PAGE 2   VOUCHER

	DATE	PAYEE	VCHR. NO.	PAID DATE	CK. NO.	VOUCHERS PAYABLE CREDIT	
1							1
2							2
3							3
4							4
5							5
6							6
7							7
8							8
9							9
10							10
11							11
12							12

Extra form

PAGE   VOUCHER

	DATE	PAYEE	VCHR. NO.	PAID DATE	CK. NO.	VOUCHERS PAYABLE CREDIT	
1							1
2							2
3							3
4							4
5							5
6							6
7							7
8							8
9							9
10							10
11							11

5-3 APPLICATION PROBLEM (concluded)

REGISTER

	PURCHASES DEBIT	SUPPLIES— SALES DEBIT	SUPPLIES— ADMIN. DEBIT	GENERAL			
	2	3	4	ACCOUNT TITLE	POST. REF.	DEBIT (5)	CREDIT (6)
1							
2							
3							
4							
5							
6							
7							
8							
9							
10							
11							
12							

Extra form

REGISTER

PAGE

	PURCHASES DEBIT	SUPPLIES— SALES DEBIT	SUPPLIES— ADMIN. DEBIT	GENERAL			
	2	3	4	ACCOUNT TITLE	POST. REF.	DEBIT (5)	CREDIT (6)
1							
2							
3							
4							
5							
6							
7							
8							
9							
10							
11							

[This page left blank intentionally.]

5-4 APPLICATION PROBLEM, p. 162

Preparing and journalizing a voucher for payroll [1, 2]

(Note: The inside of the voucher appears on page 232.)

Vchr.
No. **51**

Date _____ Due
Date _____ Payment
Date _____

To _____

Address _____
Street

_____
City   State   ZIP

ACCOUNTS DEBITED	AMOUNT	
PURCHASES		
SUPPLIES—SALES		
SUPPLIES—ADMIN.		
MISCELLANEOUS EXPENSE—SALES		
MISCELLANEOUS EXPENSE—ADMIN.		
RENT EXPENSE		
SALARY EXPENSE—SALES		
SALARY EXPENSE—ADMIN.		
TOTAL DEBITS		

ACCOUNTS CREDITED	AMOUNT	
VOUCHERS PAYABLE		
EMPLOYEE INC. TAX PAY.—FEDERAL		
EMPLOYEE INC. TAX PAY.—STATE		
SOCIAL SECURITY TAX PAYABLE		
MEDICARE TAX PAYABLE		
TOTAL CREDITS		

Voucher Approved by _____

Recorded in Voucher
Register Page _____ by _____

Paid
{ Date _____
{ Check No. _____ Amount $ _____
{ Approved by _____

PAGE 5

VOUCHER

	DATE		PAYEE	VCHR. NO.	PAID		VOUCHERS PAYABLE CREDIT	
					DATE	CK. NO.		
1								1
2								2
3								3
4								4
5								5
6								6
7								7
8								8
9								9
10								10

Extra form

PAGE

VOUCHER

	DATE		PAYEE	VCHR. NO.	PAID		VOUCHERS PAYABLE CREDIT	
					DATE	CK. NO.		
1								1
2								2
3								3
4								4
5								5
6								6
7								7
8								8
9								9
10								10

5-4 APPLICATION PROBLEM (continued)

[2]

REGISTER   PAGE 5

	PURCHASES DEBIT	SUPPLIES—SALES DEBIT	SUPPLIES—ADMIN. DEBIT	GENERAL				
				ACCOUNT TITLE	POST. REF.	DEBIT	CREDIT	
1								1
2								2
3								3
4								4
5								5
6								6
7								7
8								8
9								9
10								10

Extra form

REGISTER   PAGE

	PURCHASES DEBIT	SUPPLIES—SALES DEBIT	SUPPLIES—ADMIN. DEBIT	GENERAL				
				ACCOUNT TITLE	POST. REF.	DEBIT	CREDIT	
1								1
2								2
3								3
4								4
5								5
6								6
7								7
8								8
9								9
10								10

VOUCHER		Vchr. No. **51**

Payment Date _____ 20 _____

Date _____ 20 _____ Terms _____   Due _____ 20 _____

To _____

Address _____

City _____ State _____ ZIP _____

For the following: Enclose all invoices or other papers.

DATE	VOUCHER DETAILS	AMOUNT

5-5 MASTERY PROBLEM, p. 163

Journalizing transactions in a voucher system

[1–3]

CHECK REGISTER

	DATE		PAYEE	CK. NO.	VCHR. NO.	VOUCHERS PAYABLE DEBIT	PURCHASES DISCOUNT CREDIT	CASH CREDIT	BANK DEPOSITS	BANK BALANCE	
						1	2	3	4	5	
1											1
2											2
3											3
4											4
5											5
6											6
7											7
8											8
9											9
10											10
11											11
12											12
13											13
14											14
15											15
16											16
17											17
18											18
19											19
20											20
21											21
22											22
23											23
24											24
25											25
26											26
27											27
28											28
29											29
30											30
31											31

PAGE 22

VOUCHER

	DATE	PAYEE	VCHR. NO.	PAID		VOUCHERS PAYABLE CREDIT	
				DATE	CK. NO.		
1							1
2							2
3							3
4							4
5							5
6							6
7							7
8							8
9							9
10							10
11							11
12							12
13							13
14							14
15							15
16							16
17							17
18							18
19							19
20							20
21							21
22							22
23							23
24							24
25							25
26							26
27							27
28							28
29							29
30							30
31							31

5-5 **MASTERY PROBLEM (concluded)**

[2, 3]

REGISTER   PAGE 22

	PURCHASES DEBIT (2)	SUPPLIES— SALES DEBIT (3)	SUPPLIES— ADMIN. DEBIT (4)	GENERAL			
				ACCOUNT TITLE	POST. REF.	DEBIT (5)	CREDIT (6)
1								1
2								2
3								3
4								4
5								5
6								6
7								7
8								8
9								9
10								10
11								11
12								12
13								13
14								14
15								15
16								16
17								17
18								18
19								19
20								20
21								21
22								22
23								23
24								24
25								25
26								26
27								27
28								28
29								29
30								30
31								31

[This page left blank intentionally.]

5-6 CHALLENGE PROBLEM, p. 163

Journalizing purchases invoices at the net amount in a voucher system [1–3]

					VOUCHERS PAYABLE DEBIT	CASH CREDIT	BANK	
	DATE	PAYEE	CK. NO.	VCHR. NO.	1	2	DEPOSITS 3	BALANCE 4
1								
2								
3								
4								
5								
6								
7								
8								
9								
10								
11								
12								
13								
14								
15								
16								
17								
18								
19								
20								
21								
22								
23								
24								
25								
26								
27								
28								
29								
30								
31								

CHECK REGISTER — PAGE 20

[2, 3]

VOUCHER

1

	DATE		PAYEE	VCHR. NO.	PAID DATE	CK. NO.	VOUCHERS PAYABLE CREDIT	
1								1
2								2
3								3
4								4
5								5
6								6
7								7
8								8
9								9
10								10
11								11
12								12
13								13
14								14
15								15
16								16
17								17
18								18
19								19
20								20
21								21
22								22
23								23
24								24
25								25
26								26
27								27
28								28
29								29
30								30
31								31

5-6 CHALLENGE PROBLEM (concluded)

[2, 3]

REGISTER

PAGE 25

	PURCHASES DEBIT	DISCOUNTS LOST DEBIT	SUPPLIES DEBIT	GENERAL				
	2	3	4	ACCOUNT TITLE	POST. REF.	DEBIT	CREDIT	
1								1
2								2
3								3
4								4
5								5
6								6
7								7
8								8
9								9
10								10
11								11
12								12
13								13
14								14
15								15
16								16
17								17
18								18
19								19
20								20
21								21
22								22
23								23
24								24
25								25
26								26
27								27
28								28
29								29
30								30
31								31

Study Guide 6

Name	Perfect Score	Your Score
Identifying Accounting Terms	14 Pts.	
Analyzing Concepts and Practices Related to Inventory Control	22 Pts.	
Total	36 Pts.	

Part One—Identifying Accounting Terms

Directions: Select the one term in Column I that best fits each definition in Column II. Print the letter identifying your choice in the Answers column.

Column I	Column II	Answers
A. average number of days' sales in merchandise inventory	**1.** A form used during a periodic inventory to record information about each item of merchandise on hand. (p. 174)	1. _____
	2. The person or business who gives goods on consignment. (p. 172)	2. _____
B. consignee	**3.** The period of time needed to sell an average amount of merchandise inventory. (p. 184)	3. _____
C. consignment		
D. consignor	**4.** A form used to show the kind of merchandise, quantity received, quantity sold, and balance on hand. (p. 173)	4. _____
E. first-in, first-out inventory costing method	**5.** A file of stock records for all merchandise on hand. (p. 173)	5. _____
	6. Using the price of merchandise purchased first to calculate the cost of merchandise sold first. (p. 176)	6. _____
F. inventory record		
G. last-in, first-out inventory costing method	**7.** Using the price of merchandise purchased last to calculate the cost of merchandise sold first. (p. 177)	7. _____
	8. Using the average cost of beginning inventory plus merchandise purchased during a fiscal period to calculate the cost of merchandise sold. (p. 178)	8. _____
H. lower of cost or market inventory costing method	**9.** Using the lower of cost or market price to calculate the cost of ending merchandise inventory. (p. 180)	9. _____
I. merchandise inventory turnover ratio	**10.** Estimating inventory by using a percentage based on both cost and retail prices. (p. 183)	10. _____
J. purchase order	**11.** The number of times the average amount of merchandise inventory is sold during a specific period of time. (p. 184)	11. _____
K. retail method of estimating inventory	**12.** Goods which are given to a business to sell, but for which title to the goods remains with the vendor. (p. 172)	12. _____
L. stock ledger	**13.** A completed form authorizing a seller to deliver goods with payment to be made later. (p. 173)	13. _____
M. stock record		
N. weighted-average inventory costing method	**14.** The person or business who receives goods on consignment. (p. 172)	14. _____

Part Two—Analyzing Concepts and Practices Related to Inventory Control

Directions: Place a *T* for True or *F* for False in the Answers column to show whether each of the following statements is true or false.

Answers

1. The cost of merchandise available for sale consists of the cost of the beginning inventory and the purchases added to inventory during the fiscal period. (p. 171)

     1. _____

2. If the cost of the ending merchandise inventory is overstated, the net income will be understated. (p. 171)

     2. _____

3. If the cost of ending merchandise inventory is understated, the cost of merchandise sold will be overstated. (p. 171)

     3. _____

4. If the cost of ending merchandise inventory is understated, the total stockholders' equity will be overstated. (p. 171)

     4. _____

5. Calculating an accurate merchandise inventory cost in order to adequately report a business's financial progress and condition is an application of the accounting concept Adequate Disclosure. (p. 171)

     5. _____

6. At the end of each fiscal period, the cost of merchandise available for sale is divided into the ending inventory and net purchases. (p. 171)

     6. _____

7. Typically, a business counts as part of its inventory all goods for sale legally owned by the business. (p. 172)

     7. _____

8. When the terms of sale for goods in transit are FOB shipping point, the title to the goods passes to the buyer when the goods are received by the buyer. (p. 172)

     8. _____

9. When the terms of sale for goods in transit are FOB destination, the title to the goods passes to the buyer when the goods are received by the buyer. (p. 172)

     9. _____

10. When goods are sent to a business on consignment, title to the goods passes to the business accepting the consignment when the consignor delivers the goods to a transportation business. (p. 172)

     10. _____

11. A perpetual inventory provides day-to-day records about the quantity of merchandise on hand. (p. 173)

     11. _____

12. Because of the expense, many businesses take a periodic inventory only once a year. (p. 174)

     12. _____

13. Businesses using a perpetual inventory method never need to take a periodic inventory. (p. 174)

     13. _____

14. The weighted-average inventory costing method is based on the assumption that each item in the ending inventory has a cost equal to the average price paid for similar items. (p. 178)

     14. _____

15. In the lower of cost or market inventory costing method, if the unit price is higher than the current market price, the inventory cost is reduced to the market price. (p. 180)

     15. _____

16. During a period of increasing prices, the weighted-average inventory costing method usually will give the lowest total inventory cost. (p. 179)

     16. _____

17. During a period of decreasing prices, the fifo inventory costing method usually will give the lowest total inventory cost. (p. 179)

     17. _____

18. Taking a periodic inventory once a month for interim monthly financial statements is usually too expensive to be worthwhile. (p. 182)

     18. _____

19. Businesses that need an ending inventory cost for monthly interim financial statements usually take a monthly periodic inventory. (p. 182)

     19. _____

20. A business keeping a perpetual inventory and also preparing monthly interim financial statements will need to estimate monthly ending inventory. (p. 182)

     20. _____

21. Using the retail method of estimating inventory is more expensive than the gross profit method because more records must be kept. (p. 183)

     21. _____

22. A merchandise inventory turnover ratio expresses a relationship between an average inventory and the cost of merchandise sold. (p. 184)

     22. _____

6-1 WORK TOGETHER
ON YOUR OWN, p. 175

Completing a stock record for a perpetual inventory system and   **[1–2]**
comparing it to an inventory record

INVENTORY RECORD

DATE ___9/30/--_____ ITEM ___Televisions_____

1	2	3	4	5
STOCK NUMBER	DESCRIPTION	NO. OF UNITS ON HAND	UNIT PRICE	TOTAL COST
K087	19″ color television	85	$175.00	$14,875.00

STOCK RECORD

Description _____ Stock No. _____

Reorder _____ Minimum _____ Location _____

1	2	3	4	5	6	7
	INCREASES			DECREASES		BALANCE
DATE	PURCHASE INVOICE NO.	QUANTITY	DATE	SALES INVOICE NO.	QUANTITY	QUANTITY

WT 6-1

OYO 6-1

WORK TOGETHER
ON YOUR OWN, p. 181

Costing ending inventory using fifo, lifo, and weighted average   [1]

Fifo:

Lifo:

Weighted-average:

                                                                                    [1]

Fifo:

Lifo:

Weighted-average:

6-3 WORK TOGETHER, p. 186

Estimating inventory using the gross profit and retail methods [1]

ESTIMATED MERCHANDISE INVENTORY SHEET
Gross Profit Method

COMPANY _____ DATE _____

1	Beginning inventory, April 1	$_____
2	Net purchases to date	_____
3	Merchandise available for sale	$_____
4	Net sales to date . . . . $_____	
5	Less estimated gross profit . . . . _____	
	(Net sales × Estimated gross profit ____%)	
6	Estimated cost of merchandise sold	_____
7	Estimated ending inventory	$_____

---

[2]

ESTIMATED MERCHANDISE INVENTORY SHEET
Retail Method

COMPANY _____ DATE _____

		Cost	Retail
1			
2	Beginning inventory, April 1	$_____	$_____
3	Net purchases to date	_____	_____
4	Merchandise available for sale	$_____	$_____
5	Net sales to date		_____
	Estimated ending inventory at retail		$_____
6	Estimated ending inventory at cost	$_____	
7	(Inventory at Retail × percentage____%)		

Estimating inventory using the gross profit and retail methods [1]

ESTIMATED MERCHANDISE INVENTORY SHEET
Gross Profit Method

COMPANY _____   DATE _____

1	Beginning inventory, October 1	$ _____
2	Net purchases to date	_____
3	Merchandise available for sale	$ _____
4	Net sales to date . . . . $ _____	
5	Less estimated gross profit . . . . _____	
	(Net sales × Estimated gross profit ____%)	
6	Estimated cost of merchandise sold	_____
7	Estimated ending inventory	$ _____

---

[2]

ESTIMATED MERCHANDISE INVENTORY SHEET
Retail Method

COMPANY _____   DATE _____

		Cost	Retail
1			
2	Beginning inventory, October 1	$ _____	$ _____
3	Net purchases to date	_____	_____
4	Merchandise available for sale	$ _____	$ _____
5	Net sales to date		_____
	Estimated ending inventory at retail		$ _____
6	Estimated ending inventory at cost	$ _____	
7	(Inventory at Retail × percentage____%)		

6-1 APPLICATION PROBLEM, p. 188

Keeping perpetual inventory records [1, 2]

STOCK RECORD

Description _____ Stock No. _____

Reorder _____ Minimum _____ Location _____

1	2	3	4	5	6	7
INCREASES			DECREASES			BALANCE
DATE	PURCHASE INVOICE NO.	QUANTITY	DATE	SALES INVOICE NO.	QUANTITY	QUANTITY

STOCK RECORD

Description _____ Stock No. _____

Reorder _____ Minimum _____ Location _____

1	2	3	4	5	6	7
INCREASES			DECREASES			BALANCE
DATE	PURCHASE INVOICE NO.	QUANTITY	DATE	SALES INVOICE NO.	QUANTITY	QUANTITY

Determining inventory cost using fifo, lifo, weighted-average, and lower of cost or market

Inventory Costing Method

Stock No.	Dec. 31 Inventory	Market Price	Fifo			Lifo			Weighted-Average		
			Unit Price	Total Cost	Lower of Cost or Market	Unit Price	Total Cost	Lower of Cost or Market	Unit Price	Total Cost	Lower of Cost or Market

Highest Method: _____

Lowest Method: _____

6-3 APPLICATION PROBLEM, p. 189

Estimating cost of merchandise inventory using estimating methods [1]

ESTIMATED MERCHANDISE INVENTORY SHEET
Gross Profit Method

COMPANY _____ DATE _____

1	Beginning inventory, January 1		$ _____
2	Net purchases to date		_____
3	Merchandise available for sale		$ _____
4	Net sales to date	$ _____	
5	Less estimated gross profit	_____	
	(Net sales × Estimated gross profit ____%)		
6	Estimated cost of merchandise sold		_____
7	Estimated ending inventory		$ _____

---

[2]

ESTIMATED MERCHANDISE INVENTORY SHEET
Retail Method

COMPANY _____ DATE _____

		Cost	Retail
1		Cost	Retail
2	Beginning inventory, January 1	$ _____	$ _____
3	Net purchases to date	_____	_____
4	Merchandise available for sale	$ _____	$ _____
5	Net sales to date		_____
	Estimated ending inventory at retail		$ _____
6	Estimated ending inventory at cost	$ _____	
7	(Inventory at Retail × percentage ____%)		

APPLICATION PROBLEM, p. 190

Calculating merchandise inventory turnover ratio and [1]
average number of days' sales in merchandising inventory

Corporation A:

Corporation B:

Corporation C:

[2]

Corporation A:

Corporation B:

Corporation C:

[3]

Best Turnover Ratio: _____

6-5 MASTERY PROBLEM, p. 190

Determining cost of merchandise inventory; estimating cost of merchandise
inventory using estimating methods; calculating merchandise inventory turnover
ratio and average number of days' sales in merchandising inventory

[1, 2]

Stock No.	Dec. 31 Inventory	Inventory Costing Method					
		Fifo		Lifo		Weighted-Average	
		Unit Price	Total Cost	Unit Price	Total Cost	Unit Price	Total Cost
Total Cost							

[3]

Stock No.	Lifo Cost	Market Price			Lower of Cost or Market
		Inventory	Unit Price	Total Cost	

[6]

[7]

[4]

ESTIMATED MERCHANDISE INVENTORY SHEET
Gross Profit Method

COMPANY _____ DATE _____

1	Beginning inventory, January 1		$ _____
2	Net purchases to date		_____
3	Merchandise available for sale		$ _____
4	Net sales to date	$ _____	
5	Less estimated gross profit	_____	
	(Net sales × Estimated gross profit _____%)		
6	Estimated cost of merchandise sold		_____
7	Estimated ending inventory		$ _____

[5]

ESTIMATED MERCHANDISE INVENTORY SHEET
Retail Method

COMPANY _____ DATE _____

		Cost	Retail
1			
2	Beginning inventory, January 1	$ _____	$ _____
3	Net purchases to date	_____	_____
4	Merchandise available for sale	$ _____	$ _____
5	Net sales to date		_____
	Estimated ending inventory at retail		$ _____
6	Estimated ending inventory at cost	$ _____	
7	(Inventory at Retail × percentage_____%)		

6-6 CHALLENGE PROBLEM, p. 191

Determining the unit price of merchandise inventory purchases　　　　　　　　　　[1]

[2, 3]

Stock No.	Quantity	Unit Price	Total Cost	Adjusted Unit Price	Adjusted Total Cost
A69	50	$2.00	$100.00		
V56	15	6.00	90.00		
X28	30	4.00	120.00		
W12	20	3.00	60.00		
S92	5	8.00	40.00		

Extra space for calculations

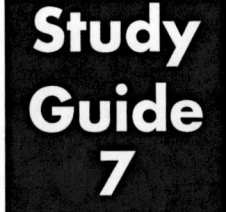
Name	Perfect Score	Your Score
Identifying Accounting Terms	7 Pts.	
Analyzing Entries for Uncollectible Accounts Expense	8 Pts.	
Analyzing Practices Involved in Journalizing Uncollectible Accounts Expense	20 Pts.	
Total	35 Pts.	

Part One—Identifying Accounting Terms

Directions: Select the one term in Column I that best fits each definition in Column II. Print the letter identifying your choice in the Answers column.

Column I	Column II	Answers
A. accounts receivable turnover ratio	1. Accounts receivable that cannot be collected. (p. 200)	1. _____
B. aging accounts receivable	2. Canceling the balance of a customer account because the customer does not pay. (p. 200)	2. _____
C. allowance method of recording losses from uncollectible accounts	3. Recording uncollectible accounts expense only when an amount is actually known to be uncollectible. (p. 201)	3. _____
D. book value of accounts receivable	4. Crediting the estimated value of uncollectible accounts to a contra account. (p. 204)	4. _____
E. direct write-off method of recording losses from uncollectible accounts	5. Analyzing accounts receivable according to when they are due. (p. 206)	5. _____
F. uncollectible accounts	6. The difference between the balance of Accounts Receivable and its contra account, Allowance for Uncollectible Accounts. (p. 211)	6. _____
G. writing off an account	7. The number of times the average amount of accounts receivable is collected during a specified period. (p. 211)	7. _____

Part Two—Analyzing Entries for Uncollectible Accounts Expense

Directions: For each entry below, print in the proper Answers column the letters identifying which accounts are to be debited and credited.

Account Titles	Transaction	Answers Debit	Credit
A. Accounts Receivable	*(a) Direct write-off method:*		
	1. Wrote off customer's account as uncollectible. (p. 201)	1. _____	_____
B. Allowance for Uncollectible Accounts	2. Reopened customer account previously written off as uncollectible. (p. 202)	2. _____	_____
	3. Received cash in full payment of customer account, described in question 2. (p. 202)	3. _____	_____
C. Cash	*(b) Allowance method:*		
D. Collection of Uncollectible Accounts	4. Recorded adjustment for uncollectible accounts expense. (p. 205)	4. _____	_____
E. Uncollectible Accounts Expense	5. Recorded adjustment for uncollectible accounts expense when using aging accounts receivable method to calculate the amount. (p. 206)	5. _____	_____
	6. Recorded adjustment for uncollectible accounts expense when using the percentage of accounts receivable account balance to calculate the amount. (p. 207)	6. _____	_____
	7. Wrote off customer account as uncollectible. (p. 208)	7. _____	_____
	8. Reopened customer account previously written off as uncollectible. (p. 209)	8. _____	_____

Part Three—Analyzing Practices Involved in Journalizing Uncollectible Accounts Expense

Directions: Place a *T* for True or *F* for False in the Answers column to show whether each of the following statements is true or false.

1. Uncollectible accounts are sometimes referred to as bad debts. (p. 200)   1. _____

2. When a sale on account is made, the amount is recorded in Allowance for Uncollectible Accounts. (p. 200)   2. _____

3. Until a specific amount is actually known to be uncollectible, the amount remains recorded in Accounts Receivable. (p. 200)   3. _____

4. When a customer account is known to be uncollectible, the account is no longer an asset. (p. 200)   4. _____

5. When a customer account is known to be uncollectible, the amount becomes a business expense. (p. 201)   5. _____

6. Because an uncollectible account may be collected in the future, the account should remain as part of the accounts receivable of a business. (p. 201)   6. _____

7. Amounts owed by customers are recorded in a general ledger account titled Accounts Receivable. (p. 200)   7. _____

8. When using the allowance method, an uncollectible account is closed by transferring the balance to a general ledger account titled Allowance for Uncollectible Accounts. (p. 208)   8. _____

9. A business with very few uncollectible accounts should probably use the allowance method of recording uncollectible accounts expense. (p. 201)   9. _____

10. One disadvantage of the direct write-off method of recording uncollectible accounts expense is that the expense may not be recorded in the same fiscal period as the revenue for the sale. (p. 204)   10. _____

11. Recording uncollectible accounts expense in the same fiscal period in which the original sale on account was made is an application of the Matching Expenses with Revenue accounting concept. (p. 204)   11. _____

12. Because there is no way of knowing for sure which customer accounts will become uncollectible, an estimate is made based on past history of uncollectible accounts expense. (p. 204)   12. _____

13. The formula for calculating the amount of uncollectible accounts expense based on a percentage of net sales is: Net sales *times* percentage *equals* estimated uncollectible accounts expense. (p. 205)   13. _____

14. An adjusting entry is made at the end of a fiscal period to record the estimated uncollectible accounts expense. (p. 205)   14. _____

15. Two accounts used for the uncollectible accounts expense adjustment are Uncollectible Accounts Expense and Accounts Receivable. (p. 205)   15. _____

16. Some businesses base their estimate of uncollectible accounts expense on a percentage of the total sales on account made during a fiscal period. (p. 205)   16. _____

17. The formula for calculating the amount of estimated uncollectible accounts expense when using a percentage of total sales on account is: Total sales on account *times* percentage *equals* estimated uncollectible accounts expense. (p. 205)   17. _____

18. When using the allowance method of recording estimated uncollectible accounts expense, regardless of the method used to calculate the amount, the adjusting entry affects the same two accounts. (p. 204)   18. _____

19. Businesses that sell on n/30 terms make a special effort to collect accounts receivable that are more than 60 days old. (p. 206)   19. _____

20. Regardless of the care taken in granting credit, some customers will not pay the amounts owed. (p. 204)   20. _____

7-1 WORK TOGETHER, p. 203

Journalizing entries to write off uncollectible accounts—direct write-off method   [1]

GENERAL JOURNAL   PAGE 2

	DATE	ACCOUNT TITLE	DOC. NO.	POST. REF.	DEBIT	CREDIT	
1							1
2							2
3							3
4							4
5							5
6							6
7							7
8							8
9							9
10							10
11							11
12							12
13							13
14							14
15							15
16							16
17							17
18							18
19							19
20							20
21							21
22							22
23							23
24							24
25							25
26							26
27							27
28							28
29							29
30							30
31							31

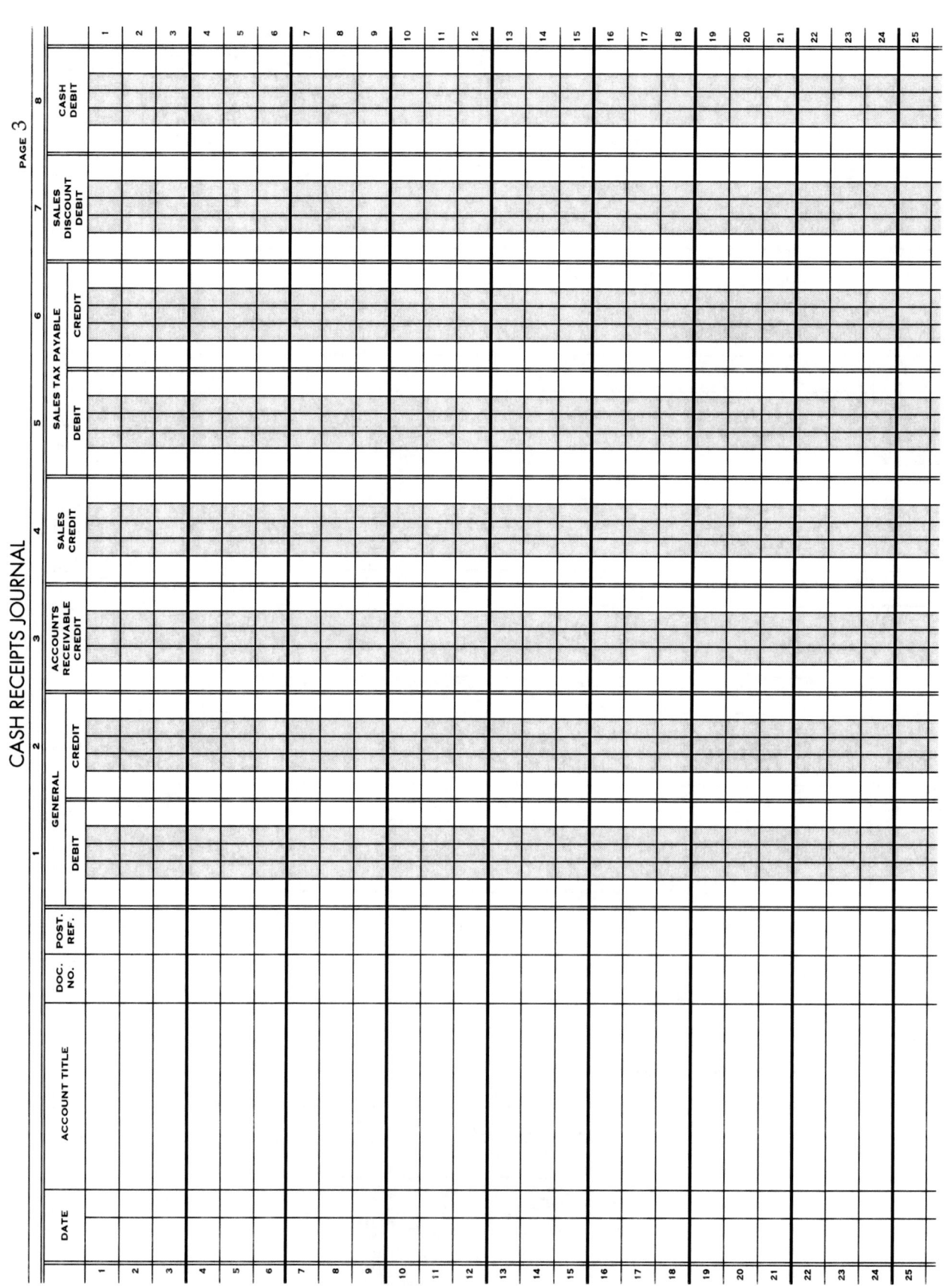

7-1 ON YOUR OWN, p. 203

Journalizing entries to write off uncollectible accounts—direct write-off method [1]

GENERAL JOURNAL

PAGE 2

	DATE	ACCOUNT TITLE	DOC. NO.	POST. REF.	DEBIT	CREDIT	
1							1
2							2
3							3
4							4
5							5
6							6
7							7
8							8
9							9
10							10
11							11
12							12
13							13
14							14
15							15
16							16
17							17
18							18
19							19
20							20
21							21
22							22
23							23
24							24
25							25
26							26
27							27
28							28
29							29
30							30
31							31

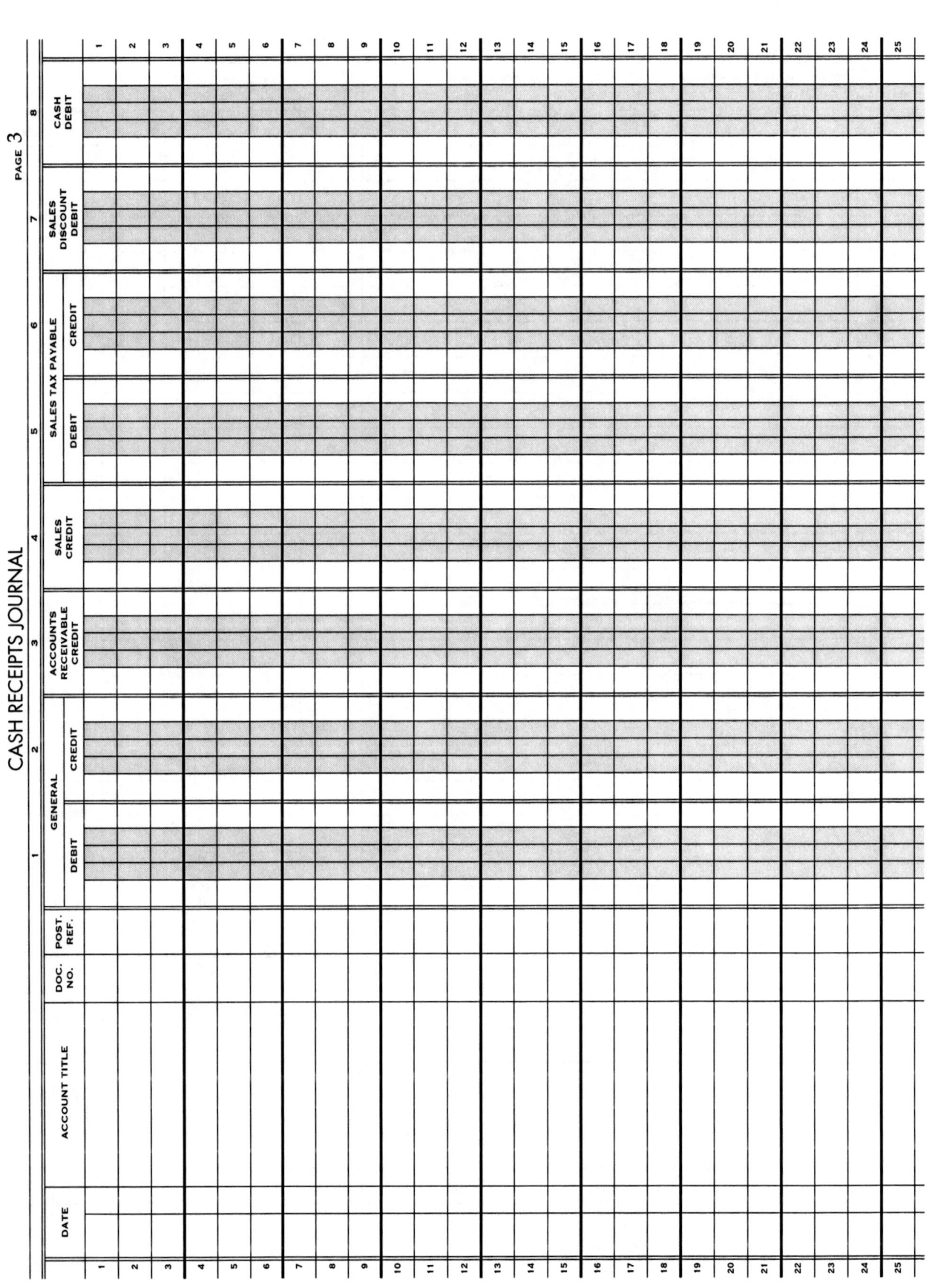

7-2 WORK TOGETHER, p. 210

Estimating amount of uncollectible accounts expense; journalizing the adjusting entry   [1]

GENERAL JOURNAL   PAGE 12

	DATE		ACCOUNT TITLE	DOC. NO.	POST. REF.	DEBIT	CREDIT	
1								1
2								2
3								3
4								4
5								5
6								6
7								7
8								8
9								9
10								10
11								11
12								12
13								13
14								14
15								15
16								16
17								17
18								18
19								19
20								20
21								21
22								22
23								23
24								24
25								25
26								26
27								27
28								28
29								29
30								30
31								31

Age Group	Amount	Percentage	Uncollectible
Not yet due	$ 8,619.18	0.1%	
1–30 days	2,254.83	0.2%	
31–60 days	862.57	0.3%	
61–90 days	2,574.57	0.8%	
Over 90 days	350.90	50.0%	
Totals	$14,662.05		
Current Balance of Allowance for Uncollectible Accounts			
Estimated Addition to Allowance for Uncollectible Accounts			

GENERAL JOURNAL

PAGE 14

	DATE	ACCOUNT TITLE	DOC. NO.	POST. REF.	DEBIT	CREDIT	
1							1
2							2
3							3
4							4
5							5
6							6
7							7
8							8
9							9
10							10
11							11
12							12
13							13
14							14
15							15
16							16
17							17

7-2 **ON YOUR OWN, p. 210**

Estimating amount of uncollectible accounts expense; journalizing the adjusting entry   [1]

GENERAL JOURNAL   PAGE 18

	DATE	ACCOUNT TITLE	DOC. NO.	POST. REF.	DEBIT	CREDIT	
1							1
2							2
3							3
4							4
5							5
6							6
7							7
8							8
9							9
10							10
11							11
12							12
13							13
14							14
15							15
16							16
17							17
18							18
19							19
20							20
21							21
22							22
23							23
24							24
25							25
26							26
27							27
28							28
29							29
30							30
31							31

Age Group	Amount	Percentage	Uncollectible
Not yet due	$16,453.18	0.1%	
1–30 days	5,354.12	0.5%	
31–60 days	645.15	10.0%	
61–90 days	3,458.01	20.0%	
Over 90 days	894.28	50.0%	
Totals	$26,804.74		
Current Balance of Allowance for Uncollectible Accounts			
Estimated Addition to Allowance for Uncollectible Accounts			

GENERAL JOURNAL

PAGE 16

	DATE	ACCOUNT TITLE	DOC. NO.	POST. REF.	DEBIT	CREDIT	
1							1
2							2
3							3
4							4
5							5
6							6
7							7
8							8
9							9
10							10
11							11
12							12
13							13
14							14
15							15
16							16
17							17

7-3 WORK TOGETHER, p. 213

Calculating accounts receivable turnover ratios [1]

Accounts receivable turnover ratio:

[2]

Average number of days for payment:

[3]

Is Milliken Industries effective in collecting accounts receivable?

_____

_____

_____

_____

Calculating accounts receivable turnover ratios [1]

Accounts receivable turnover ratio:

[2]

Average number of days for payment:

[3]

Is Stokes Building Supply effective in collecting accounts receivable?

_____

_____

_____

_____

7-1 APPLICATION PROBLEM, p. 215

Journalizing entries to write off uncollectible accounts—direct write-off method

GENERAL JOURNAL

PAGE 3

	DATE	ACCOUNT TITLE	DOC. NO.	POST. REF.	DEBIT	CREDIT	
1							1
2							2
3							3
4							4
5							5
6							6
7							7
8							8
9							9
10							10
11							11
12							12
13							13
14							14
15							15
16							16
17							17
18							18
19							19
20							20
21							21
22							22
23							23
24							24
25							25
26							26
27							27
28							28
29							29
30							30
31							31

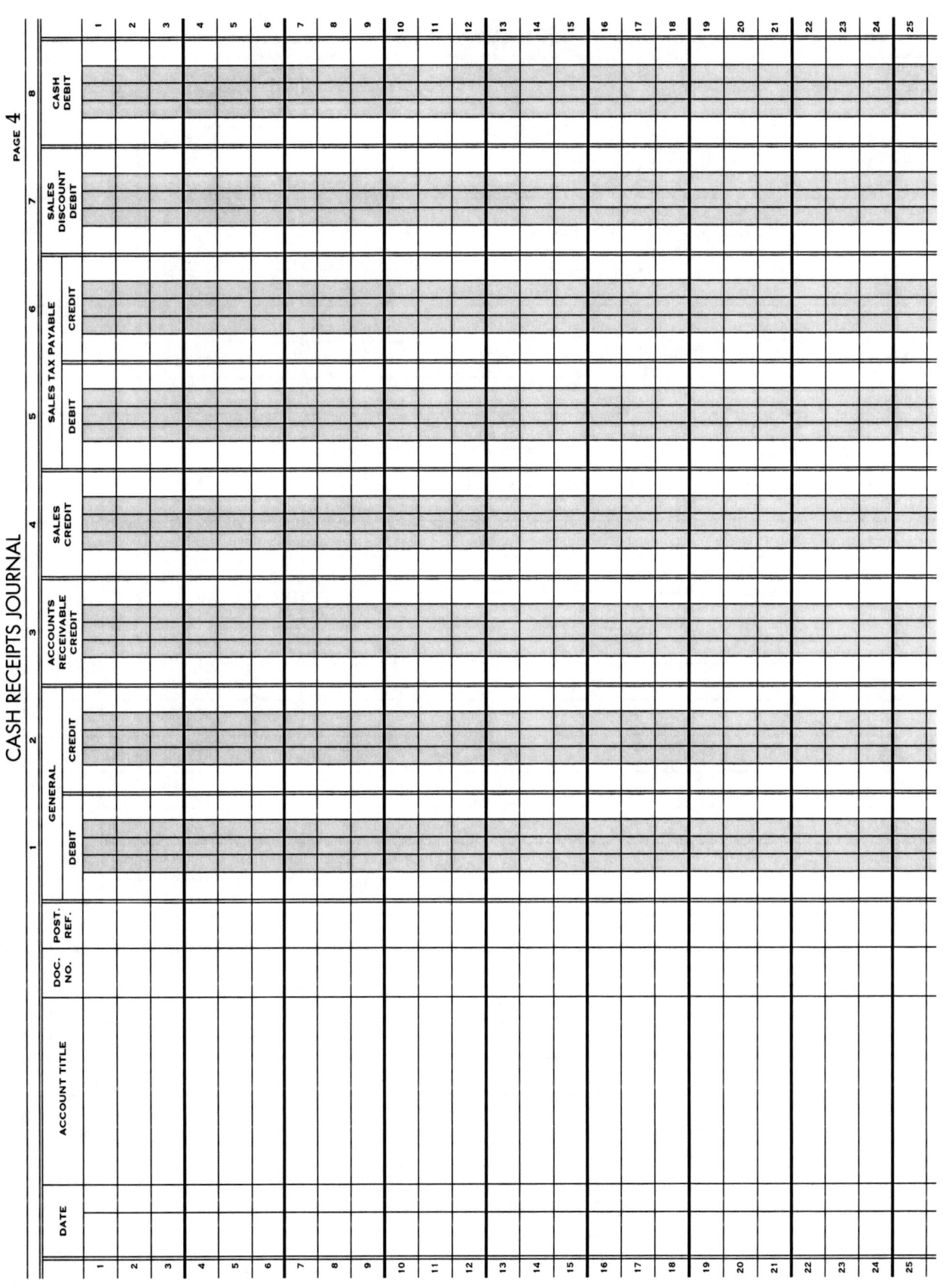

CASH RECEIPTS JOURNAL

PAGE 4

				GENERAL		ACCOUNTS RECEIVABLE CREDIT	SALES CREDIT	SALES TAX PAYABLE		SALES DISCOUNT DEBIT	CASH DEBIT
DATE	ACCOUNT TITLE	DOC. NO.	POST. REF.	DEBIT	CREDIT			DEBIT	CREDIT		
				1	2	3	4	5	6	7	8

7-2 APPLICATION PROBLEM, p. 215

Estimating amount of uncollectible accounts expense by using a percentage of net sales—allowance method; journalizing the adjusting entry

GENERAL JOURNAL   PAGE 24

	DATE	ACCOUNT TITLE	DOC. NO.	POST. REF.	DEBIT	CREDIT	
1							1
2							2
3							3
4							4
5							5
6							6
7							7
8							8
9							9
10							10
11							11
12							12

Extra space for calculations

Estimating the balance of Allowance for Uncollectible Accounts by aging accounts receivable—allowance method; journalizing the adjusting entry [1]

Age Group	Amount	Percentage	Uncollectible
Not yet due			
1–30 days			
31–60 days			
61–90 days			
Over 90 days			
Totals			
Current Balance of Allowance for Uncollectible Accounts			
Estimated Addition to Allowance for Uncollectible Accounts			

[2]

GENERAL JOURNAL   PAGE 12

	DATE	ACCOUNT TITLE	DOC. NO.	POST. REF.	DEBIT	CREDIT	
1							1
2							2
3							3
4							4
5							5
6							6
7							7
8							8
9							9
10							10
11							11
12							12
13							13
14							14
15							15
16							16

7-4 APPLICATION PROBLEM, p. 216

Journalizing entries to write off uncollectible accounts and collect written-off accounts—allowance method

GENERAL JOURNAL PAGE 3

	DATE		ACCOUNT TITLE	DOC. NO.	POST. REF.	DEBIT	CREDIT	
1								1
2								2
3								3
4								4
5								5
6								6
7								7
8								8
9								9
10								10
11								11
12								12
13								13
14								14
15								15
16								16
17								17
18								18
19								19
20								20
21								21
22								22
23								23
24								24
25								25
26								26
27								27
28								28
29								29
30								30
31								31

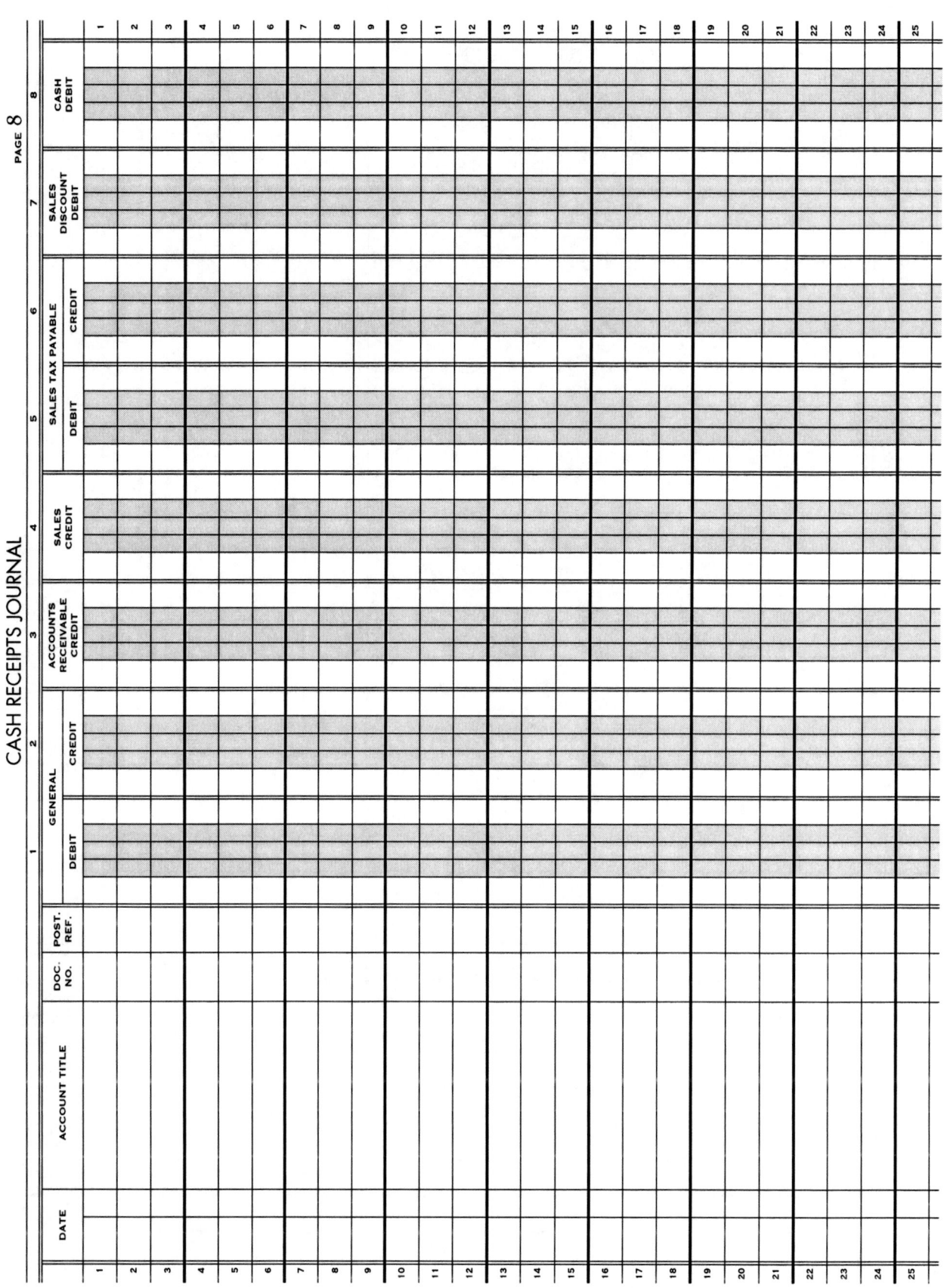

CASH RECEIPTS JOURNAL

PAGE 8

			GENERAL		ACCOUNTS RECEIVABLE CREDIT	SALES CREDIT	SALES TAX PAYABLE		SALES DISCOUNT DEBIT	CASH DEBIT
DATE	ACCOUNT TITLE	DOC. NO.	POST. REF.	DEBIT	CREDIT			DEBIT	CREDIT		

7-5 APPLICATION PROBLEM, p. 216

Calculating accounts receivable turnover ratios [1]

Accounts receivable turnover ratio:

[2]

Average number of days for payment:

[3]

Is Fleming Company effective in collecting its accounts receivable?

_____

_____

_____

_____

Accounts receivable transactions using the allowance method

GENERAL JOURNAL   PAGE 4

	DATE		ACCOUNT TITLE	DOC. NO.	POST. REF.	DEBIT	CREDIT	
1								1
2								2
3								3
4								4
5								5
6								6
7								7
8								8
9								9
10								10
11								11
12								12
13								13
14								14
15								15
16								16
17								17
18								18
19								19
20								20
21								21
22								22
23								23
24								24
25								25
26								26
27								27
28								28
29								29
30								30
31								31

7-6 APPLICATION PROBLEM (concluded)

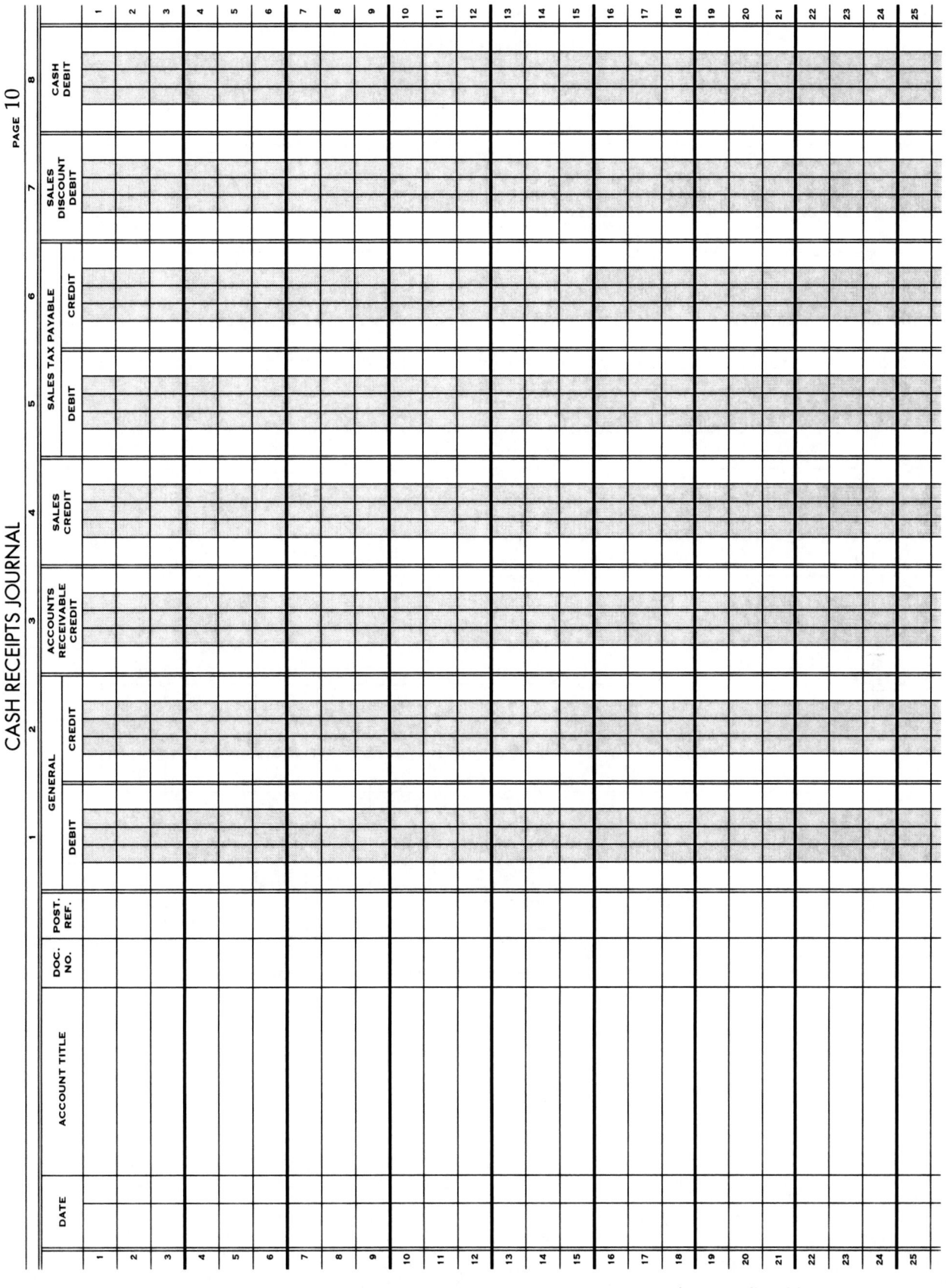

CASH RECEIPTS JOURNAL

PAGE 10

Journalizing entries for uncollectible accounts—allowance method; calculating and journalizing the adjusting entry for uncollectible accounts expense [1, 2]

GENERAL JOURNAL

PAGE 1

	DATE		ACCOUNT TITLE	DOC. NO.	POST. REF.	DEBIT	CREDIT	
1								1
2								2
3								3
4								4
5								5
6								6
7								7
8								8
9								9
10								10
11								11
12								12
13								13
14								14
15								15
16								16
17								17
18								18
19								19
20								20
21								21
22								22
23								23
24								24

[2]

7-7 MASTERY PROBLEM (concluded)

[1]

CASH RECEIPTS JOURNAL

PAGE 1

DATE	ACCOUNT TITLE	DOC. NO.	POST. REF.	GENERAL DEBIT	GENERAL CREDIT	ACCOUNTS RECEIVABLE CREDIT	SALES CREDIT	SALES TAX PAYABLE DEBIT	SALES TAX PAYABLE CREDIT	SALES DISCOUNT DEBIT	CASH DEBIT	
												1
												2
												3
												4
												5
												6
												7

[3]

Average number of days for payment:

Accounts receivable turnover ratio:

Estimating and journalizing uncollectible accounts expense by aging accounts receivable—allowance method; calculating and journalizing the adjusting entry for uncollectible accounts expense

[1]

Customer	Account Balance	Not Yet Due	Days Account Balance Past Due			
			1–30	31–60	61–90	Over 90
Atkins Co.	$ 2,523.64					
Bankhead Supply	2,435.75					
Coffman Distributing	943.74					
Fleet Trucking	2,643.23					
Griffin Industries	7,896.54					
Miskelly & Sons	2,754.48					
Oswalt, Inc.	8,723.54					
Rice Shipping Co.	4,363.27					
Smith Stores	1,324.76					
Totals	$33,608.95					

[2]

Age Group	Amount	Percentage	Uncollectible
Not yet due			
1–30 days			
31–60 days			
61–90 days			
Over 90 days			
Totals			
Current Balance of Allowance for Uncollectible Accounts			
Estimated Addition to Allowance for Uncollectible Accounts			

7-8 **CHALLENGE PROBLEM (concluded)**

[3]

GENERAL JOURNAL

PAGE 12

	DATE		ACCOUNT TITLE	DOC. NO.	POST. REF.	DEBIT	CREDIT	
1								1
2								2
3								3
4								4
5								5
6								6
7								7
8								8
9								9
10								10
11								11
12								12
13								13
14								14
15								15
16								16
17								17
18								18
19								19
20								20
21								21
22								22
23								23
24								24
25								25
26								26
27								27
28								28
29								29
30								30
31								31

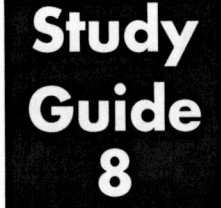

Study Guide 8

Name	Perfect Score	Your Score
Analyzing Depreciation and Disposing of Plant Assets Transactions	15 Pts.	
Identifying Accounting Terms	11 Pts.	
Analyzing Plant Asset Transactions	9 Pts.	
Total	35 Pts.	

Part One—Analyzing Depreciation and Disposing of Plant Assets Transactions

Directions: Place a *T* for True or *F* for False in the Answers column to show whether each of the following statements is true or false.

Answers

1. Plant assets are any asset that will be consumed within a year. (p. 224)

    1. _____

2. At the time a plant asset is bought, the salvage value is only an estimated amount. (p. 229)

    2. _____

3. Depreciation expense is a business operating expense. (p. 229)

    3. _____

4. When a plant asset is discarded, no notation needs to be made on the plant asset record. (p. 235)

    4. _____

5. The straight-line method of depreciation is used most often because it best meets the IRS regulations. (p. 230)

    5. _____

6. Because of land's permanent nature, it is not subject to depreciation. (p. 229)

    6. _____

7. Recording depreciation expense at the end of each fiscal period is an application of the accounting concept Matching Expenses with Revenue. (p. 229)

    7. _____

8. The actual value and book value of a plant asset are usually the same amount. (p. 231)

    8. _____

9. A gain or loss on plant assets is not recorded when one plant asset is traded for a similar plant asset. (p. 238)

    9. _____

10. Original cost, estimated useful life, and miles driven in a year are the three factors considered when calculating annual depreciation expense. (p. 229)

    10. _____

11. The actual cash paid is all that is ever considered as a plant asset's original cost. (p. 238)

    11. _____

12. The formula for calculating a plant asset's annual straight-line depreciation expense is: Original cost *minus* estimated salvage value *divided* by years of estimated useful life *equals* annual depreciation expense. (p. 230)

    12. _____

13. Three common ways of disposing of plant assets are discarding, selling, and trading. (p. 235)

    13. _____

14. If a plant asset is disposed of during a fiscal year, depreciation expense for part of a year is recorded. (p. 232)

    14. _____

15. All plant assets depreciate an equal amount each year. (p. 229)

    15. _____

Part Two—Identifying Accounting Terms

Directions: Select the one term in Column I that best fits each definition in Column II. Print the letter identifying your choice in the Answers column.

Column I	Column II	Answers
A. assessed value	1. All property not classified as real property. (p. 227)	1. _____
B. book value of a plant asset	2. An accounting form on which a business records information about each plant asset. (p. 225)	2. _____
C. declining-balance method of depreciation	3. The original cost of a plant asset minus accumulated depreciation. (p. 231)	3. _____
D. depletion	4. Charging an equal amount of depreciation expense for a plant asset in each year of useful life. (p. 230)	4. _____
E. modified accelerated cost recovery system	5. Multiplying the book value at the end of each fiscal period by a constant depreciation rate. (p. 242)	5. _____
F. personal property	6. Using fractions based on years of a plant asset's useful life. (p. 243)	6. _____
G. plant asset record	7. Calculating estimated annual depreciation expense based on the amount of production expected from a plant asset. (p. 245)	7. _____
H. production-units method of depreciation	8. The decrease in the value of a plant asset because of the removal of a natural resource. (p. 247)	8. _____
I. real property	9. Land and anything attached to the land. (p. 227)	9. _____
J. straight-line method of depreciation	10. The value of an asset determined by tax authorities for the purpose of calculating taxes. (p. 227)	10. _____
K. sum-of-the-year's-digits method of depreciation	11. A depreciation method required by the Internal Revenue Service to be used for income tax calculation purposes for most plant assets placed in service after 1986. (p. 246)	11. _____

Part Three—Analyzing Plant Asset Transactions

Directions: For each transaction below, print in the proper Answers columns the identifying letter of the accounts to be debited and credited.

Account Titles	Transactions	Answers Debit	Credit
A. Accum. Depr.—Equip.	1. Paid cash for new equipment. (p. 226)	1. _____	_____
B. Cash	2. Recorded annual depreciation on equipment. (p. 232)	2. _____	_____
C. Depr. Exp.—Equip.	3. Discarded equipment with no book value. (p. 235)	3. _____	_____
	4. Recorded depreciation for part of year. (p. 232)	4. _____	_____
D. Gain on Plant Assets	5. Discarded equipment with book value, all depreciation recorded. (p. 236)	5. _____	_____
E. Loss on Plant Assets	6. Sold equipment for less than book value, all depreciation recorded. (p. 237)	6. _____	_____
F. Equipment	7. Sold equipment for more than book value, all depreciation recorded. (p. 237)	7. _____	_____
G. Property Tax Expense	8. Paid cash plus old equipment for new equipment, $3,500.00: original cost of old equipment, $2,500.00; total accumulated depreciation recorded to date of trade, $500.00. (p. 238)	8. _____	_____
	9. Paid cash for property tax. (p. 227)	9. _____	_____

8-1 WORK TOGETHER, p. 228

Journalizing asset purchase and property tax transactions [1]

CASH PAYMENTS JOURNAL PAGE 1

	DATE	ACCOUNT TITLE	CK. NO.	POST. REF.	GENERAL DEBIT	GENERAL CREDIT	ACCOUNTS PAYABLE DEBIT	PURCHASES DISCOUNT CREDIT	CASH CREDIT	
1										1
2										2
3										3
4										4
5										5
6										6
7										7
8										8
9										9
10										10
11										11
12										12
13										13

[1]

GENERAL JOURNAL PAGE 1

	DATE	ACCOUNT TITLE	DOC. NO.	POST. REF.	DEBIT	CREDIT	
1							1
2							2
3							3
4							4
5							5
6							6
7							7
8							8
9							9
10							10
11							11
12							12
13							13

(Note: These records are needed to complete Work Together 8-2.)

PLANT ASSET RECORD, No. _____   General Ledger Account No. _____

Description _____   General Ledger Account _____

Date Bought _____   Serial Number _____   Original Cost _____

Estimated Useful Life _____   Estimated Salvage Value _____   Depreciation _____

WT 8-1

Disposed of: Discarded _____   Sold _____   Traded _____

Date _____   Disposal Amount _____

WT 8-3

YEAR	ANNUAL DEPRECIATION EXPENSE	ACCUMULATED DEPRECIATION	ENDING BOOK VALUE

WT 8-2

[2]

PLANT ASSET RECORD, No. _____   General Ledger Account No. _____

Description _____   General Ledger Account _____

Date Bought _____   Serial Number _____   Original Cost _____

Estimated Useful Life _____   Estimated Salvage Value _____   Depreciation _____

WT 8-1

Disposed of: Discarded _____   Sold _____   Traded _____

Date _____   Disposal Amount _____

WT 8-3

YEAR	ANNUAL DEPRECIATION EXPENSE	ACCUMULATED DEPRECIATION	ENDING BOOK VALUE

WT 8-2

8-1 ON YOUR OWN, p. 228

Journalizing asset purchase and property tax transactions [1]

GENERAL JOURNAL PAGE 1

	DATE	ACCOUNT TITLE	DOC. NO.	POST. REF.	DEBIT	CREDIT	
1							1
2							2
3							3
4							4
5							5
6							6
7							7
8							8
9							9
10							10
11							11
12							12
13							13

[1]

CASH PAYMENTS JOURNAL PAGE 1

	DATE	ACCOUNT TITLE	CK. NO.	POST. REF.	GENERAL DEBIT	GENERAL CREDIT	ACCOUNTS PAYABLE DEBIT	PURCHASES DISCOUNT CREDIT	CASH CREDIT	
					1	2	3	4	5	
1										1
2										2
3										3
4										4
5										5
6										6
7										7
8										8
9										9
10										10
11										11
12										12
13										13

[2]

(Note: These records are needed to complete On Your Own 8-2.)

PLANT ASSET RECORD, No. _____   General Ledger Account No. _____

Description _____   General Ledger Account _____

Date Bought _____   Serial Number _____   Original Cost _____

Estimated Useful Life _____   Estimated Salvage Value _____   Depreciation _____

OYO 8-1

Disposed of: Discarded _____   Sold _____   Traded _____

Date _____   Disposal Amount _____

OYO 8-3

YEAR	ANNUAL DEPRECIATION EXPENSE	ACCUMULATED DEPRECIATION	ENDING BOOK VALUE

OYO 8-2

[2]

PLANT ASSET RECORD, No. _____   General Ledger Account No. _____

Description _____   General Ledger Account _____

Date Bought _____   Serial Number _____   Original Cost _____

Estimated Useful Life _____   Estimated Salvage Value _____   Depreciation _____

OYO 8-1

Disposed of: Discarded _____   Sold _____   Traded _____

Date _____   Disposal Amount _____

OYO 8-3

YEAR	ANNUAL DEPRECIATION EXPENSE	ACCUMULATED DEPRECIATION	ENDING BOOK VALUE

OYO 8-2

8-2 WORK TOGETHER, p. 234

Calculating and journalizing depreciation [1]

(Note: The plant asset records from Work Together 8-1 are needed to complete this problem.
The records from Work Together 8-2 are needed to complete Work Together 8-3.)

Plant asset: _____   Original cost: _____

Depreciation method: _____   Estimated salvage value: _____

Estimated useful life: _____

YEAR	BEGINNING BOOK VALUE	ANNUAL DEPRECIATION	ACCUMULATED DEPRECIATION	ENDING BOOK VALUE

[1]

Plant asset: _____   Original cost: _____

Depreciation method: _____   Estimated salvage value: _____

Estimated useful life: _____

YEAR	BEGINNING BOOK VALUE	ANNUAL DEPRECIATION	ACCUMULATED DEPRECIATION	ENDING BOOK VALUE

GENERAL JOURNAL   PAGE 6

	DATE	ACCOUNT TITLE	DOC. NO.	POST. REF.	DEBIT	CREDIT	
1							1
2							2
3							3
4							4
5							5
6							6
7							7
8							8
9							9
10							10
11							11
12							12
13							13
14							14
15							15
16							16
17							17
18							18
19							19
20							20
21							21
22							22
23							23
24							24
25							25
26							26
27							27
28							28
29							29
30							30
31							31

8-2 ON YOUR OWN, p. 234

Calculating and journalizing depreciation   [1]

(Note: The plant asset records from On Your Own 8-1 are needed to complete this problem.
The records from On Your Own 8-2 are needed to complete On Your Own 8-3.)

Plant asset: _____   Original cost: _____

Depreciation method: _____   Estimated salvage value: _____

                                            Estimated useful life: _____

YEAR	BEGINNING BOOK VALUE	ANNUAL DEPRECIATION	ACCUMULATED DEPRECIATION	ENDING BOOK VALUE

[1]

Plant asset: _____   Original cost: _____

Depreciation method: _____   Estimated salvage value: _____

                                            Estimated useful life: _____

YEAR	BEGINNING BOOK VALUE	ANNUAL DEPRECIATION	ACCUMULATED DEPRECIATION	ENDING BOOK VALUE

GENERAL JOURNAL   PAGE 12

	DATE		ACCOUNT TITLE	DOC. NO.	POST. REF.	DEBIT	CREDIT	
1								1
2								2
3								3
4								4
5								5
6								6
7								7
8								8
9								9
10								10
11								11
12								12
13								13
14								14
15								15
16								16
17								17
18								18
19								19
20								20
21								21
22								22
23								23
24								24
25								25
26								26
27								27
28								28
29								29
30								30
31								31

8-3   WORK TOGETHER, p. 241

Recording the disposal of plant assets   [2]

(Note: The plant asset records from Work Together 8-2 are needed to complete this problem.)

PLANT ASSET RECORD, No. __127__   General Ledger Account No. __1225__

Description __Desk__   General Ledger Account __Office Equipment__

Date Bought __Apr. 4, 20X2__   Serial Number __EF26796__   Original Cost __$700.00__

Estimated Useful Life __5 years__   Estimated Salvage Value __$200.00__   Depreciation __Straight-line method__

Disposed of: Discarded _____   Sold _____   Traded _____

Date _____   Disposal Amount _____

YEAR	ANNUAL DEPRECIATION EXPENSE	ACCUMULATED DEPRECIATION	ENDING BOOK VALUE
20X2	$ 75.00	$ 75.00	$625.00
20X3	100.00	175.00	525.00
20X4	100.00	275.00	425.00
20X5	50.00	325.00	375.00

[2]

PLANT ASSET RECORD, No. __116__   General Ledger Account No. __1245__

Description __Truck__   General Ledger Account __Warehouse Equipment__

Date Bought __July 3, 20X1__   Serial Number __01E16742XL42__   Original Cost __$38,000.00__

Estimated Useful Life __5 years__   Estimated Salvage Value __$3,000.00__   Depreciation __Straight-line method__

Disposed of: Discarded _____   Sold _____   Traded _____

Date _____   Disposal Amount _____

YEAR	ANNUAL DEPRECIATION EXPENSE	ACCUMULATED DEPRECIATION	ENDING BOOK VALUE
20X1	$3,500.00	$ 3,500.00	$34,500.00
20X2	7,000.00	10,500.00	27,500.00
20X3	7,000.00	17,500.00	20,500.00
20X4	7,000.00	24,500.00	13,500.00
20X5	7,000.00	31,500.00	6,500.00

PLANT ASSET RECORD, No. __106__   General Ledger Account No. __1215__

Description __Lansing Store__   General Ledger Account __Building__

Date Bought __Jan. 6, 19X7__   Serial Number __n/a__   Original Cost __$60,000.00__

Estimated Useful Life __25 years__   Estimated Salvage Value __$10,000.00__   Depreciation __Straight-line method__

Disposed of: Discarded _____   Sold _____   Traded _____

Date _____   Disposal Amount _____

YEAR	ANNUAL DEPRECIATION EXPENSE	ACCUMULATED DEPRECIATION	ENDING BOOK VALUE
19X7	$2,000.00	$ 2,000.00	$58,000.00
19X8	2,000.00	4,000.00	56,000.00
19X9	2,000.00	6,000.00	54,000.00
20X0	2,000.00	8,000.00	52,000.00
20X1	2,000.00	10,000.00	50,000.00
20X2	2,000.00	12,000.00	48,000.00
20X3	2,000.00	14,000.00	46,000.00
20X4	2,000.00	16,000.00	44,000.00
20X5	2,000.00	18,000.00	42,000.00

[2]

PLANT ASSET RECORD, No. __105__   General Ledger Account No. __1205__

Description __Lansing Store__   General Ledger Account __Land__

Date Bought __Jan. 6, 19X7__   Serial Number __n/a__   Original Cost __$40,000.00__

Estimated Useful Life __n/a__   Estimated Salvage Value __n/a__   Depreciation __n/a__

Disposed of: Discarded _____   Sold _____   Traded _____

Date _____   Disposal Amount _____

YEAR	ANNUAL DEPRECIATION EXPENSE	ACCUMULATED DEPRECIATION	ENDING BOOK VALUE

8-3 **WORK TOGETHER (continued)**

[1]

GENERAL JOURNAL   PAGE 1

	DATE		ACCOUNT TITLE	DOC. NO.	POST. REF.	DEBIT	CREDIT	
1								1
2								2
3								3
4								4
5								5
6								6
7								7
8								8
9								9
10								10
11								11
12								12
13								13
14								14
15								15
16								16
17								17
18								18
19								19
20								20
21								21
22								22
23								23
24								24
25								25
26								26
27								27
28								28
29								29
30								30
31								31

[1]

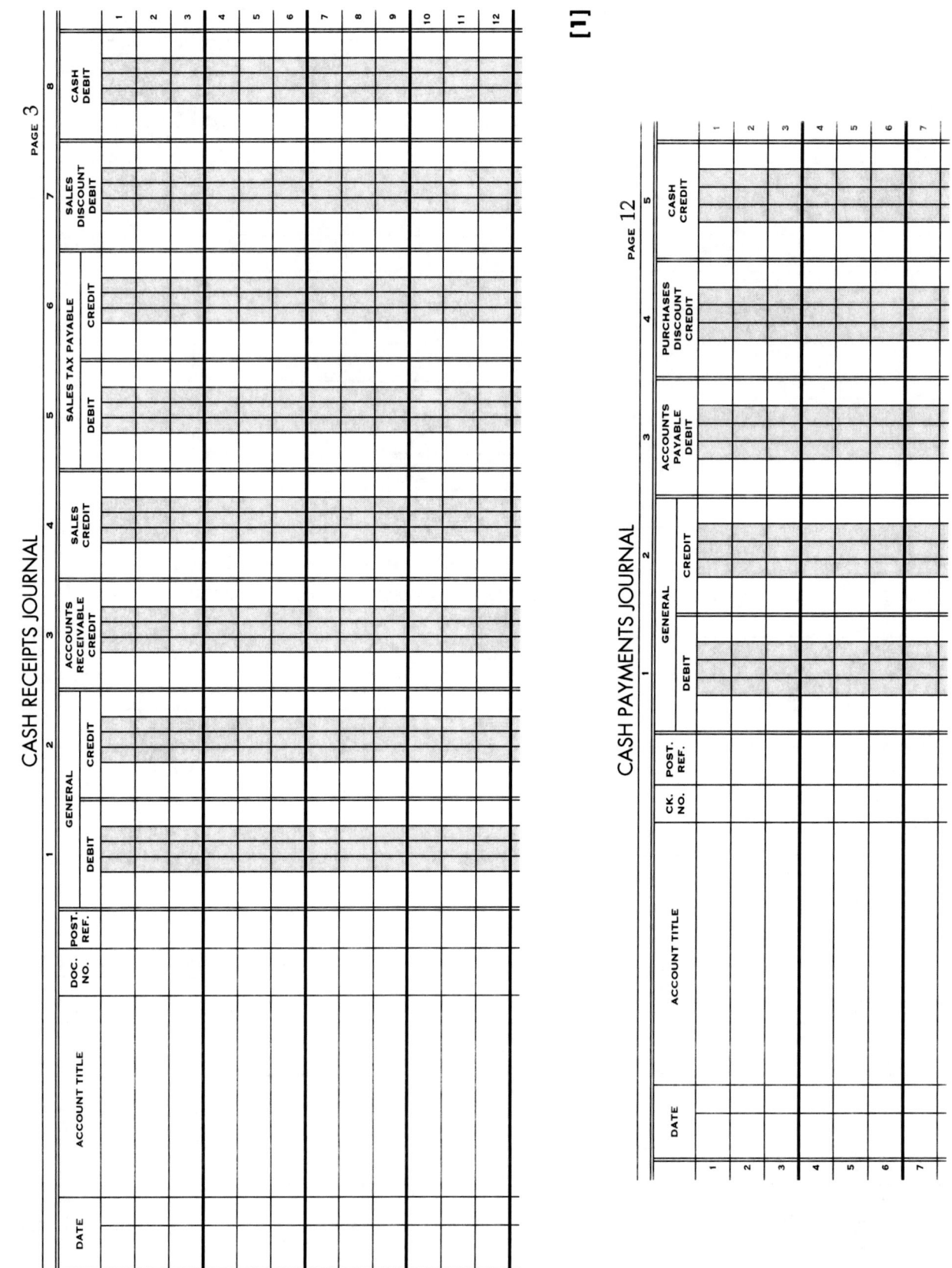

CASH RECEIPTS JOURNAL   PAGE 3

CASH PAYMENTS JOURNAL   PAGE 12

8-3 ON YOUR OWN, p. 241

Recording the disposal of plant assets   [2]

(Note: The plant asset records from On Your Own 8-2 are needed to complete this problem.)

PLANT ASSET RECORD, No. __390__   General Ledger Account No. __1205__

Description __Columbus Warehouse__   General Ledger Account __Land__

Date
Bought __Sept. 29, 20X3__   Serial
Number __n/a__   Original
Cost __$40,000.00__

Estimated
Useful Life __n/a__   Estimated
Salvage Value __n/a__   Depreciation __n/a__

Disposed of: Discarded _____   Sold _____   Traded _____

Date _____   Disposal Amount _____

YEAR	ANNUAL DEPRECIATION EXPENSE	ACCUMULATED DEPRECIATION	ENDING BOOK VALUE

[2]

PLANT ASSET RECORD, No. __391__   General Ledger Account No. __1215__

Description __Columbus Warehouse__   General Ledger Account __Building__

Date
Bought __Sept. 29, 20X3__   Serial
Number __n/a__   Original
Cost __$50,000.00__

Estimated
Useful Life __25 years__   Estimated
Salvage Value __$10,000.00__   Depreciation __Straight-line method__

Disposed of: Discarded _____   Sold _____   Traded _____

Date _____   Disposal Amount _____

YEAR	ANNUAL DEPRECIATION EXPENSE	ACCUMULATED DEPRECIATION	ENDING BOOK VALUE
20X3	$ 400.00	$ 400.00	$49,600.00
20X4	1,600.00	2,000.00	48,000.00
20X5	800.00	2,800.00	47,200.00

PLANT ASSET RECORD, No. __369__   General Ledger Account No. __1225__

Description __Office File Cabinet__   General Ledger Account __Office Equipment__

Date Bought __July 6, 20X1__   Serial Number __62B7Q76__   Original Cost __$500.00__

Estimated Useful Life __7 years__   Estimated Salvage Value __$80.00__   Depreciation __Straight-line method__

Disposed of: Discarded _____   Sold _____   Traded _____

Date _____   Disposal Amount _____

YEAR	ANNUAL DEPRECIATION EXPENSE	ACCUMULATED DEPRECIATION	ENDING BOOK VALUE
20X1	$30.00	$ 30.00	$470.00
20X2	60.00	90.00	410.00
20X3	60.00	150.00	350.00
20X4	60.00	210.00	290.00
20X5	45.00	255.00	245.00

[2]

PLANT ASSET RECORD, No. __428__   General Ledger Account No. __1225__

Description __Computer__   General Ledger Account __Office Equipment__

Date Bought __Jan. 3, 20X4__   Serial Number __62B7QX1472__   Original Cost __$2,000.00__

Estimated Useful Life __3 years__   Estimated Salvage Value __$500.00__   Depreciation __Straight-line method__

Disposed of: Discarded _____   Sold _____   Traded _____

Date _____   Disposal Amount _____

YEAR	ANNUAL DEPRECIATION EXPENSE	ACCUMULATED DEPRECIATION	ENDING BOOK VALUE
20X4	$500.00	$ 500.00	$1,500.00
20X5	500.00	1,000.00	1,000.00

8-3 **ON YOUR OWN (continued)**

[1]

GENERAL JOURNAL   PAGE 1

	DATE		ACCOUNT TITLE	DOC. NO.	POST. REF.	DEBIT	CREDIT	
1								1
2								2
3								3
4								4
5								5
6								6
7								7
8								8
9								9
10								10
11								11
12								12
13								13
14								14
15								15
16								16
17								17
18								18
19								19
20								20
21								21
22								22
23								23
24								24
25								25
26								26
27								27
28								28
29								29
30								30
31								31

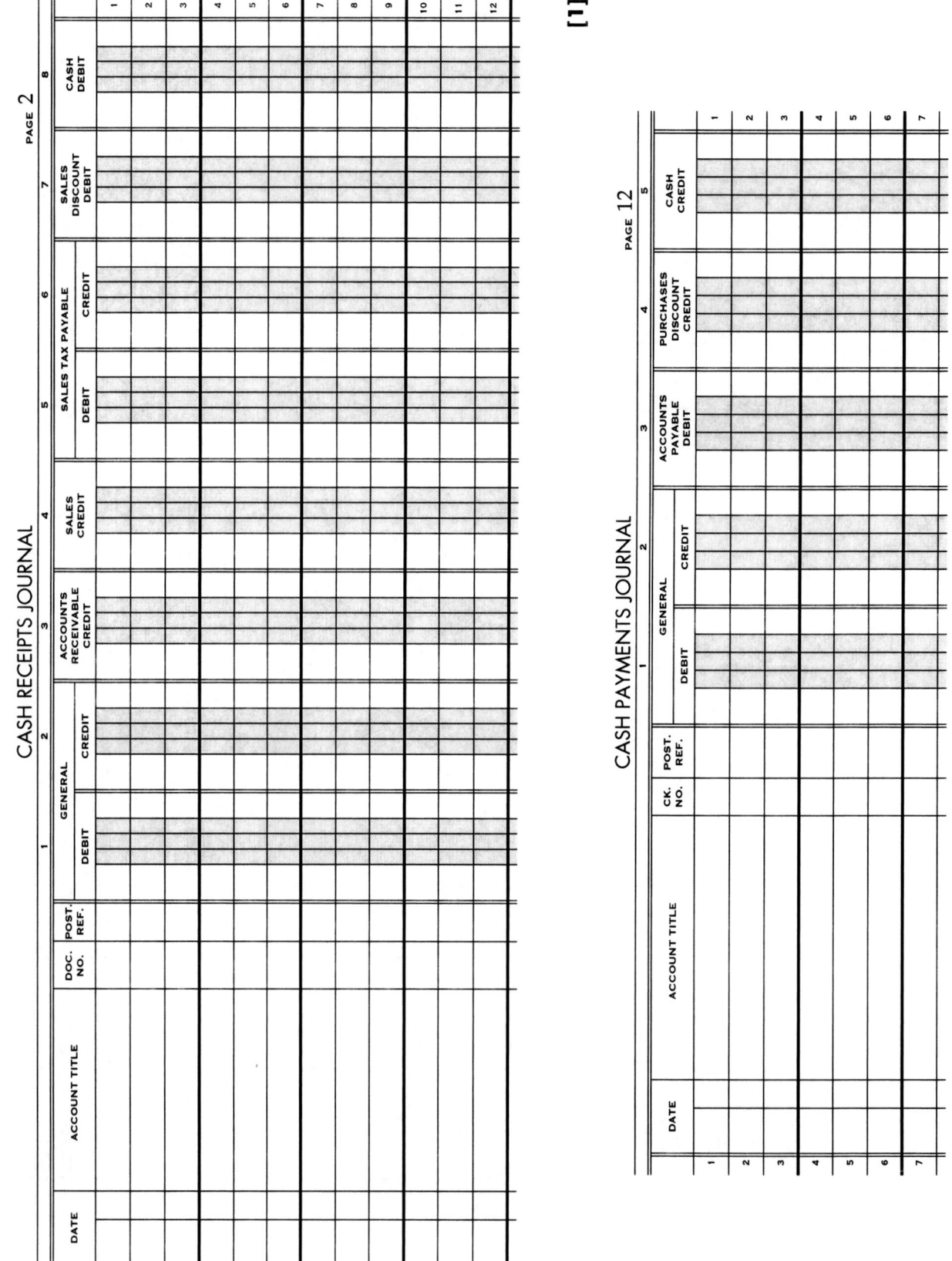

[1]

CASH RECEIPTS JOURNAL

PAGE 2

		DATE	ACCOUNT TITLE	DOC. NO.	POST. REF.	GENERAL DEBIT (1)	GENERAL CREDIT (2)	ACCOUNTS RECEIVABLE CREDIT (3)	SALES CREDIT (4)	SALES TAX PAYABLE DEBIT (5)	SALES TAX PAYABLE CREDIT (6)	SALES DISCOUNT DEBIT (7)	CASH DEBIT (8)	
1														1
2														2
3														3
4														4
5														5
6														6
7														7
8														8
9														9
10														10
11														11
12														12

[1]

CASH PAYMENTS JOURNAL

PAGE 12

	DATE	ACCOUNT TITLE	CK. NO.	POST. REF.	GENERAL DEBIT (1)	GENERAL CREDIT (2)	ACCOUNTS PAYABLE DEBIT (3)	PURCHASES DISCOUNT CREDIT (4)	CASH CREDIT (5)	
1										1
2										2
3										3
4										4
5										5
6										6
7										7

8-4 WORK TOGETHER, p. 248

Computing depreciation using various depreciation methods and calculating depletion   [1]

Plant asset: _____   Original cost: _____

Depreciation method: _Double declining-balance_   Estimated salvage value: _____

Estimated useful life: _____

YEAR	BEGINNING BOOK VALUE	DECLINING-BALANCE RATE	ANNUAL DEPRECIATION	ENDING BOOK VALUE

Plant asset: _____   Original cost: _____

Depreciation method: _Sum-of-the-years'-digits_   Estimated salvage value: _____

Estimated useful life: _____

YEAR	BEGINNING BOOK VALUE	FRACTION	ANNUAL DEPRECIATION	ENDING BOOK VALUE

Plant asset: _____   Original cost: _____

Depreciation method: _Production-units_   Estimated salvage value: _____

Estimated useful life: _____

Depreciation rate: _____

YEAR	BEGINNING BOOK VALUE	MILES DRIVEN	ANNUAL DEPRECIATION	ENDING BOOK VALUE

[1]

Plant asset: _____   Original cost: _____

Depreciation method: _MACRS_____   Property class: _____

	YEAR	DEPRECIATION RATE	ANNUAL DEPRECIATION	
		20.00%		
		32.00%		
		19.20%		
		11.52%		
		11.52%		
		5.76%		

[2]

Plant asset: _____

Depletion method: ___Production-units____   Estimated total depletion: _____

Original cost: _____   Estimated useful life: _____

Estimated salvage value: _____   Depletion rate: _____

YEAR	BEGINNING BOOK VALUE	TONS RECOVERED	ANNUAL DEPRECIATION	ENDING BOOK VALUE

8-4 ON YOUR OWN, p. 249

Computing depreciation using various depreciation methods and calculating depletion   [1]

Plant asset: _____   Original cost: _____

Depreciation method: _Double declining-balance_   Estimated salvage value: _____

Estimated useful life: _____

YEAR	BEGINNING BOOK VALUE	DECLINING-BALANCE RATE	ANNUAL DEPRECIATION	ENDING BOOK VALUE

Plant asset: _____   Original cost: _____

Depreciation method: _Sum-of-the-years'-digits_   Estimated salvage value: _____

Estimated useful life: _____

YEAR	BEGINNING BOOK VALUE	FRACTION	ANNUAL DEPRECIATION	ENDING BOOK VALUE

Plant asset: _____   Original cost: _____

Depreciation method: _Production-units_   Estimated salvage value: _____

Estimated useful life: _____

Depreciation rate: _____

YEAR	BEGINNING BOOK VALUE	PRODUCTION HOURS	ANNUAL DEPRECIATION	ENDING BOOK VALUE

[1]

Plant asset: _____   Original cost: _____

Depreciation method: _MACRS_____   Property class: _____

	YEAR	DEPRECIATION RATE	ANNUAL DEPRECIATION	

[2]

Plant asset: _____

Depletion method: _____Production-units_____   Estimated total depletion: _____

Original cost: _____   Estimated useful life: _____

Estimated salvage value: _____   Depletion rate: _____

YEAR	BEGINNING BOOK VALUE	MCF RECOVERED	ANNUAL DEPRECIATION	ENDING BOOK VALUE

8-1 APPLICATION PROBLEM, p. 251

Journalizing entries to record buying plant assets

[1]

GENERAL JOURNAL

PAGE 1

	DATE		ACCOUNT TITLE	DOC. NO.	POST. REF.	DEBIT	CREDIT	
1								1
2								2
3								3
4								4
5								5
6								6
7								7
8								8
9								9
10								10
11								11
12								12

[1]

CASH PAYMENTS JOURNAL

PAGE 1

	DATE		ACCOUNT TITLE	CK. NO.	POST. REF.	GENERAL DEBIT	GENERAL CREDIT	ACCOUNTS PAYABLE DEBIT	PURCHASES DISCOUNT CREDIT	CASH CREDIT	
						1	2	3	4	5	
1											1
2											2
3											3
4											4
5											5
6											6
7											7
8											8
9											9
10											10
11											11
12											12
13											13

(Note: These plant asset records are needed to complete Application Problems 8-3, 8-4, and 8-5.)

PLANT ASSET RECORD, No. _____   General Ledger Account No. _____

Description _____   General Ledger Account _____

Date
Bought _____   Serial
Number _____   Original
Cost _____

Estimated
Useful Life _____   Estimated
Salvage Value _____   Depreciation _____

Disposed of: Discarded _____   Sold _____   Traded _____

Date _____   Disposal Amount _____

YEAR	ANNUAL DEPRECIATION EXPENSE	ACCUMULATED DEPRECIATION	ENDING BOOK VALUE

PLANT ASSET RECORD, No. _____   General Ledger Account No. _____

Description _____   General Ledger Account _____

Date
Bought _____   Serial
Number _____   Original
Cost _____

Estimated
Useful Life _____   Estimated
Salvage Value _____   Depreciation _____

Disposed of: Discarded _____   Sold _____   Traded _____

Date _____   Disposal Amount _____

YEAR	ANNUAL DEPRECIATION EXPENSE	ACCUMULATED DEPRECIATION	ENDING BOOK VALUE

8-1 **APPLICATION PROBLEM (continued)**

PLANT ASSET RECORD, No. _____ General Ledger Account No. _____

Description _____ General Ledger Account _____

Date
Bought _____ Serial
Number _____ Original
Cost _____

Estimated
Useful Life _____ Estimated
Salvage Value _____ Depreciation _____

Disposed of: Discarded _____   Sold _____   Traded _____

Date _____   Disposal Amount _____

YEAR	ANNUAL DEPRECIATION EXPENSE	ACCUMULATED DEPRECIATION	ENDING BOOK VALUE

PLANT ASSET RECORD, No. _____ General Ledger Account No. _____

Description _____ General Ledger Account _____

Date
Bought _____ Serial
Number _____ Original
Cost _____

Estimated
Useful Life _____ Estimated
Salvage Value _____ Depreciation _____

Disposed of: Discarded _____   Sold _____   Traded _____

Date _____   Disposal Amount _____

YEAR	ANNUAL DEPRECIATION EXPENSE	ACCUMULATED DEPRECIATION	ENDING BOOK VALUE

PLANT ASSET RECORD, No. _____   General Ledger Account No. _____

Description _____   General Ledger Account _____

Date
Bought _____   Serial
Number _____   Original
Cost _____

Estimated
Useful Life _____   Estimated
Salvage Value _____   Depreciation _____

Disposed of: Discarded _____   Sold _____   Traded _____

Date _____   Disposal Amount _____

YEAR	ANNUAL DEPRECIATION EXPENSE	ACCUMULATED DEPRECIATION	ENDING BOOK VALUE

Extra form

PLANT ASSET RECORD, No. _____   General Ledger Account No. _____

Description _____   General Ledger Account _____

Date
Bought _____   Serial
Number _____   Original
Cost _____

Estimated
Useful Life _____   Estimated
Salvage Value _____   Depreciation _____

Disposed of: Discarded _____   Sold _____   Traded _____

Date _____   Disposal Amount _____

YEAR	ANNUAL DEPRECIATION EXPENSE	ACCUMULATED DEPRECIATION	ENDING BOOK VALUE

8-2 APPLICATION PROBLEM, p. 251

Calculating and journalizing property tax   [1]

Annual property tax calculation:

[2]

CASH PAYMENTS JOURNAL PAGE 3

	DATE	ACCOUNT TITLE	CK. NO.	POST. REF.	GENERAL DEBIT	GENERAL CREDIT	ACCOUNTS PAYABLE DEBIT	PURCHASES DISCOUNT CREDIT	CASH CREDIT	
1										1
2										2
3										3
4										4
5										5
6										6
7										7
8										8
9										9
10										10
11										11
12										12
13										13
14										14
15										15

Calculating depreciation using the straight-line method

The plant asset records used in Application Problem 8-1 are needed to complete Application Problem 8-3. The depreciation tables completed in Application Problem 8-3 are needed to complete Application Problem 8-4.

Plant asset: __File Cabinet__

Depreciation method: _____

Original cost: _____

Estimated salvage value: _____

Estimated useful life: _____

YEAR	BEGINNING BOOK VALUE	ANNUAL DEPRECIATION	ACCUMULATED DEPRECIATION	ENDING BOOK VALUE

Plant asset: __Word Processor__

Depreciation method: _____

Original cost: _____

Estimated salvage value: _____

Estimated useful life: _____

YEAR	BEGINNING BOOK VALUE	ANNUAL DEPRECIATION	ACCUMULATED DEPRECIATION	ENDING BOOK VALUE

Plant asset: __Hand Truck__

Depreciation method: _____

Original cost: _____

Estimated salvage value: _____

Estimated useful life: _____

YEAR	BEGINNING BOOK VALUE	ANNUAL DEPRECIATION	ACCUMULATED DEPRECIATION	ENDING BOOK VALUE

8-3   APPLICATION PROBLEM (concluded)

Plant asset: _Truck_____

Depreciation method: _____

Original cost: _____

Estimated salvage value: _____

Estimated useful life: _____

YEAR	BEGINNING BOOK VALUE	ANNUAL DEPRECIATION	ACCUMULATED DEPRECIATION	ENDING BOOK VALUE

Plant asset: _Shelving_____

Depreciation method: _____

Original cost: _____

Estimated salvage value: _____

Estimated useful life: _____

YEAR	BEGINNING BOOK VALUE	ANNUAL DEPRECIATION	ACCUMULATED DEPRECIATION	ENDING BOOK VALUE

Journalizing annual depreciation expense [2, 4]

GENERAL JOURNAL

PAGE 12

	DATE		ACCOUNT TITLE	DOC. NO.	POST. REF.	DEBIT	CREDIT	
1								1
2								2
3								3
4								4
5								5
6								6
7								7
8								8
9								9
10								10
11								11
12								12
13								13
14								14
15								15
16								16
17								17
18								18
19								19
20								20
21								21
22								22
23								23
24								24
25								25
26								26
27								27
28								28
29								29
30								30
31								31

8-5 APPLICATION PROBLEM, p. 252

Recording disposal of plant assets [1, 3]

The plant asset records used in Application Problem 8-4 are needed to complete Application Problem 8-5.

	DATE		ACCOUNT TITLE	DOC. NO.	POST. REF.	DEBIT	CREDIT	
1								1
2								2
3								3
4								4
5								5
6								6
7								7
8								8
9								9
10								10
11								11
12								12
13								13
14								14
15								15
16								16
17								17
18								18
19								19
20								20
21								21
22								22
23								23
24								24
25								25
26								26
27								27
28								28
29								29
30								30
31								31

GENERAL JOURNAL PAGE 1

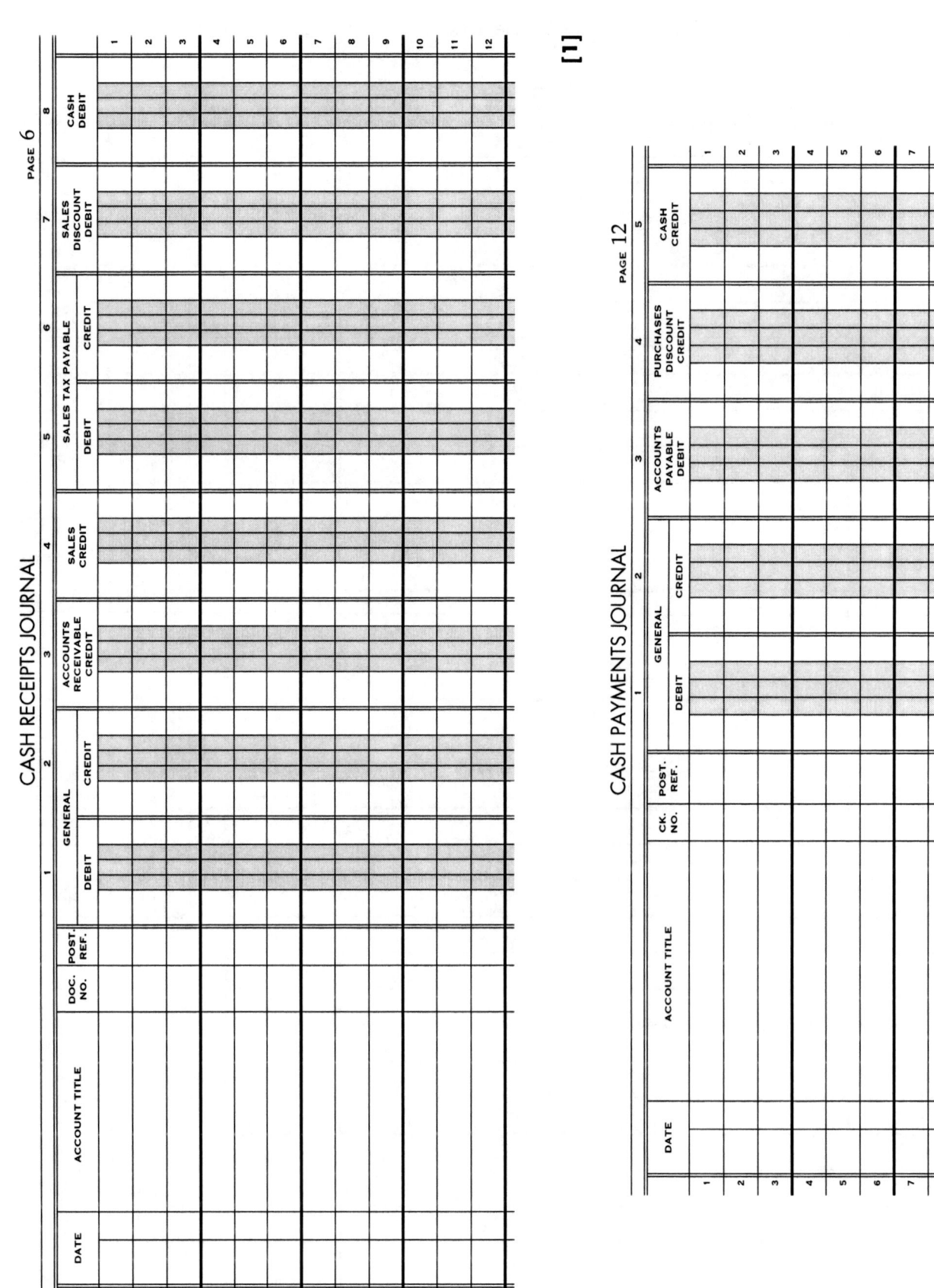

[1, 3]

CASH RECEIPTS JOURNAL

PAGE 6

[1]

CASH PAYMENTS JOURNAL

PAGE 12

8-6 APPLICATION PROBLEM, p. 252

Recording the sale of land and building [1]

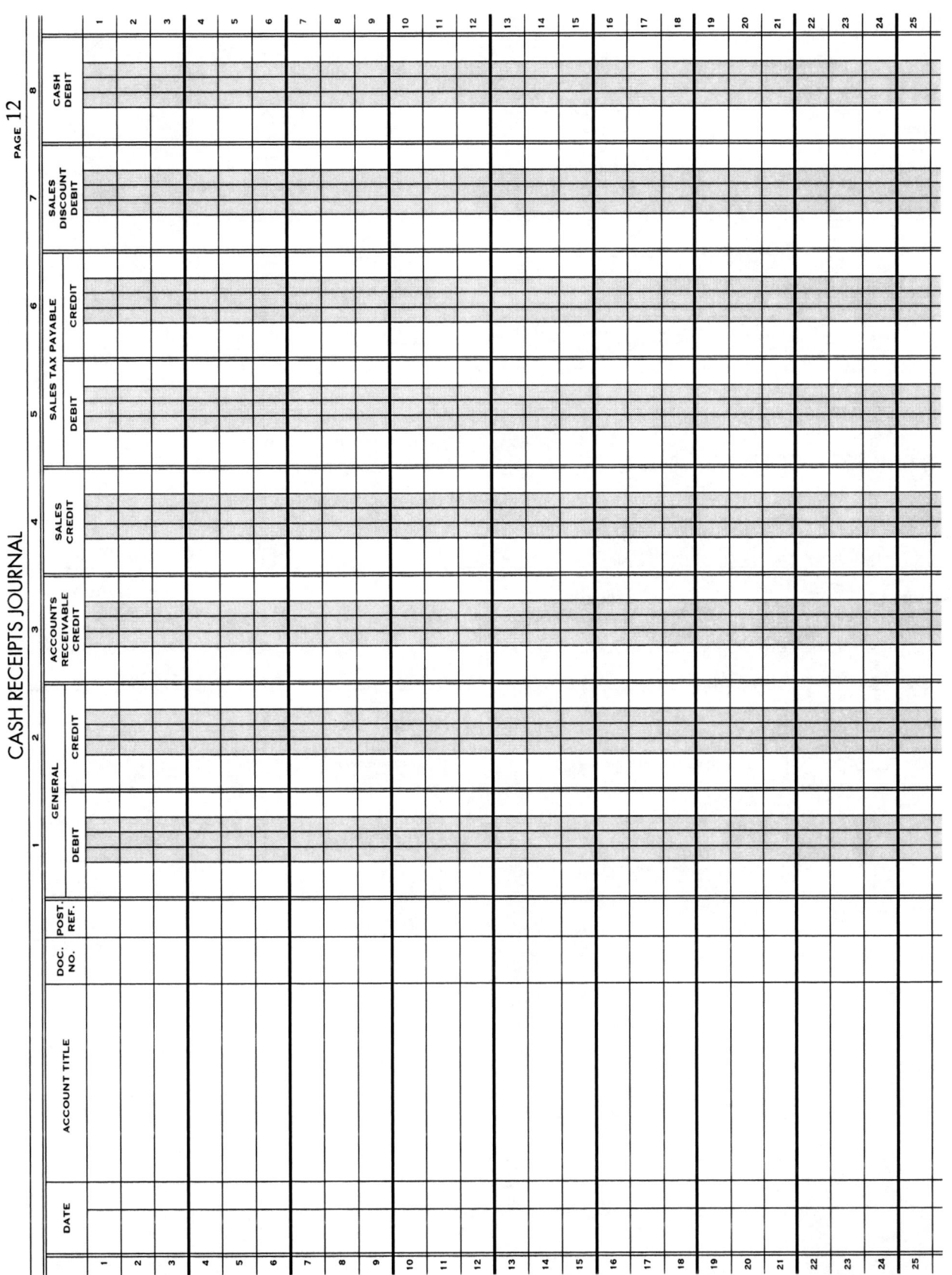

CASH RECEIPTS JOURNAL

PAGE 12

	DATE	ACCOUNT TITLE	DOC. NO.	POST. REF.	GENERAL DEBIT	GENERAL CREDIT	ACCOUNTS RECEIVABLE CREDIT	SALES CREDIT	SALES TAX PAYABLE DEBIT	SALES TAX PAYABLE CREDIT	SALES DISCOUNT DEBIT	CASH DEBIT	
1													1
2													2
3													3
4													4
5													5
6													6
7													7
8													8
9													9
10													10
11													11
12													12
13													13
14													14
15													15
16													16
17													17
18													18
19													19
20													20
21													21
22													22
23													23
24													24
25													25

PLANT ASSET RECORD, No. __61__   General Ledger Account No. __1205__

Description __Jackson Warehouse__   General Ledger Account __Land__

Date Bought __Jan. 1, 20--__   Serial Number __n/a__   Original Cost __$20,000.00__

Estimated Useful Life __Indefinite__   Estimated Salvage Value __n/a__   Depreciation __n/a__

Disposed of: Discarded _____   Sold _____   Traded _____

Date _____   Disposal Amount _____

YEAR	ANNUAL DEPRECIATION EXPENSE	ACCUMULATED DEPRECIATION	ENDING BOOK VALUE

PLANT ASSET RECORD, No. __62__   General Ledger Account No. __1215__

Description __Jackson Warehouse__   General Ledger Account __Building__

Date Bought __Jan. 1, 20--__   Serial Number __None__   Original Cost __$100,000.00__

Estimated Useful Life __25 years__   Estimated Salvage Value __$10,000.00__   Depreciation __Straight-line method__

Disposed of: Discarded _____   Sold _____   Traded _____

Date _____   Disposal Amount _____

YEAR	ANNUAL DEPRECIATION EXPENSE	ACCUMULATED DEPRECIATION	ENDING BOOK VALUE
20X5	$3,600.00	$61,200.00	$38,800.00

8-7 APPLICATION PROBLEM, p. 253

Calculating depreciation expense using the straight-line, declining-balance, and sum-of-the-years'-digits method

Plant asset: _____   Original cost: _____

Depreciation method: _Straight-line_   Estimated salvage value: _____

Estimated useful life: _____

YEAR	BEGINNING BOOK VALUE	ANNUAL DEPRECIATION	ACCUMULATED DEPRECIATION	ENDING BOOK VALUE

Plant asset: _____   Original cost: _____

Depreciation method: _Double declining-balance_   Estimated salvage value: _____

Estimated useful life: _____

YEAR	BEGINNING BOOK VALUE	DECLINING-BALANCE RATE	ANNUAL DEPRECIATION	ENDING BOOK VALUE

Plant asset: _____   Original cost: _____

Depreciation method: _Sum-of-the-years'-digits_   Estimated salvage value: _____

Estimated useful life: _____

YEAR	BEGINNING BOOK VALUE	FRACTION	ANNUAL DEPRECIATION	ENDING BOOK VALUE

Extra form

Plant asset: _____   Original cost: _____

Depreciation method: _____   Estimated salvage value: _____

Estimated useful life: _____

YEAR	BEGINNING BOOK VALUE	ANNUAL DEPRECIATION	ACCUMULATED DEPRECIATION	ENDING BOOK VALUE

8-8 APPLICATION PROBLEM, p. 253

Calculating depreciation expense using the production-unit method   [1]

Depreciation rate calculation:

[2]

Plant asset: _____

Depletion method: Production-unit

Original cost: _____   Estimated useful life: _____

Estimated salvage value: _____   Depletion rate: _____ per mile driven

YEAR	BEGINNING BOOK VALUE	MILES DRIVEN	ANNUAL DEPRECIATION	ENDING BOOK VALUE
		27,500		
		26,000		
		25,000		
		21,000		
		19,000		

Calculating depreciation expense using MACRS

Plant asset: _____   Original cost: _____

Depreciation method: _MACRS_____   Property class: _____

	YEAR	DEPRECIATION RATE	ANNUAL DEPRECIATION	
		20.00%		
		32.00%		
		19.20%		
		11.52%		
		11.52%		
		5.76%		
		100.00%		

Extra form

Plant asset: _____   Original cost: _____

Depreciation method: _____   Property class: _____

	YEAR	DEPRECIATION RATE	ANNUAL DEPRECIATION	

8-10 APPLICATION PROBLEM, p. 254

Calculating depletion expense using production-unit method

Plant asset: Mine _____

Depletion method: _____   Estimated total value of coal: _____

Original cost: _____   Estimated tons of recoverable coal: _____

Estimated salvage value: _____   Depletion rate: _____ per ton mined

YEAR	BEGINNING BOOK VALUE	TONS MINED	ANNUAL DEPLETION	ENDING BOOK VALUE
		9,000		
		9,400		
		7,000		
		12,500		
		8,200		
		46,100		

Extra form

Plant asset: _____

Depletion method: _____   Estimated total value of coal: _____

Original cost: _____   Estimated tons of recoverable coal: _____

Estimated salvage value: _____   Depletion rate: _____ per ton mined

YEAR	BEGINNING BOOK VALUE	TONS MINED	ANNUAL DEPLETION	ENDING BOOK VALUE

Recording entries for plant assets

[1]

GENERAL JOURNAL

PAGE 1

	DATE		ACCOUNT TITLE	DOC. NO.	POST. REF.	DEBIT	CREDIT	
1								1
2								2
3								3
4								4
5								5
6								6
7								7
8								8
9								9
10								10
11								11
12								12
13								13
14								14
15								15
16								16
17								17
18								18
19								19
20								20
21								21
22								22
23								23
24								24
25								25
26								26
27								27
28								28
29								29
30								30
31								31

8-11 MASTERY PROBLEM (continued)

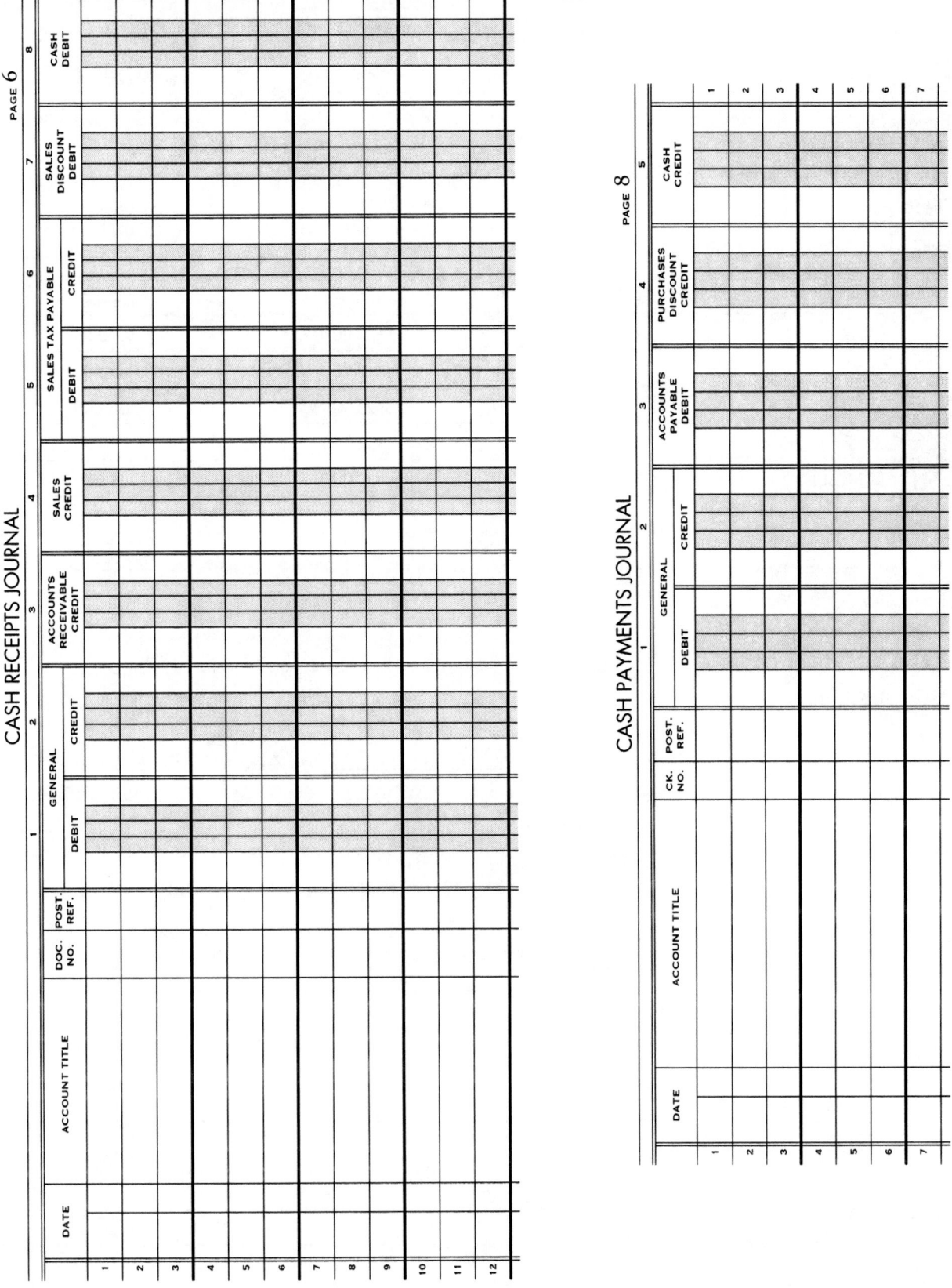

[1]

CASH RECEIPTS JOURNAL — PAGE 6

[1]

CASH PAYMENTS JOURNAL — PAGE 8

PLANT ASSET RECORD, No. 167   General Ledger Account No. 1230

Description Desk   General Ledger Account Office Equipment

Date Bought Jan. 5, 20X4   Serial Number D3481   Original Cost $720.00

Estimated Useful Life 5 years   Estimated Salvage Value $120.00   Depreciation Straight-line method

Disposed of: Discarded _____   Sold _____   Traded _____

Date _____   Disposal Amount _____

YEAR	ANNUAL DEPRECIATION EXPENSE	ACCUMULATED DEPRECIATION	ENDING BOOK VALUE
20X4	$120.00	$120.00	$600.00
20X5	120.00	240.00	480.00
20X6	120.00	360.00	360.00
20X7	120.00	480.00	240.00
20X8	120.00	600.00	120.00

PLANT ASSET RECORD, No. 168   General Ledger Account No. 1230

Description Table   General Ledger Account Office Equipment

Date Bought Mar. 29, 20X4   Serial Number T3929   Original Cost $425.00

Estimated Useful Life 5 years   Estimated Salvage Value $25.00   Depreciation Straight-line method

Disposed of: Discarded _____   Sold _____   Traded _____

Date _____   Disposal Amount _____

YEAR	ANNUAL DEPRECIATION EXPENSE	ACCUMULATED DEPRECIATION	ENDING BOOK VALUE
20X4	$60.00	$ 60.00	$365.00
20X5	80.00	140.00	285.00
20X6	80.00	220.00	205.00
20X7	80.00	300.00	125.00
20X8	80.00	380.00	45.00

8-11   MASTERY PROBLEM (continued)

[2]

PLANT ASSET RECORD, No. __169__   General Ledger Account No. __1230__

Description __Filing Cabinet__   General Ledger Account __Office Equipment__

Date Bought __June 28, 20X0__   Serial Number __FC125__   Original Cost __$400.00__

Estimated Useful Life __10 years__   Estimated Salvage Value __$50.00__   Depreciation __Straight-line method__

Disposed of: Discarded _____   Sold _____   Traded _____

Date _____   Disposal Amount _____

YEAR	ANNUAL DEPRECIATION EXPENSE	ACCUMULATED DEPRECIATION	ENDING BOOK VALUE
20X0	$17.50	$ 17.50	$382.50
20X1	35.00	52.50	347.50
20X2	35.00	87.50	312.50
20X3	35.00	122.50	277.50
20X4	35.00	157.50	242.50
20X5	35.00	192.50	207.50
20X6	35.00	227.50	172.50
20X7	35.00	262.50	137.50
20X8	35.00	297.50	102.50

PLANT ASSET RECORD, No. __170__   General Ledger Account No. __1230__

Description __Word Processor__   General Ledger Account __Office Equipment__

Date Bought __Apr. 6, 20X3__   Serial Number __TM48194H32__   Original Cost __$750.00__

Estimated Useful Life __6 years__   Estimated Salvage Value __$150.00__   Depreciation __Straight-line method__

Disposed of: Discarded _____   Sold _____   Traded _____

Date _____   Disposal Amount _____

YEAR	ANNUAL DEPRECIATION EXPENSE	ACCUMULATED DEPRECIATION	ENDING BOOK VALUE
20X3	$ 75.00	$ 75.00	$675.00
20X4	100.00	175.00	575.00
20X5	100.00	275.00	475.00
20X6	100.00	375.00	375.00
20X7	100.00	475.00	275.00
20X8	100.00	575.00	175.00

PLANT ASSET RECORD, No. __171__   General Ledger Account No. __1230__

Description __Copying Machine__   General Ledger Account __Office Equipment__

Date Bought __July 1, 20X4__   Serial Number __C56M203__   Original Cost __$800.00__

Estimated Useful Life __5 years__   Estimated Salvage Value __$50.00__   Depreciation __Straight-line method__

Disposed of: Discarded _____   Sold _____   Traded _____

Date _____   Disposal Amount _____

YEAR	ANNUAL DEPRECIATION EXPENSE	ACCUMULATED DEPRECIATION	ENDING BOOK VALUE
20X4	$ 75.00	$ 75.00	$725.00
20X5	150.00	225.00	575.00
20X6	150.00	375.00	425.00
20X7	150.00	525.00	275.00
20X8	150.00	675.00	125.00

PLANT ASSET RECORD, No. _____   General Ledger Account No. _____

Description _____   General Ledger Account _____

Date Bought _____   Serial Number _____   Original Cost _____

Estimated Useful Life _____   Estimated Salvage Value _____   Depreciation _____

Disposed of: Discarded _____   Sold _____   Traded _____

Date _____   Disposal Amount _____

YEAR	ANNUAL DEPRECIATION EXPENSE	ACCUMULATED DEPRECIATION	ENDING BOOK VALUE

PLANT ASSET RECORD, No. _____   General Ledger Account No. _____

Description _____   General Ledger Account _____

Date Bought _____   Serial Number _____   Original Cost _____

Estimated Useful Life _____   Estimated Salvage Value _____   Depreciation _____

Disposed of: Discarded _____   Sold _____   Traded _____

Date _____   Disposal Amount _____

Name _____ Date _____ Class _____

8-12 CHALLENGE PROBLEM, p. 254

Recording entries for plant assets

GENERAL JOURNAL

PAGE 7

	DATE		ACCOUNT TITLE	DOC. NO.	POST. REF.	DEBIT	CREDIT	
1								1
2								2
3								3
4								4
5								5
6								6
7								7
8								8
9								9
10								10
11								11
12								12
13								13
14								14
15								15
16								16
17								17
18								18
19								19
20								20
21								21
22								22
23								23
24								24
25								25
26								26
27								27
28								28
29								29
30								30
31								31

CASH PAYMENTS JOURNAL   PAGE 12

				1	2	3	4	5	
	DATE	ACCOUNT TITLE	CK. NO.	POST. REF.	GENERAL		ACCOUNTS PAYABLE DEBIT	PURCHASES DISCOUNT CREDIT	CASH CREDIT	
					DEBIT	CREDIT				
1										1
2										2
3										3
4										4
5										5
6										6
7										7
8										8
9										9
10										10
11										11
12										12
13										13
14										14
15										15
16										16
17										17
18										18
19										19
20										20
21										21
22										22
23										23
24										24
25										25
26										26
27										27
28										28
29										29
30										30

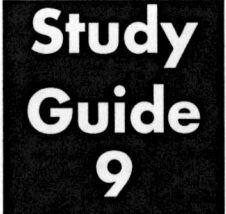

Study Guide 9

Name	Perfect Score	Your Score
Analyzing Procedures for Notes Payable, Prepaid Expenses, and Accrued Expenses	12 Pts.	
Identifying Accounting Terms	12 Pts.	
Analyzing Entries for Notes Payable, Prepaid Expenses, and Accrued Expenses	9 Pts.	
Total	33 Pts.	

Part One—Analyzing Procedures for Notes Payable, Prepaid Expenses, and Accrued Expenses

Directions: Place a *T* for True or *F* for False in the Answers column to show whether each of the following statements is true or false.

Answers

1. Showing in accounting records all information needed to prepare the financial statements of a business is an application of the accounting concept Adequate Disclosure. (p. 260)

   1. _____

2. When a note payable is issued for cash, Cash is debited and Notes Payable is credited. (p. 261)

   2. _____

3. The length of time to maturity of a note may be expressed in months or in days or in years. (p. 262)

   3. _____

4. When a note's time is expressed in months, the time from a date in one month to the same date in the next month is counted as one month. (p. 262)

   4. _____

5. When a note's time is expressed in days, the time from a date in one month to the same date in the next month is counted as 30 days. (p. 262)

   5. _____

6. Reporting as expenses only that portion of prepaid expenses that has been used in the current fiscal period is an application of the accounting concept Historical Cost. (p. 266)

   6. _____

7. An adjusting entry is made at the end of a fiscal period to separate the expense from the asset portion of prepaid expenses. (p. 266)

   7. _____

8. After adjusting entries are journalized and posted, the interest expense account balance includes all interest received or paid for the fiscal period. (p. 272)

   8. _____

9. Recording accrued payroll is an application of the accounting concept Matching Expenses with Revenue. (p. 274)

   9. _____

10. An adjusting entry for employer payroll taxes is not made at the end of a fiscal period because the accrued payroll has not yet been paid. (p. 274)

    10. _____

11. An adjusting entry for accrued employee federal income taxes is made at the end of a fiscal period. (p. 274)

    11. _____

12. A reversing entry is usually the opposite of the adjusting entry made to the same accounts. (p. 273)

    12. _____

Part Two—Identifying Accounting Terms

Directions: Select the one term in Column I that best fits each definition in Column II. Print the letter identifying your choice in the Answers column.

Column I	Column II	Answers
A. accrued expenses	1. The interest accrued on money borrowed. (p. 263)	1. _____
B. date of a note	2. The amount that is due on the maturity date of a note. (p. 263)	2. _____
C. interest	3. The day a note is issued. (p. 261)	3. _____
D. interest expense	4. The original amount of a note. (p. 261)	4. _____
E. interest rate of a note	5. The date a note is due. (p. 261)	5. _____
	6. An amount paid for the use of money for a period of time. (p. 261)	6. _____
F. maturity date of a note	7. The percentage of the principal that is paid for use of the money. (p. 261)	7. _____
G. maturity value	8. A written and signed promise to pay a sum of money at a specified time. (p. 261)	8. _____
H. notes payable		
I. prepaid expenses	9. Promissory notes signed by a business and given to creditors. (p. 261)	9. _____
J. principal of a note	10. Expenses paid in one fiscal period but not reported as expenses until a later fiscal period. (p. 266)	10. _____
K. promissory note	11. An entry made at the beginning of one fiscal period to reverse an adjusting entry made in the previous fiscal period. (p. 269)	11. _____
L. reversing entry	12. Expenses incurred in one fiscal period but not paid until a later fiscal period. (p. 272)	12. _____

Part Three—Analyzing Entries for Notes Payable, Prepaid Expenses, and Accrued Expenses

Directions: For each transaction below, print in the proper Answers columns the identifying letter of the accounts to be debited and credited.

Account Titles	Transaction	Answers Debit	Credit
A. Cash	1. Issued a 3-month note to the bank. (p. 261)	1. _____	_____
B. Insurance Expense	2. Issued a 60-day note to the bank. (p. 261)	2. _____	_____
C. Interest Expense	3. Paid cash for the maturity value of a note payable. (p. 263)	3. _____	_____
D. Interest Payable	4. Adjusting entry for accrued interest expense. (p. 272)	4. _____	_____
E. Notes Payable	5. Reversing entry for accrued interest expense. (p. 273)	5. _____	_____
F. Prepaid Insurance	6. Adjusting entry for sales supplies. (p. 268)	6. _____	_____
G. Supplies—Sales	7. Adjusting entry for prepaid insurance. (p. 270)	7. _____	_____
H. Supplies Expense—Sales	8. Reversing entry for sales supplies expense. (p. 269)	8. _____	_____
	9. Reversing entry for prepaid insurance expense. (p. 270)	9. _____	_____

9-1 WORK TOGETHER, p. 265

Journalizing notes payable transactions

[1]

CASH RECEIPTS JOURNAL

PAGE 15

			GENERAL		ACCOUNTS RECEIVABLE CREDIT	SALES CREDIT	SALES TAX PAYABLE		SALES DISCOUNT DEBIT	CASH DEBIT
DATE	ACCOUNT TITLE	DOC. NO.	POST. REF.	DEBIT	CREDIT			DEBIT	CREDIT		

[3]

CASH PAYMENTS JOURNAL

PAGE 18

				GENERAL		ACCOUNTS PAYABLE DEBIT	PURCHASES DISCOUNT CREDIT	CASH CREDIT
DATE	ACCOUNT TITLE	CK. NO.	POST. REF.	DEBIT	CREDIT			

[2]

Maturity dates:

[2]

Interest due at maturity:

Note signed May 14:

Note signed June 5:

9-1 ON YOUR OWN, p. 265

Journalizing notes payable transactions

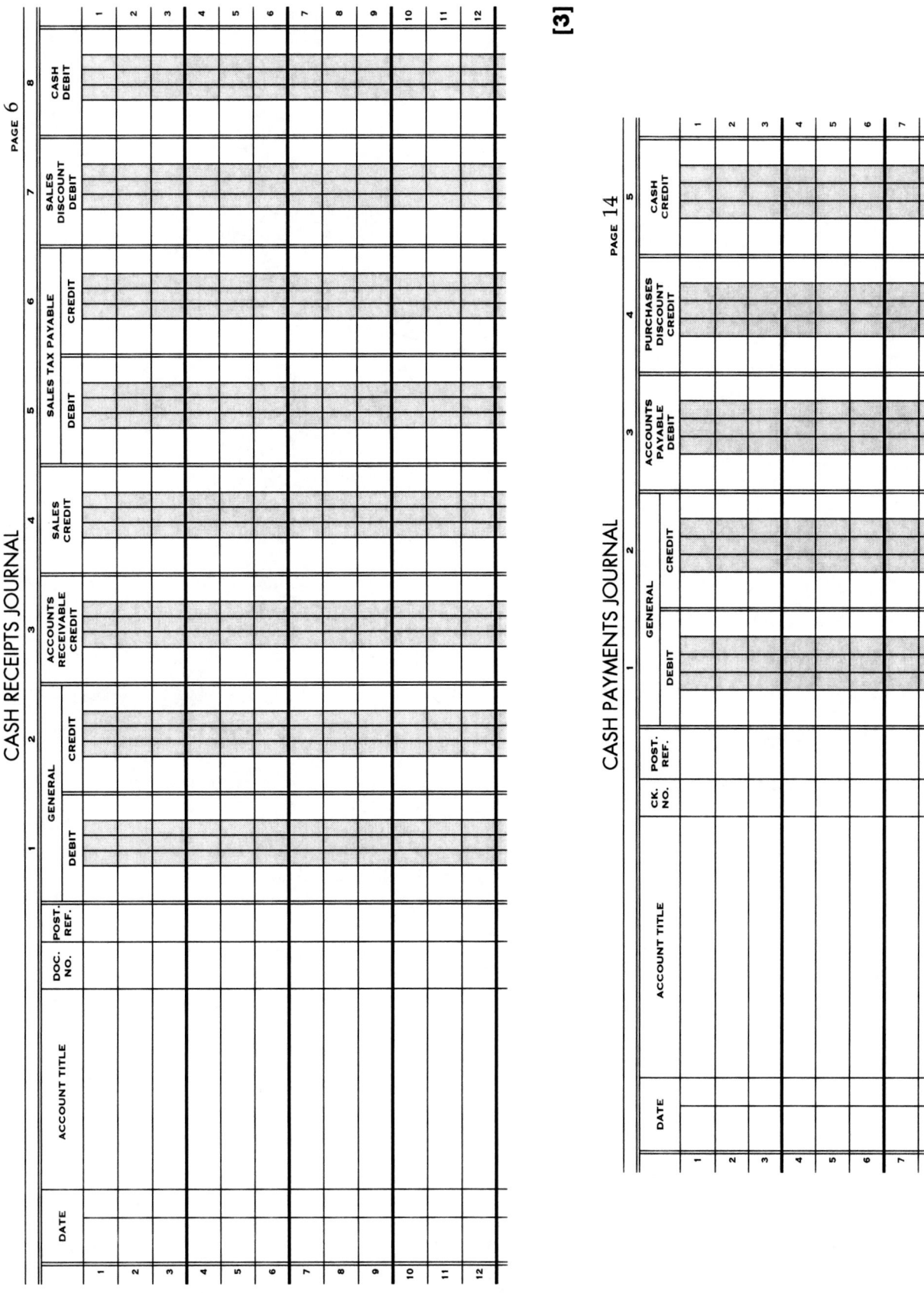

[1]

CASH RECEIPTS JOURNAL

PAGE 6

			GENERAL		ACCOUNTS RECEIVABLE CREDIT	SALES CREDIT	SALES TAX PAYABLE		SALES DISCOUNT DEBIT	CASH DEBIT
DATE	ACCOUNT TITLE	DOC. NO.	POST. REF.	DEBIT	CREDIT			DEBIT	CREDIT		

[3]

CASH PAYMENTS JOURNAL

PAGE 14

				GENERAL		ACCOUNTS PAYABLE DEBIT	PURCHASES DISCOUNT CREDIT	CASH CREDIT
DATE	ACCOUNT TITLE	CK. NO.	POST. REF.	DEBIT	CREDIT			

[2]

Maturity dates:

[2]

Interest due at maturity:

   Note signed March 23:

   Note signed July 12:

9-2 **WORK TOGETHER, p. 271**

**Journalizing adjusting and reversing entries for prepaid expenses
initially recorded as expenses**

[1]

GENERAL JOURNAL

PAGE 15

	DATE		ACCOUNT TITLE	DOC. NO.	POST. REF.	DEBIT	CREDIT	
1								1
2								2
3								3
4								4
5								5
6								6
7								7
8								8
9								9
10								10
11								11
12								12
13								13
14								14
15								15
16								16
17								17
18								18
19								19
20								20
21								21
22								22
23								23
24								24
25								25
26								26
27								27
28								28
29								29
30								30
31								31

[2]

GENERAL JOURNAL

PAGE 16

	DATE	ACCOUNT TITLE	DOC. NO.	POST. REF.	DEBIT	CREDIT	
1							1
2							2
3							3
4							4
5							5
6							6
7							7
8							8
9							9
10							10
11							11
12							12
13							13
14							14
15							15
16							16
17							17
18							18
19							19
20							20
21							21
22							22
23							23
24							24
25							25
26							26
27							27
28							28
29							29
30							30
31							31

9-2   ON YOUR OWN, p. 271

Journalizing adjusting and reversing entries for prepaid expenses   **[1]**
initially recorded as expenses

GENERAL JOURNAL   PAGE 13

	DATE		ACCOUNT TITLE	DOC. NO.	POST. REF.	DEBIT	CREDIT	
1								1
2								2
3								3
4								4
5								5
6								6
7								7
8								8
9								9
10								10
11								11
12								12
13								13
14								14
15								15
16								16
17								17
18								18
19								19
20								20
21								21
22								22
23								23
24								24
25								25
26								26
27								27
28								28
29								29
30								30
31								31

GENERAL JOURNAL PAGE 14

	DATE		ACCOUNT TITLE	DOC. NO.	POST. REF.	DEBIT	CREDIT	
1								1
2								2
3								3
4								4
5								5
6								6
7								7
8								8
9								9
10								10
11								11
12								12
13								13
14								14
15								15
16								16
17								17
18								18
19								19
20								20
21								21
22								22
23								23
24								24
25								25
26								26
27								27
28								28
29								29
30								30
31								31

9-3 WORK TOGETHER, p. 279

Journalizing adjusting and reversing entries for accrued expenses

a. One note payable is outstanding on December 31: 180-day, 12% note with First National Bank, $10,000, dated October 15.

b. Payroll information from the December 31 payroll:

Payroll and Employee Payroll Taxes		Employer Payroll Taxes	
Salaries—administrative	$1,200.00	Social Security tax	$143.00
Salaries—sales	1,000.00	Medicare tax	33.00
Federal income tax withheld	340.00	Federal unemployment tax	17.60
Social Security tax	143.00	State unemployment tax	118.80
Medicare tax	33.00		

c. Additional federal income tax, $1,500.00.

[1]

GENERAL JOURNAL   PAGE 13

	DATE		ACCOUNT TITLE	DOC. NO.	POST. REF.	DEBIT	CREDIT	
1								1
2								2
3								3
4								4
5								5
6								6
7								7
8								8
9								9
10								10
11								11
12								12
13								13
14								14
15								15
16								16
17								17

[2]

GENERAL JOURNAL   PAGE 14

	DATE	ACCOUNT TITLE	DOC. NO.	POST. REF.	DEBIT	CREDIT	
1							1
2							2
3							3
4							4
5							5
6							6
7							7
8							8
9							9
10							10
11							11
12							12
13							13
14							14
15							15
16							16
17							17
18							18
19							19
20							20
21							21
22							22
23							23
24							24
25							25
26							26
27							27
28							28
29							29
30							30
31							31

9-3 ON YOUR OWN, p. 279

Journalizing adjusting and reversing entries for accrued expenses

a. One note payable is outstanding on December 31: 90-day, 10% note with American National Bank, $20,000, dated November 29.

b. Payroll information from the December 31 payroll:

Payroll and Employee Payroll Taxes		Employer Payroll Taxes	
Salaries—administrative	$1,500.00	Social Security tax	$214.50
Salaries—sales	1,800.00	Medicare tax	49.50
Federal income tax withheld	740.00	Federal unemployment tax	9.60
Social Security tax	214.50	State unemployment tax	64.80
Medicare tax	49.50		

c. Additional federal income tax, $1,500.00.

[1]

GENERAL JOURNAL   PAGE 13

	DATE	ACCOUNT TITLE	DOC. NO.	POST. REF.	DEBIT	CREDIT	
1							1
2							2
3							3
4							4
5							5
6							6
7							7
8							8
9							9
10							10
11							11
12							12
13							13
14							14
15							15
16							16
17							17

GENERAL JOURNAL   PAGE 14

	DATE		ACCOUNT TITLE	DOC. NO.	POST. REF.	DEBIT	CREDIT	
1								1
2								2
3								3
4								4
5								5
6								6
7								7
8								8
9								9
10								10
11								11
12								12
13								13
14								14
15								15
16								16
17								17
18								18
19								19
20								20
21								21
22								22
23								23
24								24
25								25
26								26
27								27
28								28
29								29
30								30
31								31

9-1 **APPLICATION PROBLEM, p. 281**

Journalizing notes payable transactions

[1]

CASH RECEIPTS JOURNAL

				1 GENERAL	2	3 ACCOUNTS RECEIVABLE CREDIT	4 SALES CREDIT	5 SALES TAX PAYABLE	6	7 SALES DISCOUNT DEBIT	8 CASH DEBIT
DATE	ACCOUNT TITLE	DOC. NO.	POST. REF.	DEBIT	CREDIT			DEBIT	CREDIT		
1											
2											
3											
4											
5											
6											
7											
8											
9											
10											
11											
12											

[4]

CASH PAYMENTS JOURNAL

				1 GENERAL	2	3 ACCOUNTS PAYABLE DEBIT	4 PURCHASES DISCOUNT CREDIT	5 CASH CREDIT
DATE	ACCOUNT TITLE	CK. NO.	POST. REF.	DEBIT	CREDIT			
1								
2								
3								
4								
5								
6								
7								

[2]

Maturity dates:

August 1 note:

September 12 note:

October 21 note:

[3]

Interest due at maturity:

Note   Interest at Maturity

9-2 APPLICATION PROBLEM, p. 281

**Journalizing adjusting and reversing entries for prepaid expenses
initially recorded as expenses**

[1]

GENERAL JOURNAL

PAGE 13

	DATE		ACCOUNT TITLE	DOC. NO.	POST. REF.	DEBIT	CREDIT	
1								1
2								2
3								3
4								4
5								5
6								6
7								7
8								8
9								9
10								10
11								11
12								12
13								13
14								14
15								15
16								16
17								17
18								18
19								19
20								20
21								21
22								22
23								23
24								24
25								25
26								26
27								27
28								28
29								29
30								30
31								31

GENERAL JOURNAL

PAGE 1

	DATE		ACCOUNT TITLE	DOC. NO.	POST. REF.	DEBIT	CREDIT	
1								1
2								2
3								3
4								4
5								5
6								6
7								7
8								8
9								9
10								10
11								11
12								12
13								13
14								14
15								15
16								16
17								17
18								18
19								19
20								20
21								21
22								22
23								23
24								24
25								25
26								26
27								27
28								28
29								29
30								30
31								31

9-3 APPLICATION PROBLEM, p. 282

Journalizing adjusting and reversing entries for accrued expenses [1]

GENERAL JOURNAL

PAGE 13

	DATE		ACCOUNT TITLE	DOC. NO.	POST. REF.	DEBIT	CREDIT	
1								1
2								2
3								3
4								4
5								5
6								6
7								7
8								8
9								9
10								10
11								11
12								12
13								13
14								14
15								15
16								16
17								17
18								18
19								19
20								20
21								21
22								22
23								23
24								24
25								25
26								26
27								27
28								28
29								29
30								30
31								31

GENERAL JOURNAL   PAGE 1

	DATE	ACCOUNT TITLE	DOC. NO.	POST. REF.	DEBIT	CREDIT	
1							1
2							2
3							3
4							4
5							5
6							6
7							7
8							8
9							9
10							10
11							11
12							12
13							13
14							14
15							15
16							16
17							17
18							18
19							19
20							20
21							21
22							22
23							23
24							24
25							25
26							26
27							27
28							28
29							29
30							30
31							31

9-4 MASTERY PROBLEM, p. 282

Journalizing adjusting and reversing entries for prepaid expenses initially recorded as expenses and for accrued expenses [1]

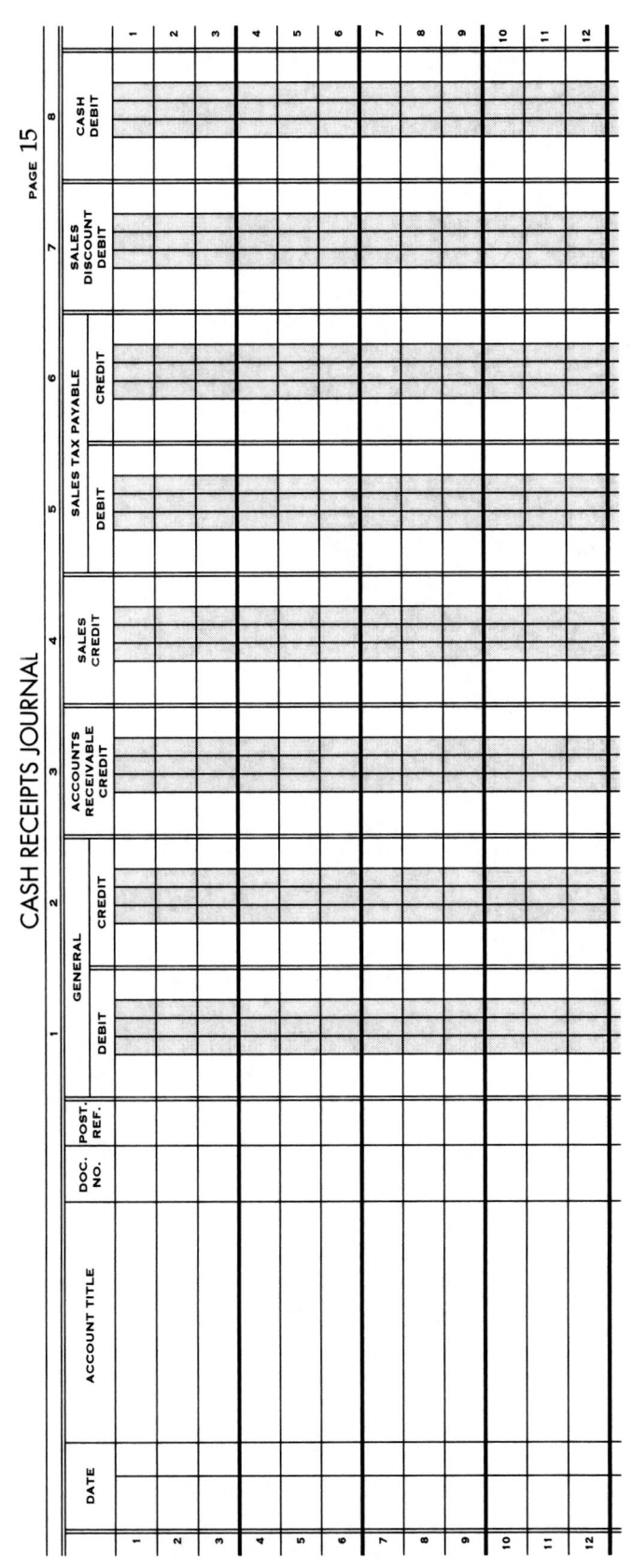

[1]

CASH RECEIPTS JOURNAL PAGE 15

[3]

CASH PAYMENTS JOURNAL PAGE 21

Maturity dates:

July 1 note:

October 10 note:

November 1 note:

9-4　**MASTERY PROBLEM (continued)**

[4]

GENERAL JOURNAL

PAGE 13

	DATE		ACCOUNT TITLE	DOC. NO.	POST. REF.	DEBIT	CREDIT	
1								1
2								2
3								3
4								4
5								5
6								6
7								7
8								8
9								9
10								10
11								11
12								12
13								13
14								14
15								15
16								16
17								17
18								18
19								19
20								20
21								21
22								22
23								23
24								24
25								25
26								26
27								27
28								28
29								29
30								30
31								31

GENERAL JOURNAL

PAGE 1

	DATE	ACCOUNT TITLE	DOC. NO.	POST. REF.	DEBIT	CREDIT	
1							1
2							2
3							3
4							4
5							5
6							6
7							7
8							8
9							9
10							10
11							11
12							12
13							13
14							14
15							15
16							16
17							17
18							18
19							19
20							20
21							21
22							22
23							23
24							24
25							25
26							26
27							27
28							28
29							29
30							30
31							31

9-5 **CHALLENGE PROBLEM, p. 283**

Journalizing entries for notes payable when no reversing entries are recorded

[1]

Cash		Income Summary

Interest Payable		Interest Expense

Notes Payable		Retained Earnings

[1]

GENERAL JOURNAL

PAGE 13

	DATE	ACCOUNT TITLE	DOC. NO.	POST. REF.	DEBIT	CREDIT	
1							1
2							2
3							3
4							4
5							5
6							6
7							7
8							8
9							9
10							10
11							11

[1]

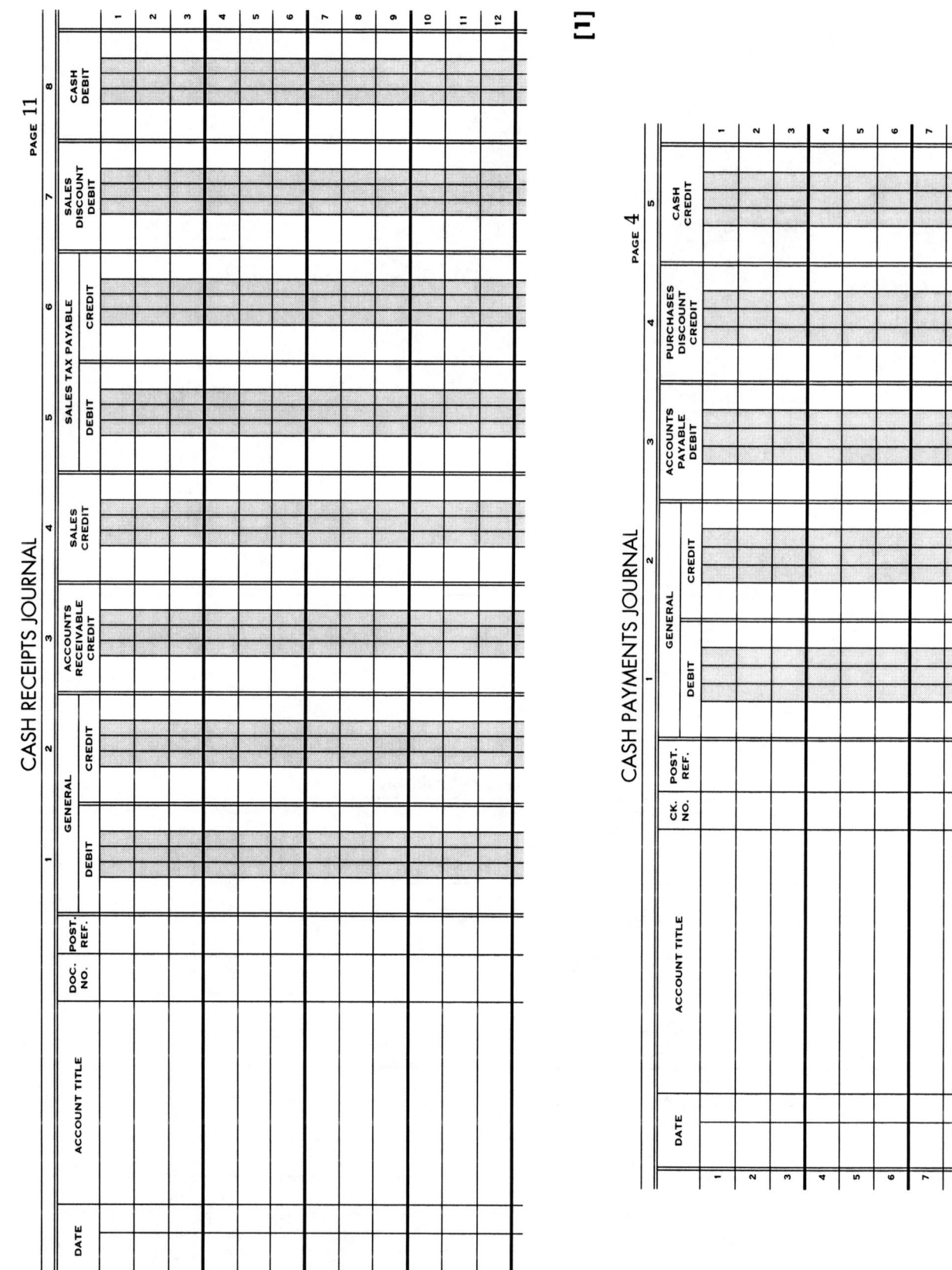

CASH RECEIPTS JOURNAL   PAGE 11

CASH PAYMENTS JOURNAL   PAGE 4

[1]

9-5 CHALLENGE PROBLEM (continued)

[2]

Cash		Income Summary

Interest Payable		Interest Expense

Notes Payable		Retained Earnings

[2]

GENERAL JOURNAL

PAGE 13

	DATE	ACCOUNT TITLE	DOC. NO.	POST. REF.	DEBIT	CREDIT	
1							1
2							2
3							3
4							4
5							5
6							6
7							7
8							8
9							9
10							10
11							11

[2]

CASH RECEIPTS JOURNAL

PAGE 11

			1	2	3	4	5	6	7	8
			GENERAL		ACCOUNTS RECEIVABLE CREDIT	SALES CREDIT	SALES TAX PAYABLE		SALES DISCOUNT DEBIT	CASH DEBIT
DATE	ACCOUNT TITLE	DOC. NO.	POST. REF.	DEBIT	CREDIT			DEBIT	CREDIT		

[2]

CASH PAYMENTS JOURNAL

PAGE 4

				1	2	3	4	5
				GENERAL		ACCOUNTS PAYABLE DEBIT	PURCHASES DISCOUNT CREDIT	CASH CREDIT
DATE	ACCOUNT TITLE	CK. NO.	POST. REF.	DEBIT	CREDIT			

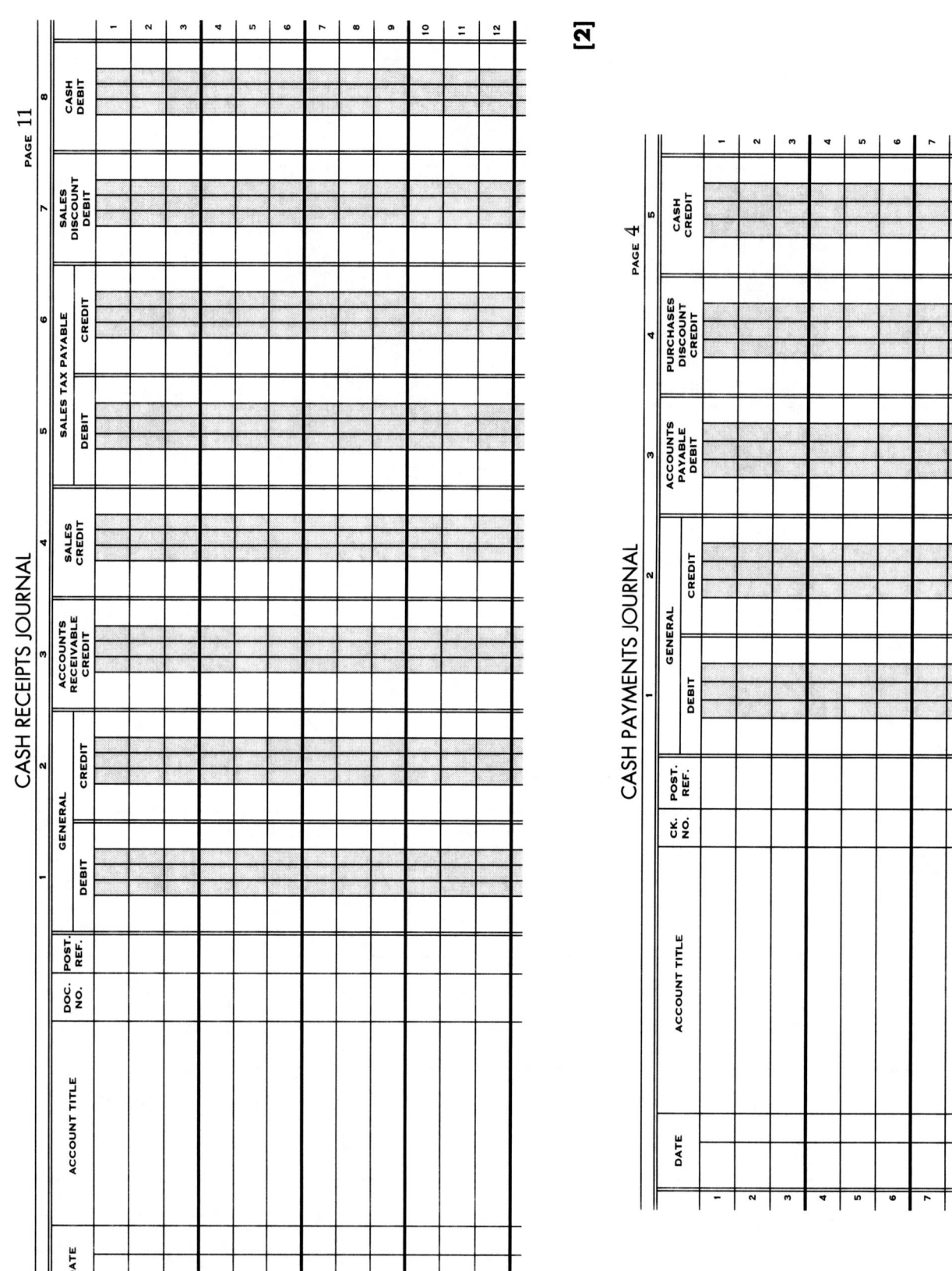

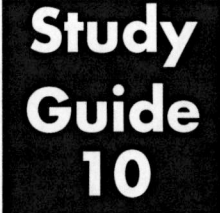

Name	Perfect Score	Your Score
Identifying Accounting Terms	4 Pts.	
Analyzing Entries for Notes Receivable, Unearned Revenue, and Accrued Revenue	8 Pts.	
Analyzing Procedures for Notes Receivable, Unearned Revenue, and Accrued Revenue	9 Pts.	
Total	21 Pts.	

Part One—Identifying Accounting Terms

Directions: Select the one term in Column I that best fits each definition in Column II. Print the letter identifying your choice in the Answers column.

Column I	Column II	Answers
A. accrued revenue	**1.** Promissory notes that a business accepts from customers. (p. 291)	**1.** _____
B. dishonored note	**2.** A note that is not paid when due. (p. 293)	**2.** _____
C. notes receivable	**3.** Revenue received in one fiscal period but not earned until the next fiscal period. (p. 297)	**3.** _____
D. unearned revenue	**4.** Revenue earned in one fiscal period but not received until a later fiscal period. (p. 299)	**4.** _____

Part Two—Analyzing Entries for Notes Receivable, Unearned Revenue, and Accrued Revenue

Directions: For each transaction below, print in the proper Answers column the identifying letters of the accounts to be debited and credited.

Account Titles	Transactions	Answers Debit	Credit
A. Accounts Receivable	**1.** Received a 30-day, 10% note for an extension of time to pay on account. (p. 291)	**1.** _____	_____
B. Cash	**2.** A note receivable is dishonored. (p. 293)	**2.** _____	_____
C. Interest Income	**3.** Received cash for the maturity value of a note receivable. (p. 292)	**3.** _____	_____
D. Interest Receivable	**4.** Received cash for a previously dishonored note receivable. (p. 294)	**4.** _____	_____
E. Notes Receivable	*Unearned revenue initially recorded as revenue:*		
	5. Adjusting entry for unearned rent income. (p. 297)	**5.** _____	_____
F. Rent Income	**6.** Reversing entry for unearned rent income. (p. 298)	**6.** _____	_____
G. Unearned Rent	*Accrued revenue:*		
	7. Adjusting entry for accrued interest income. (p. 299)	**7.** _____	_____
	8. Reversing entry for accrued interest income. (p. 300)	**8.** _____	_____

Part Three—Analyzing Procedures for Notes Receivable, Unearned Revenue, and Accrued Revenue

Directions: For each item below, select the choice that best completes the sentence. Print the letter identifying your choice in the Answers column.

1. Rent received in advance is a liability until the rented space is actually (p. 297)
   - (A) paid for
   - (B) used
   - (C) rented
   - (D) none of these

   1. _____

2. At the end of a fiscal period, a business must show how much rent received in advance has become (p. 297)
   - (A) an expense
   - (B) a revenue
   - (C) an asset
   - (D) none of these

   2. _____

3. When a business actually receives cash in advance for rent, the amount is recorded as (p. 297)
   - (A) a liability
   - (B) a revenue
   - (C) either a liability or a revenue
   - (D) none of these

   3. _____

4. When a business actually receives cash in advance for rent, and initially records unearned revenue as revenue, the account credited is (p. 297)
   - (A) Cash
   - (B) Rent Income
   - (C) Notes Receivable
   - (D) none of these

   4. _____

5. Recording an adjusting entry for accrued interest income is an application of the accounting concept (p. 299)
   - (A) Objective Evidence
   - (B) Historical Cost
   - (C) Consistent Reporting
   - (D) Matching Expenses with Revenue

   5. _____

6. If a note is dishonored, the account debited is (p. 293)
   - (A) Notes Receivable
   - (B) Accounts Receivable
   - (C) Interest Income
   - (D) Allowance for Notes Receivable

   6. _____

7. When a dishonored note is paid, the additional interest is calculated on the (p. 294)
   - (A) principal of the note
   - (B) original value of the note
   - (C) maturity value of the note
   - (D) none of these

   7. _____

8. The interest on a 3-month, 10%, $1,000.00 note receivable is (p. 292)
   - (A) $25.00
   - (B) $100.00
   - (C) $24.66
   - (D) none of these

   8. _____

9. The interest on a 90-day, 10%, $2,000.00 note receivable is (p. 292)
   - (A) $50.00
   - (B) $200.00
   - (C) $49.32
   - (D) none of these

   9. _____

10-1 WORK TOGETHER, p. 296

Journalizing notes receivable transactions [1]

GENERAL JOURNAL   PAGE 5

	DATE	ACCOUNT TITLE	DOC. NO.	POST. REF.	DEBIT	CREDIT	
1							1
2							2
3							3
4							4
5							5
6							6
7							7
8							8
9							9
10							10
11							11
12							12
13							13
14							14
15							15
16							16
17							17
18							18
19							19
20							20
21							21
22							22
23							23
24							24
25							25
26							26
27							27
28							28
29							29
30							30
31							31

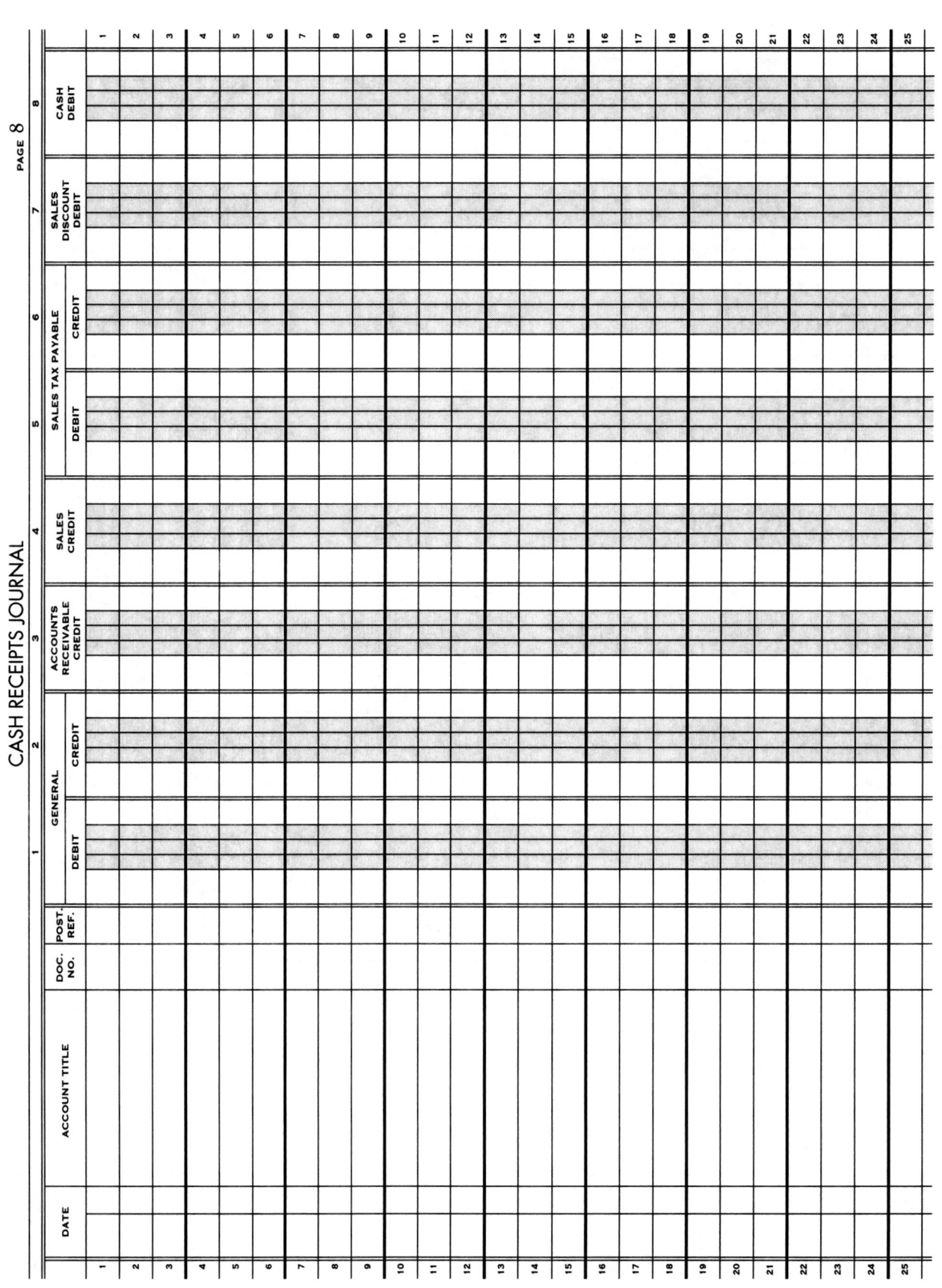

CASH RECEIPTS JOURNAL

PAGE 8

10-1 ON YOUR OWN, p. 296

Journalizing notes receivable transactions [1]

GENERAL JOURNAL

PAGE 6

	DATE	ACCOUNT TITLE	DOC. NO.	POST. REF.	DEBIT	CREDIT	
1							1
2							2
3							3
4							4
5							5
6							6
7							7
8							8
9							9
10							10
11							11
12							12
13							13
14							14
15							15
16							16
17							17
18							18
19							19
20							20
21							21
22							22
23							23
24							24
25							25
26							26
27							27
28							28
29							29
30							30
31							31

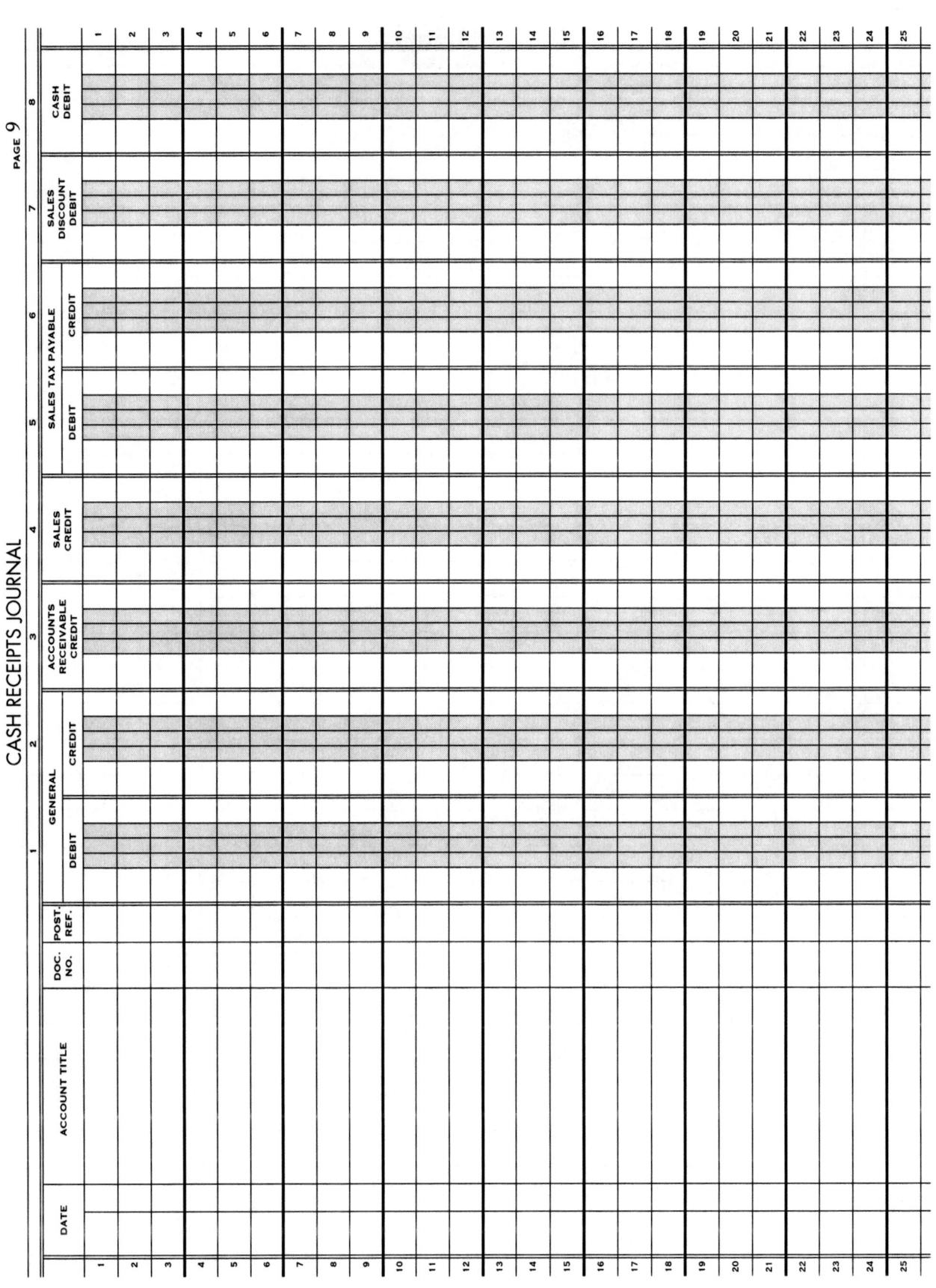

10-2 **WORK TOGETHER, p. 302**

Journalizing adjusting and reversing entries for unearned revenue
initially recorded as revenue and for accrued revenue

[1, 3]

GENERAL JOURNAL

PAGE 13

	DATE	ACCOUNT TITLE	DOC. NO.	POST. REF.	DEBIT	CREDIT	
1							1
2							2
3							3
4							4
5							5
6							6
7							7
8							8
9							9
10							10
11							11
12							12
13							13
14							14
15							15
16							16
17							17
18							18
19							19
20							20
21							21
22							22
23							23
24							24
25							25
26							26
27							27
28							28
29							29
30							30
31							31

[2, 4]

GENERAL JOURNAL

PAGE 14

	DATE	ACCOUNT TITLE	DOC. NO.	POST. REF.	DEBIT	CREDIT	
1							1
2							2
3							3
4							4
5							5
6							6
7							7
8							8
9							9
10							10
11							11
12							12

Space for calculations:

Note: Calculation not a required part of solution.

10-2 ON YOUR OWN, p. 303

Journalizing adjusting and reversing entries for unearned revenue
initially recorded as revenue and for accrued revenue   [1, 3]

GENERAL JOURNAL   PAGE 19

	DATE	ACCOUNT TITLE	DOC. NO.	POST. REF.	DEBIT	CREDIT	
1							1
2							2
3							3
4							4
5							5
6							6
7							7
8							8
9							9
10							10
11							11
12							12
13							13
14							14
15							15
16							16
17							17
18							18
19							19
20							20
21							21
22							22
23							23
24							24
25							25
26							26
27							27
28							28
29							29
30							30
31							31

[2, 4]

GENERAL JOURNAL

PAGE 20

	DATE	ACCOUNT TITLE	DOC. NO.	POST. REF.	DEBIT	CREDIT	
1							1
2							2
3							3
4							4
5							5
6							6
7							7
8							8
9							9
10							10
11							11
12							12

Space for calculations:

Note: Calculation not a required part of solution.

 **EXPLORE ACCOUNTING, p. 304**

Projection assuming no factoring

Transaction	Week	Cash	Accounts Receivable	Inventory	Sales	Cost of Goods Sold
Balance	1			10,000		
Sales			2,000	(1,000)	2,000	1,000
Collection						
Purchases						
Balance	2	0	2,000	9,000	2,000	1,000
Sales						
Collection						
Purchases						
Balance	3	0				
Sales						
Collection						
Purchases						
Balance	4	0				
Sales						
Collection						
Purchases						
Balance	5	0				
Sales						
Collection		2,000	(2,000)			
Purchases						
Balance	6					
Sales						
Collection		1,800				
Purchases						
Balance	7					
Sales						
Collection		1,620				
Purchases						
Balance	8					
Sales						
Collection		1,458				
Purchases						
Balance	9					

Sales
Cost of Goods Sold
Income

 ## EXPLORE ACCOUNTING (concluded)

Projection assuming factoring

Transaction	Week	Cash	Accounts Receivable	Inventory	Sales	Cost of Goods Sold	Factoring Expense
Balance	1			10,000			
Sales			2,000	(1,000)	2,000	1,000	
Collection							
Factoring		1,800	(2,000)				200
Purchases		(1,000)		1,000			
Balance	2	800	0	10,000	2,000	1,000	200
Sales							
Collection							
Factoring							
Purchases							
Balance	3						
Sales							
Collection							
Factoring							
Purchases							
Balance	4						
Sales							
Collection							
Factoring							
Purchases							
Balance	5						
Sales							
Collection							
Factoring							
Purchases							
Balance	6						
Sales							
Collection							
Factoring							
Purchases							
Balance	7						
Sales							
Collection							
Factoring							
Purchases							
Balance	8						
Sales							
Collection							
Factoring							
Purchases							
Balance	9						

Sales
Cost of Goods Sold
Factoring Expense
Income

Consultant's recommendation:

10-1 APPLICATION PROBLEM, p. 305

Journalizing transactions for notes receivable

GENERAL JOURNAL   PAGE 8

	DATE	ACCOUNT TITLE	DOC. NO.	POST. REF.	DEBIT	CREDIT	
1							1
2							2
3							3
4							4
5							5
6							6
7							7
8							8
9							9
10							10
11							11
12							12
13							13
14							14
15							15
16							16
17							17
18							18
19							19
20							20
21							21
22							22
23							23
24							24
25							25
26							26
27							27
28							28
29							29
30							30
31							31

CASH RECEIPTS JOURNAL

PAGE 15

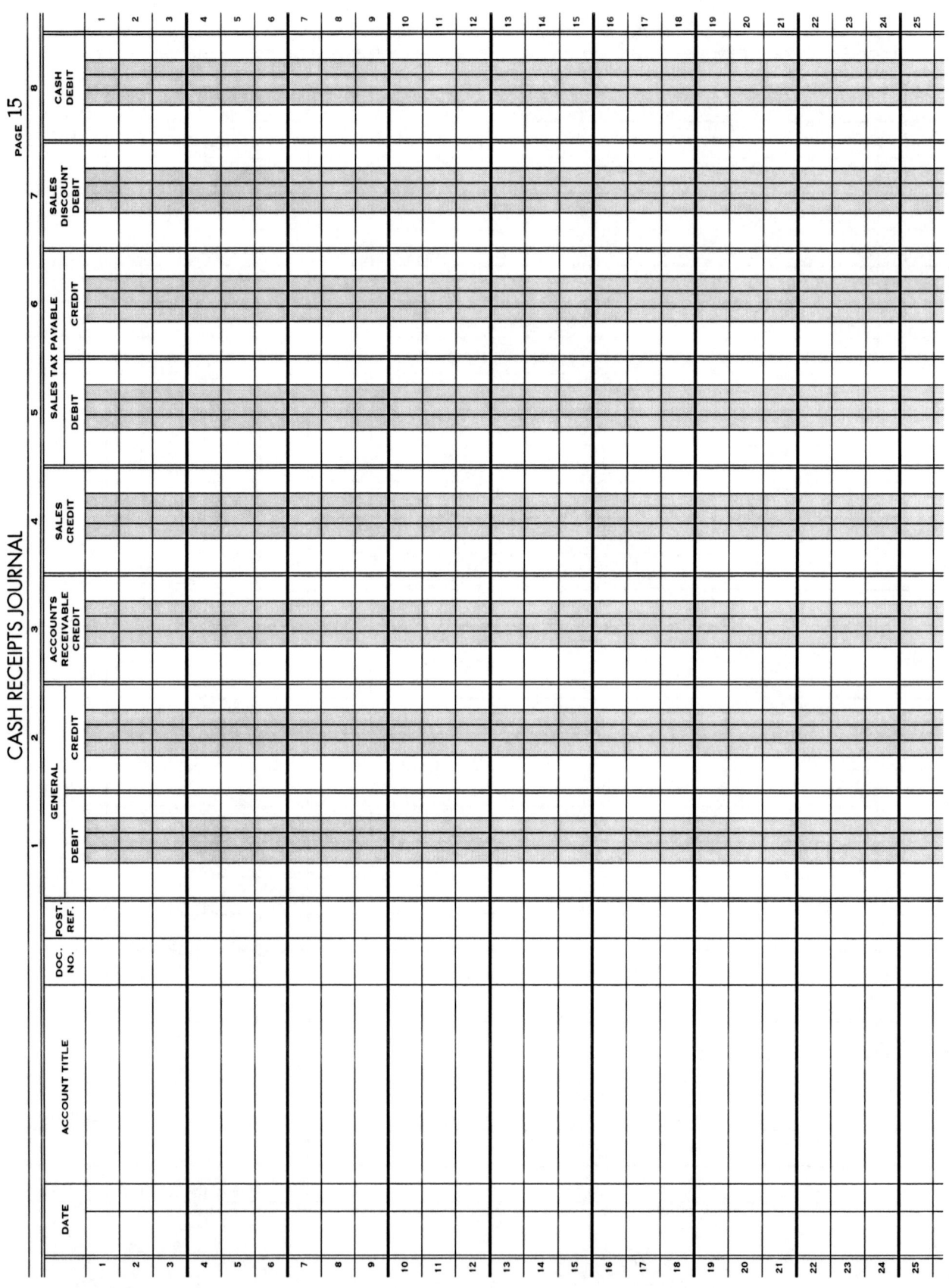

	DATE	ACCOUNT TITLE	DOC. NO.	POST. REF.	GENERAL		ACCOUNTS RECEIVABLE CREDIT	SALES CREDIT	SALES TAX PAYABLE		SALES DISCOUNT DEBIT	CASH DEBIT	
					DEBIT	CREDIT			DEBIT	CREDIT			
					1	2	3	4	5	6	7	8	

10-2 **APPLICATION PROBLEM, p. 305**

Journalizing adjusting and reversing entries for unearned revenue initially recorded as revenue [1]

GENERAL JOURNAL PAGE 13

	DATE		ACCOUNT TITLE	DOC. NO.	POST. REF.	DEBIT	CREDIT	
1								1
2								2
3								3
4								4
5								5
6								6
7								7
8								8
9								9
10								10
11								11
12								12
13								13
14								14
15								15
16								16
17								17
18								18
19								19
20								20
21								21
22								22
23								23
24								24
25								25
26								26
27								27
28								28
29								29
30								30
31								31

GENERAL JOURNAL   PAGE 1

	DATE		ACCOUNT TITLE	DOC. NO.	POST. REF.	DEBIT	CREDIT	
1								1
2								2
3								3
4								4
5								5
6								6
7								7
8								8
9								9
10								10
11								11
12								12
13								13
14								14
15								15
16								16
17								17
18								18
19								19
20								20
21								21
22								22
23								23
24								24
25								25
26								26
27								27
28								28
29								29
30								30
31								31

10-3 APPLICATION PROBLEM, p. 306

Journalizing adjusting and reversing entries for accrued revenue   [2]

GENERAL JOURNAL   PAGE 13

	DATE	ACCOUNT TITLE	DOC. NO.	POST. REF.	DEBIT	CREDIT	
1							1
2							2
3							3
4							4
5							5
6							6
7							7
8							8
9							9
10							10
11							11
12							12

[1]

Space for calculations:

Note	Accrued Interest Income
1	
2	
Total	

GENERAL JOURNAL

PAGE 1

	DATE	ACCOUNT TITLE	DOC. NO.	POST. REF.	DEBIT	CREDIT	
1							1
2							2
3							3
4							4
5							5
6							6
7							7
8							8
9							9
10							10
11							11
12							12
13							13
14							14
15							15
16							16
17							17
18							18
19							19
20							20
21							21
22							22
23							23
24							24
25							25
26							26
27							27
28							28
29							29
30							30
31							31

10-4 MASTERY PROBLEM, p. 306

Journalizing notes receivable, unearned revenue, and accrued revenue initially recorded as revenue transactions

[1, 2]

GENERAL JOURNAL

PAGE 7

	DATE	ACCOUNT TITLE	DOC. NO.	POST. REF.	DEBIT	CREDIT	
1							1
2							2
3							3
4							4
5							5
6							6
7							7
8							8
9							9
10							10
11							11
12							12
13							13
14							14
15							15
16							16

[3]

GENERAL JOURNAL

PAGE 1

	DATE	ACCOUNT TITLE	DOC. NO.	POST. REF.	DEBIT	CREDIT	
1							1
2							2
3							3
4							4
5							5
6							6
7							7
8							8
9							9

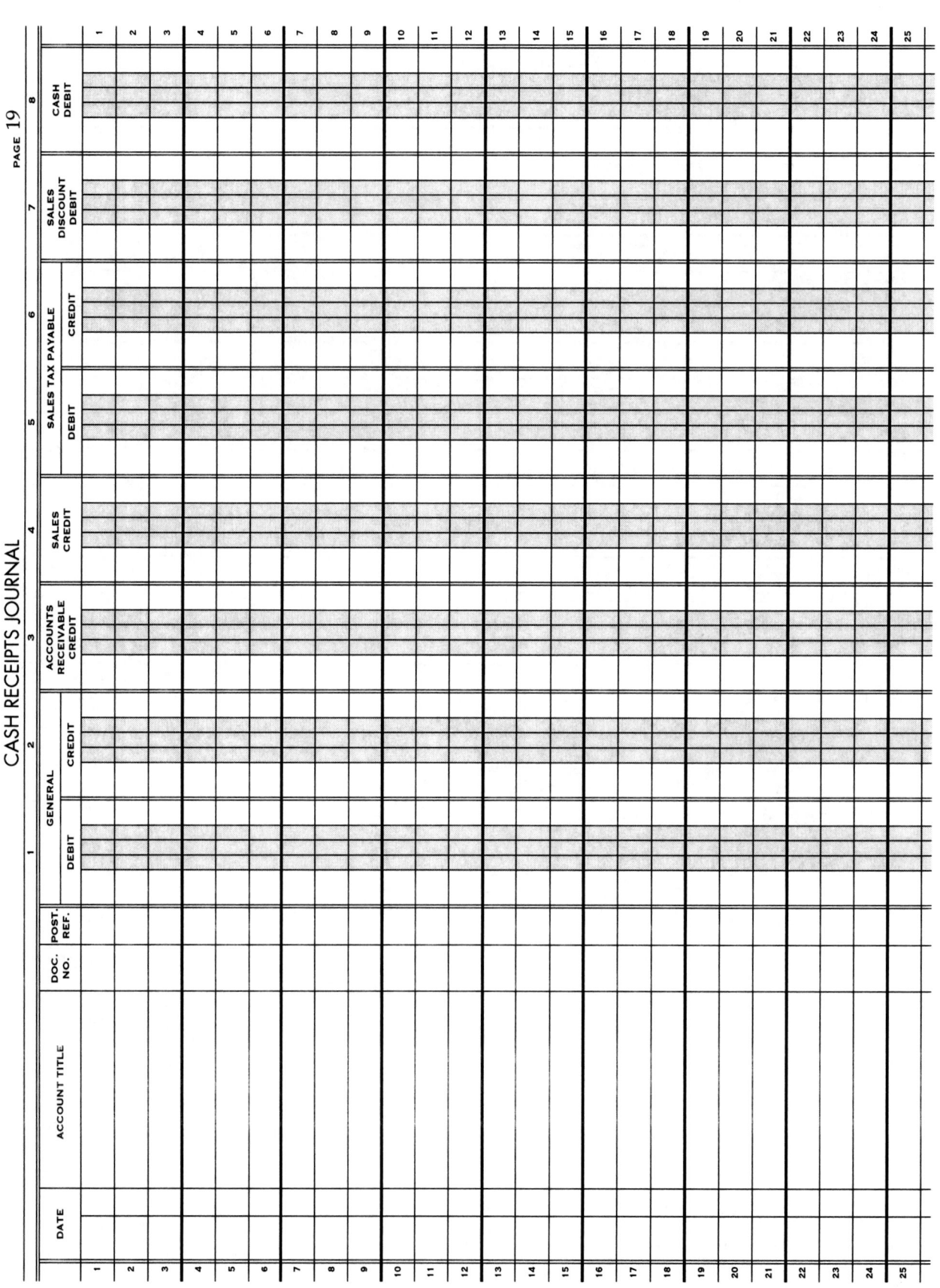

CASH RECEIPTS JOURNAL

PAGE 19

				1 GENERAL DEBIT	2 GENERAL CREDIT	3 ACCOUNTS RECEIVABLE CREDIT	4 SALES CREDIT	5 SALES TAX PAYABLE DEBIT	6 SALES TAX PAYABLE CREDIT	7 SALES DISCOUNT DEBIT	8 CASH DEBIT
DATE	ACCOUNT TITLE	DOC. NO.	POST. REF.								

10-5 CHALLENGE PROBLEM, p. 306

Journalizing accounts and notes receivable

GENERAL JOURNAL

PAGE 7

	DATE	ACCOUNT TITLE	DOC. NO.	POST. REF.	DEBIT	CREDIT	
1							1
2							2
3							3
4							4
5							5
6							6
7							7
8							8
9							9
10							10
11							11
12							12
13							13
14							14
15							15
16							16
17							17
18							18
19							19
20							20
21							21
22							22
23							23
24							24
25							25
26							26
27							27
28							28
29							29
30							30
31							31

CASH RECEIPTS JOURNAL

PAGE 7

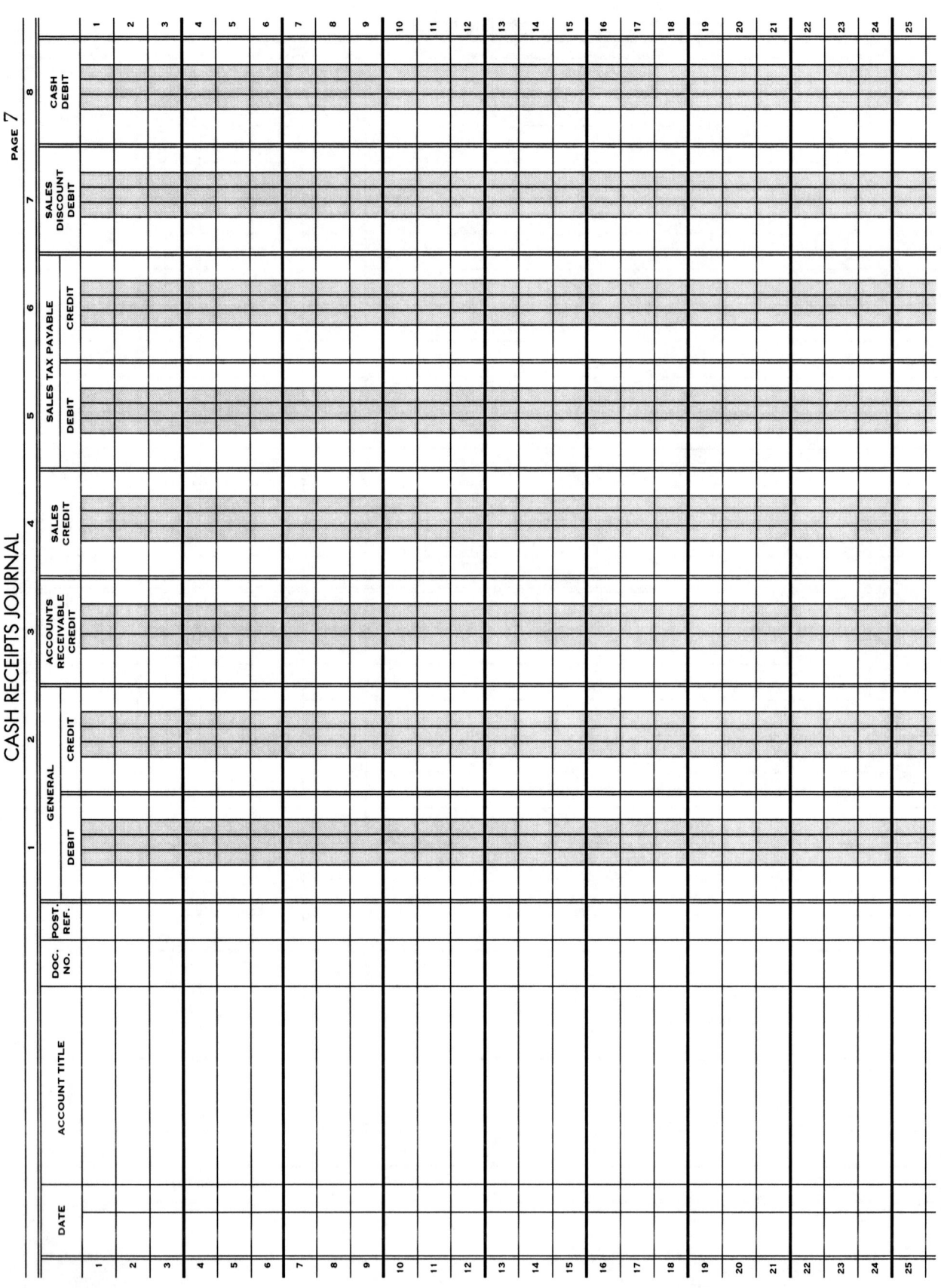

Extra Form

GENERAL LEDGER

ACCOUNT _____ ACCOUNT NO. _____

DATE	ITEM	POST. REF.	DEBIT	CREDIT	BALANCE DEBIT	BALANCE CREDIT

ACCOUNT _____ ACCOUNT NO. _____

DATE	ITEM	POST. REF.	DEBIT	CREDIT	BALANCE DEBIT	BALANCE CREDIT

PAYROLL REGISTER

PAY PERIOD ENDED

	EMPL. NO.	EMPLOYEE NAME	MARI- TAL STATUS	NO. OF ALLOW- ANCES	TOTAL HOURS	EARNINGS				
	1	2	3	4	5	REGULAR (6)	OVERTIME (7)	COMMISSION (8)	TOTAL (9)	
1										1
2										2
3										3
4										4
5										5
6										6
7										7
8										8
9										9
10										10
11										11
12										12
13										13
14										14
15										15

EARNINGS RECORD FOR QUARTER ENDED _____

EMPLOYEE NO. _____ NAME _____ SOCIAL SECURITY NO. _____

MARITAL STATUS _____ WITHHOLDING ALLOWANCES _____ HOURLY RATE _____ SALARY _____

DEPARTMENT _____ POSITION _____

PAY PERIOD		TOTAL EARNINGS	DEDUCTIONS						NET PAY	ACCUMULATED EARNINGS
NO. (1)	ENDED (2)	(3)	FEDERAL INCOME TAX (4)	STATE INCOME TAX (5)	SOC. SEC. TAX (6)	MEDICARE TAX (7)	OTHER (8)	TOTAL (9)	(10)	(11)
1										
2										
3										
4										
5										
6										
7										
8										
9										
10										

Extra Forms

PAYROLL REGISTER

DATE OF PAYMENT

	10	11	12	13	14	15	16	17	18	19	20	
	DEPARTMENT		ADMIN. SALARIES	DEDUCTIONS						PAID		
				FEDERAL INCOME TAX	STATE INCOME TAX	SOC. SEC. TAX	MEDICARE TAX	OTHER	TOTAL	NET PAY	CHECK NO.	
1												1
2												2
3												3
4												4
5												5
6												6
7												7
8												8
9												9
10												10
11												11
12												12
13												13
14												14
15												15

EARNINGS RECORD FOR QUARTER ENDED _____

EMPLOYEE NO. _____ NAME _____ SOCIAL SECURITY NO. _____

MARITAL STATUS _____ WITHHOLDING ALLOWANCES _____ HOURLY RATE _____ SALARY _____

DEPARTMENT _____ POSITION _____

	1	2	3	4	5	6	7	8	9	10	11
	PAY PERIOD		TOTAL EARNINGS	DEDUCTIONS						NET PAY	ACCUMULATED EARNINGS
	NO.	ENDED		FEDERAL INCOME TAX	STATE INCOME TAX	SOC. SEC. TAX	MEDICARE TAX	OTHER	TOTAL		
1											
2											
3											
4											
5											
6											
7											
8											
9											
10											

PLANT ASSET RECORD, No. _____   General Ledger Account No. _____

Description _____   General Ledger Account _____

Date
Bought _____   Serial
Number _____   Original
Cost _____

Estimated
Useful Life _____   Estimated
Salvage Value _____   Depreciation _____

Disposed of: Discarded _____   Sold _____   Traded _____

Date _____   Disposal Amount _____

YEAR	ANNUAL DEPRECIATION EXPENSE	ACCUMULATED DEPRECIATION	ENDING BOOK VALUE

PLANT ASSET RECORD, No. _____   General Ledger Account No. _____

Description _____   General Ledger Account _____

Date
Bought _____   Serial
Number _____   Original
Cost _____

Estimated
Useful Life _____   Estimated
Salvage Value _____   Depreciation _____

Disposed of: Discarded _____   Sold _____   Traded _____

Date _____   Disposal Amount _____

YEAR	ANNUAL DEPRECIATION EXPENSE	ACCUMULATED DEPRECIATION	ENDING BOOK VALUE

CPSIA information can be obtained
at www.ICGtesting.com
Printed in the USA
FFOW02n0334300817
39377FF